". . . and the Name Shall Be Amana."

A Change
and a Parting

MY STORY OF AMANA

by *Barbara S. Yambura*

in collaboration with

Eunice W. Bodine

illustrated by DALE BALLANTYNE

THE IOWA STATE UNIVERSITY PRESS, *Ames*, IOWA

I·O·W·A
HERITAGE
COLLECTION

BARBARA S. YAMBURA was born and raised in the Amana colonies in Iowa. She is proud of her heritage and delights in sharing the rich experiences and vivid memories of her youth, which are an authentic chronicle of the life and traditions of the Amanas. After graduating from Coe College and the University of Illinois, she eventually returned to Iowa City, a scant twenty-three miles from where she grew up. She now resides in Colorado Springs, Colo.

EUNICE WILLIS BODINE, after college, traveled in Europe and South America before locating in Iowa City, where she formed a close friendship with Barbara Yambura. These friends pooled their talents and mutual interest to create this book.

© 1960 Iowa State University Press, Ames, Iowa 50010
All rights reserved

Manufactured in the United States of America
♾ This book is printed on acid-free paper.

Authorization to photocopy items for internal or personal use, or the internal or personal use of specific clients, is granted by Iowa State University Press, provided that the base fee of $.10 per copy is paid directly to the Copyright Clearance Center, 27 Congress Street, Salem, MA 01970. For those organizations that have been granted a photocopy license by CCC, a separate system of payments has been arranged. The fee code for users of the Transactional Reporting Service is 0–8138–0261–X/90 $.10.

First edition, 1960
Iowa Heritage Collection edition, 1986
Second printing, 1988
Third printing, 1990

Library of Congress Cataloging-in-Publication Data

Yambura, Barbara S. (Barbara Schneider)
   A change and a parting.

   (Iowa heritage collection)
   1. Amana Society—History. 2. Iowa—Church history. I. Bodine,
Eunice W. (Eunice Willis) II. Title. III. Series.
HX656.A4Y3   1986   335′.9777653   86–18598
ISBN 0–8138–0261–X

To my Mother and my friends in Amana
who share these memories with me

notes and acknowledgments

This story of Amana stems from a long-standing friendship between the authors. One of us knew the Amana way of life and the other wondered—as do most visitors when they see the Amana villages for the first time—how this charming European-looking community came to be. Hence the story that lay hidden behind the peaceful façade of stone house and country garden was gradually unfolded.

Many questions arose—and were answered truly—about the history of Amana, its home life, religious beliefs, customs, and most of all, what it was like to be a member of a communal society where all shared alike. The story proved so interesting that it seemed well worth the telling for others.

The characters in this book are composites, typical

of people in the Amanas. They are not intended to represent any particular persons, nor are the names those of actual people. Any similarity to persons living or dead is purely coincidental.

Translations from the original German are Mrs. Yambura's except when otherwise indicated.

The authors wish to thank their friends in Amana for the valuable information they so generously contributed toward the authenticity of the story.

We also wish to thank Mr. Dale Ballantyne who so aptly captured the spirit of Amana in his illustrations, and Mr. Howard Yambura for his tireless assistance in the preparation of the manuscript.

We acknowledge with appreciation the many helpful suggestions of Mr. Marshall Townsend, Mrs. Rowena James, and others of the Iowa State University Press. Their vision of the book as a whole made possible the unity that is so necessary for a work of this kind.

BARBARA S. YAMBURA

EUNICE WILLIS BODINE

contents

Introduction 11

AMANA HERITAGE

How Amana Came to Be 17
Once Upon a Morning 39
Dinner for Uncle Albert 49
Schooldays 67
"Give Us This Day Our Daily Bread" 79
Hobo Helpers 91
The Pleasant Hours 101
George, the Whitewasher 117

FAITH OF OUR FATHERS

The Thunderstorm 127
Religious Tradition, the "Law" of Amana 135

The Elders 143
My First Day in Church 151
A Sunday Walk With Grandpa 163
"It is Better to be Unmarried" 169
Amana Wedding 179
Unterredung 185
Liebesmahl 197
When Death Comes to Amana 213

NEW HORIZONS

Henry and His Paper Route 223
Money Matters 229
The Brecks, Our Friends From "Outside" 241
When Mama Went Away 247
New Adventures 257
Uncle John's Surprise 263
Forebodings 267
The "Change" is Upon Us 273

THE PARTING

The New Economy in Amana 287
Uncle John Explains 295
Emancipation Summer 303
A New Life for Mother 311
Becoming an Outsider 321
Amana Wedding, June 1942 333
The Dream Passes 343

Appendix

The Twenty-four Rules of True Godliness 355
Glossary 361

introduction

MAN'S MOST ANCIENT DREAM is his vision of an earthly utopia where an ideal way of life is pleasant, satisfying, and good. Most of us accept the dream as a dream. But there are ever a few among us who believe in its reality and seek hopefully for its fulfillment. So it is that one after another "ideal community" has come into being, flourished for a generation, or two, or three, and then faded away leaving only fragmentary evidence of having been. Yet who is to evaluate such experiments? We know only that they survive but briefly, the dreams passing with the dreamers.

The Society of True Inspirationists in Amana, Iowa, was one of the most enduring of such religious-communal enterprises. Founded a hundred years ago, under the magnetic and valid leadership of Christian Metz, it flourished for seventy-five splendid years.

11

I was born and reared in communal Amana, as were my parents. My grandparents came there to live out their lives when Christian Metz led the believers from Ebenezer, New York, in 1855. My great-grandparents crossed the Atlantic in 1843 with the 800 followers Metz brought to Ebenezer, New York, from Ronneburg in Hessen, Germany. I knew only the Amana way of life until, at age fifteen, in 1932, I left my native village to become an "outsider."

My mother could not prepare me for the new life. She had never lived away from Amana and did not know. To live in Amana in those days was to be isolated —completely. There was almost no opportunity to associate with the world beyond the boundaries of our thirty-thousand-acre tract of land and our seven villages. But this was long ago—before the days of radios, cars, and tourists and before new ideas began to erode the old order of Christian Metz.

In the years between, the communal plan has been forsaken and the Society has been reorganized on a capitalistic basis, each of the members receiving stock, signifying private ownership of a portion of the community assets.

Since leaving the Amanas, I have acquired two college degrees and am married to an "outsider." We have two children and make our home in the shadow of a modern university.

People often ask me about Amana. I can only say that my life there was a good life and the people, good people. It is a pleasure to recall my childhood as a member of the True Inspirationists. Before the spirit of Amana is gone forever, and while I still remember, I want to record my impressions of it. This is my story of Amana.

BARBARA S. YAMBURA

The title of this book is taken from one of the testimonies of the *Werkzeug* Christian Metz. It signifies the change that took place in the Society of the True Inspirationists, and the parting, or termination of their dream of an ideal way of life.

Metz, speaking for the Lord, said:

"The Lord has yet another solution to this downfall, this collapsing.... He will change His station, and there shall be a battle, a suffering, and a parting."

(Gottlieb Scheuner:
Inspirations-Historie
1817-1867, p. 517)

Amana Heritage

how Amana came to be

IF YOU HAD TRAVELED in eastern Iowa in 1917, the year of my birth, you might have found yourself in a quaint-looking village suggestive of the Old Country. Hearing the older people speak you might have imagined yourself in an out-of-the-way German *Dorf*. The *Dorf* would have been an Amana village and the language an Amana dialect.

Seven Amana villages, laid out and built up by my ancestors and other True Inspirationists back in 1855, were located within a few miles of each other, and were set "away from the world" in the midst of thirty thousand acres of choice and fertile farm land. Beauty also was there—in the sweeping hills, the shadowy woodlands, and the still Iowa River.

My home—a simple, two-storied frame building with

17

twin gables and small-paned windows—was unpainted as were all frame buildings in the Amanas. The elders (our governors) considered rebuilding to be more economical than painting since we had an abundance of free labor and free lumber but very little capital. So a visitor's first impression on sighting this rural community from a distance was the general weathered and unpainted appearance of the frame buildings. He would see, too, that the buildings were all similar. Whether of wood, native sandstone, or locally made brick, the same simple basic plan of two-storied gabled buildings with small-paned windows had been used for all. Even the neighborhood meeting halls and the larger regular church buildings matched the other buildings architecturally, looking not at all like typical churches.

The main street of each village was nothing but a country road bordered by deep open ditches and narrow wooden sidewalks. Along this street were our homes, schools, churches, and shops, though you might have had some trouble identifying them. There were no conventional store fronts, but you could find the post office or the general store or the pharmacy by the large lettered signs on the various buildings.

We had no need for retail bakeries, or groceries, or meat markets, because our food was prepared and served in community kitchens whose supplies came directly from the slaughter house, the bake shop, and the kitchen gardens. For the Amanas—Main, South, West, Middle, East, High, and Homestead—were communal villages with elders of the church responsible for the religious, social, and economic welfare of the residents. We who lived in the villages had no individual problems of housing, food, clothing, sickness or funeral expense, nor did we pay for education, recreation, church, nor for any part of our maintenance. We had no civil government, no police, no courts. The Society of Amana, into which we were born, provided for all our needs. In return, we accepted with good grace the work assigned us by the elders. At fourteen years of age, we were regarded as adults and we took our places in the scheme of community living, doing the same type of work as our parents and grandparents were doing. We wanted only to do our share honorably.

However, it was religion, rather than communal living, that distinguished the Amanas. Here was the secret of their endurance and the source of their strength as an organization. In fact, their communal living was derived from religious needs, as is shown by this paragraph taken from Article I of their Constitution and By-Laws, 1860:

> The purpose of our association as a religious Society is therefore no worldly or selfish one, but the purpose of the love of God in His vocation of grace received by us, to serve Him in the inward and outward bond of union, according to His laws and His requirements in our own consciences, and thus to work out the salvation of our souls, through the redeeming grace of Jesus Christ, in self-denial, in the obedience of our faith and in the demonstrations of our faithfulness in the inward and outward service of the Community by the power of grace, which God presents us with.

From stories of my grandparents and from the conversation of adults I learned the history and traditions of our people. The fabulous revelations of their adventures aroused in me a probing interest. My themes and reading and even my thesis in college reflected my absorption in this subject. To understand how Amana came to be, one must know something of the religious origins of the True Inspirationists:

The story begins in 18th century Germany, at that time a natural spawning ground for many sects who found fault with the practices of the Lutheran Church. The clergy of that period was preoccupied with minor points of dogma and the Bible was all but forsaken as a spiritual source. Worst of all, the clergy was known to indulge in immoral practices. Even the church buildings symbolized worldliness with their emphasis on lavish decoration and ornate architecture. Feelings of insecurity created restless yearning for spiritual reassurance.

The government, too, was criticized by weary and disgruntled citizens who objected to the endless, futile wars with their tragic casualties and burdensome taxes.

Opposing these unwholesome conditions was a handful of "rebels" known as Mystics. This spiritually discontented group searched for a closer relationship with God than could be found in the cold Lutheran rituals.

The desire for intimate communication with God soon produced a remarkable phenomenon. Certain "gifted" men and women claimed God spoke to the people through them. Therefore the testimonies they uttered were not their own thoughts but God's. They believed that as God spoke to Moses and Isaiah and Jeremiah in Biblical times, even so can He speak today, should He find persons holy enough for His divine purpose. They said:

"God can now, as well as of old, inspire men to speak and declare His Word and Will and thus act as messengers of divine teaching to the World."

It is easy to imagine the sensational quality of such performances. Who would not listen to God's spoken communications even though He used voices of men and women rather than His own? These chosen ones were called *Werkzeuge,* meaning instruments or tools of the

Lord. The idea was taken up with great enthusiasm, and many people claimed to have been visited by God until two outstanding leaders, Eberhard Ludwig Gruber and Johann Friedrich Rock, brought about order by setting up a regulated group of elders for a governing board. They formed a distinct religious sect in 1714 which came to be called the "Community of True Inspiration."

The faithfulness and devotion of the True Inspirationists through the years rested firmly on their belief in the power of the *Werkzeuge* to deliver messages directly from God. *Revelation was an accepted fact.* This one doctrine was the basis of the religion that was to lead believers to organize in Germany, migrate to Ebenezer, New York, and finally to found and sustain the Amana Colonies in Iowa.

Naturally, all testimonies were considered sacred and so were recorded by the *Werkzeuge* themselves or by their scribes. The sayings of Rock and Gruber and later Metz and Heinemann were carefully gathered together. A large number of them have been printed and bound in leather by the Amana printing shop. The *Revelations* became the "sermons" of the church services after the *Werkzeuge* passed away. Every elder owned a set of these volumes and read from them when it was his turn to preside at a service. My grandfather, who would not touch a Sunday paper or any other secular literature on the Sabbath, spent his Sundays, between church services, reading from these volumes.

It was these records that preserved the faith for future generations. Here we find the famous "Twenty-One Rules for the Examination of Our Daily Lives" (1)

---

1. Bertha Shambaugh, *Amana That Was and Amana That Is* (Iowa City, Iowa: State Historical Society, 1932).

as laid down by Gruber in 1715. The stern and sober influence of this straightforward ethical code set a pattern for living in the early days of the Inspirationists and continued to influence the habits and customs of the people of Amana in the Twentieth century. Let me illustrate with some selected rules:

1. Obey, without reasoning, God, and through God your superiors.

5. Abandon self, with all its desires, knowledge and power.

8. Live in love and pity toward your neighbor, and indulge neither anger nor impatience in your spirit.

10. Count every word, thought, and work as done in the immediate presence of God, in sleeping and waking, eating, drinking, etc., and give Him at once an account of it, to see if all is done in His fear and love.

11. Be in all things sober, without levity or laughter; and without vain and idle words, works, or thoughts; much less heedless or idle.

13. Bear all inner and outward sufferings in silence, complaining only to God; and accept all from Him in deepest reverence and obedience.

16. Have no intercourse with worldly-minded men; never seek their society; speak little with them, and never without need; and then not without fear and trembling.

17. Therefore, what you have to do with such men do in haste; do not waste time in public places and worldly society, that you be not tempted and led away.

18. Fly from the society of women-kind as much as possible, as a very highly dangerous magnet and magical fire.

20. Dinners, weddings, feasts, avoid entirely; at the best there is sin.

21. Constantly practice abstinence and temperance, so that you may be as wakeful after eating as before.

22

On July 4, 1716, the "Twenty-Four Rules for True Godliness, and Holy Conduct" were received by the community in the form of a revelation through Johann Adam Gruber, son of Eberhard Ludwig Gruber. These rules became the basis of the faith for the Inspirationists and are still the foundation on which the whole religious structure is erected. During my recent translation of them from the German, I appreciated that apparently their main objective was to keep the members faithful and at the same time provide for a training program for young people (see Appendix).

We in Amana were well aware of these Rules for they were read to us in church each year on the Sunday preceding Thanksgiving Day in order that we might give them "careful regard and sincere observation." The Thanksgiving Day service was considered a service of renewal of the Covenant which was climaxed by "hand and mouth" as each adult member proceeded to shake hands with the elders. This was considered the holiest of all church services and therefore the one from which a "sinner's" absence would be most conspicuous if he had been banned from church.

Rock and Gruber soon had many followers—men and women of all social standings. They sent missionaries throughout southern Germany and Switzerland and established many small congregations. The leaders preached in city streets, in palace yards, in inns, in courts, and even in churches while the clergymen were conducting services. They naturally suffered much persecution for this and were fined and imprisoned, stoned, and sent out of the city, province, or country. By 1720 definite meeting places were established, most of them in Hesse, which seemed to enjoy more religious freedom than the other German provinces.

23

In the meantime, wars were raging throughout Europe and a state of apathy existed everywhere. Interest began to lag after the death of Gruber in 1728 and Rock in 1749. The elders kept up the practices as long as they could, but in the absence of inspired leaders, worldly ideas took over, and the society was almost entirely lost.

Little is to be said of the True Inspirationists from the time of Rock's death in 1749 until 1817, but in that year a dramatic reawakening occurred.

It was at Bischweiler in Alsace that Michael Krausert, a journeyman tailor, became acquainted with Rock's testimonies and in them found the key to an unexplainable longing of his heart. He received the gift of inspiration in 1817 and roused the Bischweiler community from its apathy by his spirited preaching. His was the first living voice to speak directly for God since the death of Rock some seventy years before.

Krausert succeeded in sparking a remarkable reawakening, faithfully reinstating the teachings of the old-time Inspirationists. He in turn passed along the renewed faith to a young peasant maid, Barbara Heinemann, and to Christian Metz, a carpenter's son, whose grandfather had been active in the old society of Rock and Gruber. According to God's will, these two inspired "vessels" were to preserve the faith and keep it alive for the coming century. Together, they were the prophets most responsible for building and promoting the new Inspirationist communities, first in Germany, then Ebenezer, New York, and at last, in Amana, Iowa, where they died in due time and where they lie buried.

By the time Christian Metz and Barbara Heinemann became the leaders of the Inspirationists a goodly number of converts were scattered about central Europe.

24

However, these people again suffered persecution, both from the church and the state, because they were refusing to take the military oath and because they wanted their children to learn the Inspirationist's beliefs as opposed to the Lutheranism taught in the schools. As early as 1820 there was a plea to the Prince of Bavaria for more religious freedom. Annoyances were especially bad in eastern Germany, and in 1826 the Inspirationists of Schwarzenau were driven from their homes. The people at prayer meetings were stoned and their appeals for tolerance and separate schools were officially denied. When they were ordered to conform or leave the country within six months, many joined Christian Metz and the followers who had already settled in more tolerant Hesse.

Metz now became chief organizer and manager of the assembled members. He leased a castle at Marienborn as quarters for the faithful. People were attracted from all levels of society, even as was true of the original organization in the days of Rock and Gruber. The religious ideas of the sect were promoted, Metz being guided in all decisions by direct revelations from the Lord. As more room was needed, Metz contrived to lease a nearby cloister at Arnsburg in 1832.

Communal living sprang up quite naturally at these Hessian Castles—not as a religious precept but as an economic need. It became easiest to work the land together, and it was found most economical to eat together. With the Lord's direction, Metz and the elders rented woolen mills, a grist mill, and an oil mill to provide employment for the members. Rich members gave generous sums of money. Others could give only labor. Finally, some four estates were under leases to the Inspirationists, now including tradesmen, craftsmen, arti-

sans, and laborers. All were pledged to follow the teachings of the True Inspirationists.

Persecution bound the men and women together and fired their spirits for the new belief and the new way of life. They no longer existed as single combatants but as a *community*. They conducted school and religious services according to their inspired convictions. In all their vicissitudes, the Lord furnished innumerable revelations through testimonies of Christian Metz, the only active *Werkzeug* of this period. Even so, they were up against many a tough problem. Rents went up, a drought came, and the government again became uncooperative. Even liberal Hesse finally would not permit them to keep up their churches and schools. In 1841 all hope of saving the society was gone. In the midst of despair, the Lord revealed a plan (through Metz) for leading His people "towards the West, to the land which is still open to you and your faith. I am with you and shall lead you over the sea. Hold Me. Call upon Me through your prayer when the storm of temptation arises. Four may then prepare themselves. . . ."

So on September 5, 1842, a committee of four, headed by Christian Metz, sailed for New York in search of a new home. The outcome of the venture was their purchase of 5,000 acres of the Seneca Indian Reservation near Buffalo, New York. The new settlement was called Ebenezer, after the Biblical term meaning "Hitherto has God helped us."

Between 1843 and 1846 some 800 people came from Germany and Switzerland. Most of the Germans came from southwestern Germany, although there was also quite a large Saxon element. The society was formally organized under the name of "Ebenezer," with houses arranged in four villages. Later two more villages were begun in Canada and several Canadians joined the society. New members came from surrounding states, especially Ohio. Most of these people had themselves immigrated from Germany. One branch of our family came from this group.

Not all converts joined the society for religious reasons. Some were fleeing from persecution and had no better haven. Others were hard pressed for the necessities of life and this offer of spiritual as well as economic security appealed to them. They could give labor, which they had, and were not required to give cash which they had not. Others were adventurers trying out a new life and looking for a free ride to a new land where they might find wealth and excitement. A few were notorious "free loaders." One family with ten children joined, only to desert when they were safely landed in America. Actually, there were few deserters.

My paternal great-grandmother, who lived to be eighty-four, often told us fascinating stories of the migration from Germany. Some prospective members bargained with God about joining. Her own parents were in doubt as to whether to become members or not. They had a small baby and did not like to think of the long journey to America with so young a child. So when the missionary came to ask them, they said "no." Just then someone noticed that the baby had swallowed a button. His mother was frantic, fearing the baby would die, and the father, too, was frightened. Seeing the missionary praying for the baby he said they would prove their faith and their gratitude. If God saved the child they would join the colonists and go to America to help build the new home in Ebenezer, New York. The button passed through in a natural way, the baby lived, and so the parents joined the immigrants.

27

Another story tells of a widow who tried to sell her former husband's mill. There were no buyers, so she made an agreement with God that if the mill were sold she would not only come to America herself but she would bring along a poor family and pay for their passage. The mill was sold and she kept her promise.

The problem of communal ownership came up for definite settlement when the True Inspirationists sought title to land in New York. Again the Lord spoke through Christian Metz, offering an answer. Although communal possession had been sanctioned unofficially, not all of the people approved of it, especially the more well-to-do members. A plan was suggested whereby each person might buy a portion of the community real estate, according to his ability to pay, and receive interest on his investment. This plan failed before it began because of the unequal conditions of age, strength, and net worth of the members. Christian Metz and the First Brethren were alarmed over the threat of dissatisfied members to desert the society in a search for independent ways and means of their own. If the group could not be held together, Metz reflected, what would become of the religious dream of the True Inspirationists?

The outcome was a permanent constitution, drawn up in 1846. It was in German and had to be translated before it could be presented for recognition to the State Office in Albany. The new constitution called for communal sharing, all property to be owned by the society as a whole.

Now came more loud and serious protests from all sides. In vain the elders quoted St. Paul's admonition

(Acts 2:44, 45), "And all that believe were together and had all things in common; and sold their possessions and goods and parted them to all men, as every man had need." Finally, the Lord expressed His "grief and displeasure," through a testimony by Metz, over the discontent of the many members with regard to common possession. In 1854, the Lord further testified that a curse would be put upon all who refused to subscribe to communal sharing, whereas a gracious promise was offered to all who would subscribe to it. Finally the amendment was signed and the communal system adopted. It has been appropriately called "communism by revelation," for without the revelation, probably no formal agreement could have been reached.

Again, the pattern of communal living was established purely as an economic measure and not primarily as a religious practice. *Unlike Marxian communism, the system of the Inspirationists was controlled by religion.* The purpose of the communal system was to simplify the business of living so that members might have more free time for their larger calling of serving the Lord.

For the Inspirationists the solution offered by communal living proved wise and beneficial because it was a means of holding the group intact and isolated—both conditions being necessary for the survival of the religious dream. The efficient communal plan provided labor and leisure for all at a minimum cost, allowing ample time for the main objective: "a pure sacrifice to God that He may take delight in us."

With the problem of government and economic security settled, the colonists were free to develop their new communities at Ebenezer. The success of their ventures in agriculture, woolen manufacture, crafts and

29

others, speaks for the truly enterprising ability of the members.

But the outside world kept crowding in and threatened to introduce materialistic ways and ideas. Also, no more land was available for expansion in the area of Ebenezer. Realizing that the maintenance of community strength depended upon its isolation from worldliness and its ability to expand, Metz soon had another inspiration from the Lord telling him that once again the society should be moved.

Skipping pages of fascinating history of the Ebenezer community, we find that in 1854 the will of the Lord made known that the colonists, now numbering some 1,200, should migrate westward. After due exploration (including several false starts), inspiration, and negotiation, a new home was founded in Iowa, just west of Iowa City. The Ebenezer holdings were sold at considerable profit.

By 1855, the new site included some 25,000 acres of Iowa's most fertile lands, forests, rolling hills, primitive river banks and even a lotus pond. The new home was called *Amana*, meaning "believe faithfully," after a memorable song which came to Metz one day. By 1863, six villages were laid out and abuilding. In 1865, the town of Homestead was purchased for its railroad facilities and it became the seventh colony—my Amana home.

The committee of True Inspirationists who selected Amana for their new community could have found no better location had they searched the country over. They recognized that this 25,000 acre tract in Iowa County, Iowa, seemed to meet the exacting specifications

30

of Christian Metz and the elders. It promised isolation from worldly influences, being nearly inaccessible from any main traveled road. Its natural resources surpassed all other available prospective locations: The Iowa River offered a splendid source of water power; acres of heavy forest contained fine old walnut and oak trees for building homes and furniture; red and yellow clay needed only kilns to transform it into bricks; sandstone ledges along the river could be quarried for building stones; and above all, the wonderfully fertile earth laid down by the river in prior centuries waited for planting.

When the land purchase was finally consummated, the transfer of the communities from Ebenezer progressed according to careful and specific plans. Farm lands were set aside for clearing and roads were constructed to open up communication. Villages were laid out in a pattern similar to that of the former Ebenezer villages. Likewise, homes and shops were built to closely resemble those of Ebenezer. They in turn, of course, had been duplicated architecturally from the buildings the Inspirationists had known in Germany.

The dismantling and moving of the Ebenezer communities complicated the progress of operation in Iowa. The business of transferring looms from the woolen mills, farm machinery, livestock, household goods, and all sorts of furniture, fixtures, and equipment posed many a serious problem. Everything had to be loaded onto boats at Buffalo for shipping to Chicago and then reloaded for rail transport to Iowa City. Here the railroad ended. Finally oxcarts hauled the Inspirationists and their possessions onward to the Amanas.

The simultaneous process of leaving one home and establishing another progressed slowly over a period of ten years, 1855-1865. The Iowa villages were largely completed by 1860 and the society was incorporated under the state laws as an organization "not for pecuniary profit" in 1859.

The construction of the Amana canal claims special attention as a remarkable accomplishment, especially in view of the fact that the engineers who designed and dredged it were strictly amateurs. The Iowa River was tapped in such a way that the canal touched the Amanas at two spots—where the woolen mills were to be located. Horsepower was used for dredging the seven miles needed for the canal and it was graded so accurately that there was just enough fall to keep the water flowing in the right direction. Power yielded by the huge, picturesque water wheels ran the machines at the mills. The mill site is now a favorite subject for camera fans. The water from the canal is no longer required for power; however, it is still used as an auxiliary source.

Just as the colonists moved their industrial and agricultural equipment to the new communities, so did they transfer their systems of communal living. After the acceptance of the communal way of life in Ebenezer, and with the willingness of the *Werkzeuge* to give inspired direction, the problem of labor was largely solved.

Discretion seems to have played a part in regard to job assignment, for individuals worked at whatever they were best qualified to do by training and experience. Certain jobs were kept in certain families, being handed down from father to son. The elders saw to it that everyone worked, contributing to the common good a fair share of the labor. No one counted hours spent on a job. The work day lasted until the crop was in, or the rows hoed, or the lumber cut. The elders frowned on idleness, even during the evening hours. Chores, handiwork, clockmaking, furniture making and other crafts took up the leisure time.

The management of the Amana enterprise was not unlike that of modern line-staff organizations. A Council of the Brethren, made up of thirteen representatives (elders) from all the communities, served as a board of trustees and was the main governing body with authority over both temporal and spiritual affairs of the Inspirationists. Each village depended upon its own committee of elders for solutions to its local problems, such as assigning places to live, sanctioning marriages, and directing employment.

A great variety of occupations familiar to the colonists at Ebenezer reappeared in Amana. Because these villages were self-sufficient, many tasks needed doing. Everyone worked at something, as he was assigned, rendering service for the good of the society. The tinners, cabinet makers, plumbers, machinists, harness makers, and others operated little shops. They could be called upon by any of the members whenever repairs were needed, and the service was performed without charge. Major repairs had to be cleared through the Council of the Brethren. Several people worked in the village store, bakery, butcher shop, and printing shop. Other groups of workers belonged to crews like the whitewashers, who were commissioned to keep the interiors of the buildings fresh and clean with seasonal coats of Amana blue "white wash." A few members were professionally trained to be teachers, pharmacists, and doctors. Women were mainly occupied with the processing and preparing of food.

In addition to the smaller units of labor and the impressive agricultural program, the woolen mills employed large numbers of men and women and represented the main industry of the colonies. Beginning with raw wool from the sheep, all the processes of woolen manufacture were carried out, such as carding, spinning, dyeing and, finally, manufacturing the yarn into blankets and other woolen products. Amana woolens are widely distributed even today. The society depended upon profit from the operation of the woolen mills to furnish capital for necessities not produced locally.

My grandfather Guyer had charge of the shipping of the blankets and the blanket warehouse. He also made up sample cards to be shown by the salesmen. My childhood friends and I often played among the huge crates that were made and nailed shut in the warehouse. Its long corridors and many places to hide gave the warehouse top rating as a playroom.

Agriculture, too, was a business in itself, and was supervised by one man from each village, known as the "farm manager." He was assisted by a number of subordinate managers. My grandfather Schneider had charge of the farms for our village and when he died, his son (my Uncle John) replaced him, according to Amana custom.

The farm buildings were located in one end of the village and the manager lived near them. Special barns sheltered the cattle, hogs, sheep, and horses, with plenty of sheds and other storage space for the farm implements and tools. The lofts were crammed with hay.

Uncle John often allowed my brother Henry and me to play in certain parts of the barns and lots. In the winter we slid down the cattle runways on our sleds, and in the summer watched the haymaking and threshing. We sometimes had rides on the backs of the big draft horses. Amana kept no riding horses for that would

34

have been wasteful. We needed work horses to pull the plows and the delivery wagons, so we had only work horses.

In the wintertime when there was little field work to do, the crew of farm workers cut timber for the sawmill and for the wood-burning stoves. They would come through the village with big horse-drawn wagons loaded with uncut logs and dump them off, some at each house. On another day, the wood sawers would come along with a portable horse-drawn saw, leaving a pile of cut wood in our yards. The sawing of the wood was such an interesting and exciting spectacle that we all stood around the windows to watch it. It was the job of the men of the houses to chop and split the wood pieces so they could be burned in our stoves. They also stored the cut pieces in neat piles in the woodsheds. Each building had its own woodshed for that purpose.

From the time when all the members of the Society of True Inspirationists were finally moved to Amana, until the conversion to modified capitalism in 1932, known as "The Change," the communal economy proved to be most productive and successful. The co-operative system of employing all the members fully at all seasons was notably efficient and economical. Even back in Ebenezer, production methods enabled them to underprice the farmers and manufacturers in nearby Buffalo. They paid no wages and the cost of maintaining the colony was kept at a minimum, most of their food being produced right there. All expenditures were well regulated. By guarding their gains and increases in a

35

thrifty, conservative manner, the elders avoided unnecessary spending and loss of capital.

The result was that the Amana economy maintained itself in a comfortable, prosperous way, providing generously for all its members and exacting only fair labor in return. The colonies boasted a higher standard of living over a longer period than any other community on record. There were no slums; uniform housing of good quality was furnished for all. Other "free" benefits included food, clothing, medical and dental care, and even burial. No one needed life insurance, for widows and orphans were taken care of automatically. Old age problems were taken in stride; retired members were assigned apartments near their relatives and the society cared for them as usual. The Inspirationists cannot be accused of being altruistic, however, beyond the confines of their own local responsibilities. They supported no charitable institutions. Educational or cultural achievements were not incorporated in their plans for living the good life. They wanted only to insure for themselves an unhampered opportunity for worshipping God in their own way. If the motto of "work and pray" is the formula for worthwhile living, then the Inspirationists' dream was fully realized. For years, contentment abided in the Amanas. All shared the work, the material benefits, and the spiritual blessing, equally. Only a few stories point to complaints against people who shirked or did not cheerfully do as they were directed. Isolation, by geography, by a common background of European culture, by their German language, by their religious preoccupation, and by their self-sufficiency, conspired to sustain the True Inspirationists.

Into this Amana, of good earth, of prosperity, of contentment, and of True Inspiration, was I born. . . .

once upon a morning

DAYS IN COMMUNAL AMANA were pleasant, undisturbed replicas of each other.

My earliest recollections are of my mother, as she would awaken me in the morning. . . .

"Anna," mother called softly and gently. Her low-pitched voice filtered through as I lay suspended between sleeping and waking.

I opened my eyes to see her looking down at me. Her shiny black hair, neatly combed and confined in a twist at the back of her head, and her black and white calico dress covered by a large black apron, gave her the appearance of a small dark angel.

Stretching sleepily, I felt the familiar hardness of the Amana-made horse-hair mattress beneath me and sensed the friendly blueness of the tinted Amana "whitewashed" walls of the bedroom. The bright sunshine of a glorious May morning softened the color to a lovely pale blue glow. The insistent cries of baby robins came from the apple tree beneath the window, and an apple blossom fragrance scented the room.

"Are you ready to say your morning prayer?" mother asked.

With a rich sense of well-being I closed my eyes again and placed my hands together for the prayer:

"In the morning when I arise
And in the evening when I go to sleep
My eyes, Oh Lord, are looking towards Thee.
Dear Jesus, I bequeath my soul to Thee. Amen."

"Amen," she repeated after me. "Now, dress quickly so you will be ready when Grandpa comes with our breakfast."

"Yes, Mama." I learned early to be especially obedient wherever Grandpa Guyer was concerned. As I dressed, I could hear my brother, Henry, pleading with mother. It seemed that Henry was always wanting to do something mother would not allow because she was afraid Grandpa Guyer would not approve. I wondered what the argument was about this time.

I was sympathetic with Henry, for I had my own problems with mother on account of Grandpa. It seemed that whenever I wanted to do what my friends were permitted to do, mother would say,

"Oh, my no! You can't do that—Grandpa wouldn't like it!"

I was not allowed to bob my hair, even after the fashion had been accepted generally in our villages. And when my friends began wearing knee socks, I was not free to do so; it was "sinful" to show my knees, according to Grandpa.

On this particular morning I had a thought! Maybe while mother was busy with Henry she might not notice me, so I could roll my stockings. It was not easy—confining so much cottony bulk with a mere elastic garter, but at last I managed, leaving my knees feeling naked and exposed. The awkward, protruding rolls rubbed together as, with some effort, I walked sedately across the hall into our dining-living room where mother was setting the table. Henry was saying—

"But, Mama, I need money for a bicycle, and if you would let me run a paper route I could buy one. Besides, most all the fellows have a bicycle except me."

Mother did not answer. She had already had her say on this subject. At the washstand in the corner, I touched my fingers gingerly in the cold water someone had left in the basin and wet my face ever so little before wiping on the long roller towel. I gave it a quick yank, and roller and all came crashing to the floor. As I stooped over to pick up the pieces, mother spoke sharply.

"Anna, what have you done to your stockings?"

I faced her bravely. "I rolled them, Mama. All the other girls have knee stockings; I want so much to have them, too. And besides, it will probably be real hot today."

"Have you forgotten that Grandpa Guyer is an elder and does not approve of girls showing their knees? Now quickly, before he comes, go back to your room and fix those stockings."

"Oh, Mama, do I have to?" I asked hopefully.

"Yes, you have to," Henry chimed in vindictively.

41

"Hush, Henry," mother gave him a threatening look.

These humiliating situations might not have come up so often if we had not lived in the upstairs of Grandpa Guyer's house, and if he had not been an elder of our village. Of course he did not own the house for no one in the Amanas owned property personally. This house had been mother's childhood home, and when she married, the elders assigned the upstairs rooms to her and father for their home. After father died, when Henry and I were very small, we three stayed on as before. I only knew that Grandpa lived right there in our house and Henry and I were never allowed to forget it.

Back in my bedroom, I pulled the long, black stockings to the above-the-knee position, and hated them. Knowing that I had lost the battle, I took my stand at my favorite window to watch the procession going and coming through the kitchen house door.

Most of the windows in our second story rooms were large and high, fitting closely under the eaves of the roof. One small window in the gable end of our dining room came all the way to the floor. By squatting before it, I could see the yard below: Narrow bands of neatly cut lawn ran close to the walks and borders. The wide-spreading kitchen garden formed a beautiful pattern of great-leaved rhubarb, broad, crinkly kale, solid, massive potato plants, and many other richly green vegetables in converging weedless rows. Borders of red tulips, yellow daffodils, and purple iris gave a touch of welcome decoration, wherever space permitted. Then there were the grape trellises—story-high frames attached to the houses, made sturdy and wide to support the abundant growth of the grape vines. They were like huge screens, hiding the buildings, and were in keeping with the tradition that everything ornamental must also be productive.

But I was interested in the kitchen house. I had already learned to watch it at mealtimes for all our food came from there. From my window, I could see all the people hurrying to the door with their long, narrow, covered baskets, one person coming from each home to have pots and kettles filled with food to be taken back for all to eat. Then, one by one, they came forth, mostly women, their bodies bending slightly with the weight they carried. I knew them all and amused myself by calling their names as each passed in the continuing procession, day after day, year in and year out, to share the common fare.

Single men and women not belonging to families were served their meals at the kitchen house. Grandpa Guyer ate there and he always brought our breakfast to us when he had finished. The other meals mother would get. I watched for him and as soon as his tall slender figure appeared, I ran to tell mother—

"He's coming, Mama, he's coming."

"Anna, don't be noisy. Little girls should be thinking quiet, thankful thoughts early in the morning."

"Yes, Mama, but I'm hungry."

Henry had dashed for the door. He was much bigger than I, even though he was only two years older. "I get to open it today," he boasted.

"Then I get to help with the basket," I said eagerly.

Henry waited, holding the door open for Grandpa,

and I stood by, first on one foot, then the other, watching for the basket.

"Good morning," said Grandpa seriously.

"Good morning, Grandpa," we chanted.

"Put it here, Father," said mother, indicating a chair by the table. Grandpa released the basket carefully and sat in his favorite rocker. He held his hat in his long, slender hands and turned it round and round thoughtfully. The thin white fringe of hair made a neat circle around his pink bald spot.

I took the fitted covers from the little kettles and mother began reheating the coffee and fried potatoes above the blue flames of the kerosene stove.

"What is the news from the kitchen house this morning? Did you hear how Grandpa Schneider is getting along?" mother asked.

"Not good, not good," he told her. We knew from the way he spoke that there was no good news. For a week our Grandpa Schneider had been sick, sleeping night and day. We had not been allowed to visit him and had waited anxiously for the daily report, which usually traveled by way of the kitchen house.

Mother waited for Grandpa to go on. At last she asked—"What's to be done?"

"They have sent for his brother Albert."

"Our Uncle Albert?" Henry could not conceal his excitement over the possibility of seeing Uncle Albert. Even I knew about him—how he had been discontented with life in Amana and had left the colonies years ago, moving to a faraway town. From the presents he sent his sisters and my mother, we guessed that he was quite rich.

"Will he come?" Mother stopped stirring the sizzling, frying potatoes, her spoon poised in mid air.

"Yes, he will come tomorrow, and will stay several days."

No one spoke as we considered the vast importance of having Uncle Albert visit in Amana. He was practically an outsider.

"Will Aunt Ella come too?" I asked curiously.

"We think so, but we do not know."

"Where will they stay?" mother wondered. "They can't stay at Schneiders', with Grandpa so sick."

"They will stay with Albert's sisters—at their kitchen house." Grandpa cleared his throat hesitatingly.

"It would be nice for them to take some of their meals with their other relatives, so they wouldn't have to eat at the kitchen house all the time," mother protested.

"Will they eat with us too?" I asked, wondering how it would be to share a family meal with visitors.

"Yes, Anna, we will have them, too. He was father's uncle and is your great uncle," mother explained patiently, as she scraped the golden-brown potatoes from the little iron skillet into a bowl.

"We must get ready," was all she said but I knew we would be turning our house upside down in honor of such an occasion.

"Will we use the parlor?" I asked hopefully.

"Yes, Anna. We must clean and dust it."

"I'll help," I offered.

"And we will use my wedding presents—the linen, the dishes, and the silver—after all these years," she continued, as if thinking aloud.

How wonderful! Never had we used the beautiful dishes mother displayed in the dining room cabinet, for we had never entertained at mealtime.

"I wonder what day they will come to eat with us?"

45

Mother was checking over in her mind the menus we were served, according to the days of the week. The food we would serve the guests would, of course, come from the kitchen house.

"You will have to talk with Caroline and Katherine about that." This was not Grandpa's problem.

"I only hope we don't have them on Tuesday. The *Mehlspeise* meal is not good for company," said mother. "Why, we might have only pancakes or potato dumplings. They are used to more than that."

"Yes, but it could be doughnuts, or cream puffs, or even waffles," I reminded her, for my favorite of the meals was the one with waffles, served with heavily sugared strawberries or cherries. It was a game to fit the fruit into the "squares" of the waffles. We always looked forward to Tuesdays, because on this day we did not have to eat meat and potatoes. We considered the *Mehlspeise* a special treat.

"And that terrible soup." Mother made a face showing her dislike for it.

"The Tuesday soup is not always bad," said Grandpa.

"Oh, but it will most likely be pancake soup. We had pancakes last week. If you could see the cooks make it —of left-over pancakes chopped into little slivers and boiled in warmed-over broth! Well, anyway, I hope we do not have Uncle Albert for Tuesday dinner. I prefer Monday or Wednesday, when we have 'new' meat."

"Sophie, it is ungrateful to talk so. We should be thankful that we have so much to eat in Amana and are never hungry." Grandpa rose to go, his tall slender height nearly equalling that of the door. "Sophie, don't fuss too much," he added. "Albert is really one of us, even though he left us seventeen years ago."

46

"Come, children, take your places at the table," mother reminded us about our breakfast.

"Henry, let me see your hands." Reluctantly Henry brought his hands out in front, palms up. "I thought so. Now go to the washstand and wash them carefully—with soap." Henry's shoulders gave the least bit of a shrug as he slouched off to the corner. Mother poured coffee into our heavy cups.

"Put lots of milk in mine," Henry called.

"Henry, remember to say 'please.' "

"Please," he added belatedly.

"Put lots of sugar in mine, please." I did not like milk.

Grandpa was standing there, leaning restfully against the door frame and watching us with his blue, blue eyes. Even if he was an elder and strict, I liked Grandpa.

Mother waited for us to fold our hands in our laps and be quiet for the blessing.

Henry and I repeated together:

"Come Lord Jesus be our guest
And let these gifts to us be blest. Amen."

Grandpa left so quietly we did not notice.

dinner for Uncle Albert

HAVING A VISITOR was more exciting and more unusual even than Christmas, or *Liebesmahl,* or anything else that happened in Amana. Never before had an "outsider" come to our home for a meal, nor could we remember when the parlor had last been used. Just being permitted to go inside the closed, darkened, precious parlor, was itself a holiday.

"When will we dust the parlor?" I asked for the tenth time.

"Right now, Anna. I am ready. Here, take a clean cloth—and take one for Henry, too."

We rushed to the closed door, and waited. As mother pushed it back, a damp, musty, unpleasant odor struck our nostrils and we hesitated about going in. Carefully, she raised the drawn shades and opened a window. The

49

white lace curtains floated gently in the breeze. The chairs, the horsehair sofa, the pictures—everything was covered with dust and we could have drawn pictures on the "old chest." Henry stood looking at the chest, for it was our dearest treasure. It had been made in Germany as a masterwork by one of our ancestors, an apprenticed cabinet maker.

"I wish I could make a chest like this," said Henry, admiring its satiny rich brown finish. It had three large drawers and was inlaid and veneered over its entire surface with contrasting woods.

"Maybe someday you can try," said mother. "Just now we must get on with the dusting. I will take the pretty things from the top of the chest and these you must not touch." Lovingly, mother dusted the two frosted pastel green glass vases.

"Is that real gold decoration?" Henry asked.

"Yes, it's called 'gold leaf,' " said mother as she set them gingerly on a nearby table.

"Are these the vases Grandma brought from Germany?" I wanted to hear all those wonderful stories again.

"No, Anna, not Grandma, but your great-grandmother brought them from her home in Germany when she came to Ebenezer, New York, and then later to Amana."

"How old are the vases?" Henry wanted to know.

"I'm not sure, but very old—at least a hundred years. Now watch out for the swan. It came from Germany too."

The graceful white china swan "boat" carrying a lovely maiden on its back was to me the most beautiful of all.

50

"This spoon-holder set belonged to my mother's grandmother." Mother proudly held the rose-colored glass pieces, elegant with old, highly engraved silver.

"And this grape dish was a present from Uncle Albert." The bowl, shaped like a huge bunch of grapes, shimmered with the iridescence of pearls. "We will put it in front so Uncle Albert will see we like it."

Henry and I stood awed by the splendor of the gorgeous treasures.

"Now, be very careful as you dust the chest."

At last we had dusted everything in the parlor and it seemed to be a different room. I could hardly believe that it really belonged to us. Mother punched up the cross-stitched pillows on the sofa and already had her mind on her next big problem—the meal.

We had almost forgotten Grandpa Schneider and his critical condition, so interested had we become in our prospective visitors. The uncles, the aunts, Grandma, and the cooks in the neighborhood kitchen houses could talk of nothing else. Uncle Albert and Aunt Ella had been away for so long they had almost become outsiders. Had they not returned occasionally for visits we would not have known them.

They had been in town several days but I hadn't seen them. General concern for Grandpa Schneider and the anxiety of the sick room isolated Henry and me at home. It was good to have something special to think about—like a meal for visitors. Never before had mother made such elaborate preparations for anything.

As bad luck would have it, Uncle Albert and Aunt

Ella decided on Tuesday as the day for dinner with us. Mother was inconsolable.

"Tuesday! If only they would have come some other day. I am ashamed to serve them only *Mehlspeise,* and no meat or potatoes! And the soup, oh that horrible soup!"

"Nobody eats the soup anyway so I don't see why that makes any difference—and most everybody likes the *Mehlspeise."* Henry tried to be cheerful about it.

But mother went about her work as though she did not know we were there. I had never seen her so worried. That is, she was worried until she had her wonderful idea. Suddenly her face lighted up, and we could hardly wait to hear.

"I have just thought of something." She fairly beamed.

"What?" We both wanted to know.

"I remember that Uncle Albert liked salsify so well when he lived here that he used to eat all the family serving. I will give him salsify."

"Where are you going to get salsify in May?" Henry was the practical one.

"I must go talk with Mina, the kitchen boss. There might be some left." There was an air of importance and revolt about her as she tied her sunbonnet in place.

"You come with me, Anna, we may have to go to the cellar to find some salsify."

"I don't see how Uncle Albert can like that stuff." I hated this awful-tasting stringy vegetable, especially after seeing the withered, dried roots as they came from the cellar during the winter.

*   *   *

Our visit with *Baas* Mina began very casually, but finally mother got around to her topic of greatest interest.

"And what will the *Mehlspeise* be this coming Tuesday?"

"Doughnuts and applesauce will be for Tuesday," said Mina.

"I was hoping for chicken and noodles," said mother, hopefully. "I wish we could have a meat dish for Uncle Albert and Aunt Ella."

"Doughnuts and applesauce are good enough for us and they're good enough for Albert and his Ella. Just because he is an outsider now, he is not so fine that he cannot eat what his mother and father and grandparents ate." Mina bristled as if she were being criticized. But mother persisted in her quiet way.

"I remember that Uncle Albert especially liked salsify." No response from Mina, only a glum look. "Do we have any left in the cellar?"

"Sophie, you know that salsify is all shriveled and dried up by May. If Albert wants salsify, let him come to Amana in the fall." Mina went back to kneading a huge bowl of dough. The assistant cooks were now listening eagerly. Mother, though extremely shy, intended to go after that salsify.

"I think I will just take a look in the cellar and see if I can find some."

"You will have to go all the way to the back and look through the carrot bin. The salsify was buried with the carrots, and it is pitch dark in there." Mina tried to frighten mother.

"I know," said mother. "I'll take the lantern, and Anna will come with me."

Realizing that mother was not coming off too well,

I did not raise a question about weasels. Once mother had seen one in a dark cellar and it had scared her so that she had hated cellars since that day. She had impressed us, too, with her descriptions of this small furry animal "that looked like a snake."

I bravely followed mother outside to the cellar entrance. The door was flush with the ground and slanted gently from the building. It took both of us to open it.

"Mama, will we see a weasel in the cellar?" Now I was frightened.

"I don't know. We'll light a lantern and that will scare them away."

Mother took the lantern from a nail, high on the wall and prepared to light the wick with a match she had been carrying in her hand all the while. I dreaded the excursion into the damp, dark, smelly caverns and yet I was fascinated by the thrill of its possibilities.

The cellar extended under the whole expanse of the kitchen house and on even beneath the private lodgings of the Glücks. It was cut up into dozens of small rooms, each equipped with shelves and bins for keeping the winter stores needed to feed forty some people. A few of the excavated rooms had been cemented; most of them were just dirt holes.

To find the salsify, as Mina had warned, we had to explore the length of the cellar to the very end. First came the shelves, laden with hundreds of jars of fruit—reminding me of hours spent pitting cherries, shelling peas, stemming strawberries. In the lantern light the rich dark red of beets contrasted colorfully with the yellow of peach halves and the whiteness of pears.

"Stay close to me, Anna. You might get lost," said mother, as if I were not hanging on to her skirt already. Now we turned the eerie light of the lantern into the next room. A fetid, acrid smell of fermentation mingled with that of decaying fruit and vegetables. Before the light illuminated the barrels of sauerkraut with their overflowing, caked brine, we knew where we were by the sour odor. We passed that room quickly and looked in the next. Apples, shriveled and dry, lay scattered on the shelves, as though an army had been through and left only the useless ones. In turn, our lantern showed us the milkroom where troughs of cold water supposedly kept the milk cool. The sour smell oppressed and almost nauseated me. Next came the cubbyhole where the cheeses were ripening. I kept brushing cobwebs from my hair and face. Once, something seemed to run across my foot and my heart nearly stopped beating. We were far away from sunlight and lost in a cavernous black hole, but still mother kept moving from room to room, looking for the bin where carrots and other roots were kept. Finally we reached the very last one. Mother set the lantern on a protruding ledge and began digging with her hands into a pile of dirt on the floor by our feet.

"This must be the mound for the carrots and salsify." She spoke as if to herself.

Her hand came up with a shriveled, limp root. I could not be sure what it was. Mother smelled it and brought it close to the light of the lantern.

"A carrot," she commented with disgust. "Now there must be some salsify here somewhere."

She dug into another corner of the mound and showed me another specimen, looking much like the first.

"Ah, that's it. Salsify," she said. "If I can just find a few more."

She dug patiently at different points in the dirt and

soon had eight pathetic roots that resembled roots of a tree. Just as she stooped to pick up the lantern, she gave a blood-curdling yell and grabbed me frantically.

"Anna, it's the weasel."

"Where?"

"It ran across my hand. I felt it."

I froze with fear of some unknown monster and could not move. Mother recovered first—

"Come, Anna, let's get out of here." She clasped the lantern firmly in one of her hands and took hold of my hand with the other. Away we ran for the entrance. It seemed miles to the lighted opening. Out in the sunshine, our fright vanished as a nightmare. We looked at each other in the bright light of day, and behold! We had come out of the cellar without the salsify! Mother burst into hysterical laughter. Without a word, she took up the lantern again and with sheer determination we retraced our steps to recover our lost treasure.

Monday came and mother brought us our dinner from the kitchen house, as usual. Even if I had not known it was Monday, I could have guessed it by the *"Inlauf"* soup I saw in one of the little kettles. I hated this stringy mixture. It was made of egg batter run through a sieve into a boiling broth. Then Sunday's leftover rice soup was added to it. However, Monday was a good day, as menus came, for we had pot roast of beef with a creamed vegetable as the side dish.

Mother examined all the food critically.

"No," she said. "There is nothing here that we can use for Tuesday. Already, I have saved three eggs from our breakfasts and I did get a little chocolate from the store for 30¢ worth of credit." Mother thoughtfully placed the little kettles on the kerosene flames for re-heating the food, and continued.

"Tuesday morning, maybe, we will have three more eggs and that will be enough for a big chocolate pie for the company. I am putting all the butter away to make the pie crust. If we keep all our rations of butter, eggs, and milk until tomorrow, I will have about a half a pound of butter and enough of everything I need for the pie."

"It's a good thing they don't send us cooked eggs," said Henry.

"Mama, won't *Baas* Mina let you have some lard?" I asked.

"No, Anna. She cannot give me any food except our share—just what everyone else receives. Of course, she will let us have extra servings of the Tuesday dinner for Uncle Albert and Aunt Ella, but that is all."

"I wish we had all the food we wanted in our own house so we could fix a beautiful dinner for them," I said wistfully.

"Anna, we will have a good dinner. You will see. We have saved our cold ham from Sunday supper so they will have meat with the *Mehlspeise* meal. And," she added triumphantly, "Uncle Albert will have his sal-sify."

"How does it look today?" Henry asked. We had all been keeping an eye on the eight shriveled roots soaking in a bucket of water on the floor. Henry took a peek. "It sure looks terrible to me."

"It will be good when I get it fixed. You'll see. Uncle Albert will like it."

"Mama, why do we have to give Uncle Albert sal-sify?" I began to wonder if I was overlooking something.

"He liked it when he used to live in Amana. It is hard to find on the outside. If we did not raise it here we would not have it either. Besides, Uncle Albert says it tastes like oysters and he likes oysters."

Never having eaten oysters, the explanation meant nothing to me. I would go along with mother on the salsify. If she said Uncle Albert liked it, then we must have it for him.

We ate our dinner without much enthusiasm. Henry said—

"I don't like bread without butter."

"Here, use some of this nice strawberry jam," mother offered.

It seemed that Tuesday, *the Day,* would never come, but slowly time rolled around and I wakened to the wonderful aroma of chocolate as it penetrated even to my bedroom. Mother had said she would bake the pies early on Tuesday and this meant she had been up since five o'clock. Oh, this wonderful day—bringing us exciting visitors *and* chocolate pie too. Only once before had I tasted chocolate pie. It was for mother's birthday and then, too, we had hoarded our rations for several days in order to have the required ingredients.

"Mama, you made two chocolate pies!" I could not believe it.

"Yes," mother answered with real satisfaction. "We will each have a big piece."

"I hope so," said Henry, his mouth watering.

"I will leave the pies here on the table and you children must not even come near them. Do you understand?"

While we were admiring the pies, we heard Grandpa's footsteps on the stairs and Henry and I flew to the door. Even he seemed to be a little excited, though it was hard to tell about Grandpa. He was always so stern and said so little. We exchanged greetings with him as usual and waited for him to speak.

"And how is he today?" Mother referred to Grandpa Schneider. She took the basket from her father and put it on a chair.

"Just the same. He has never wakened from his sleep." Grandpa shook his head ominously. "It's ten days already."

"What did the doctor say? Will it be today?" mother inquired anxiously.

"He did not say," answered Grandpa.

I wondered whether mother really wanted to know about Grandpa Schneider or whether she wanted assurance that "the meal" would really be served after all. Grandpa regarded the pies disapprovingly. He clearly saw no reason for all mother's fussing about "outsiders."

"Come, children, take your places for breakfast. We will not reheat the food today. There is too much to do." She did not need to prod us. We stood ready to help with anything she asked. Grandpa vanished in his usual quiet way and we sat down at the table. When breakfast was over, Henry and I waited for mother's signal for the closing prayer.

> "Lord Jesus, Thee we praise and thank
> For the food we ate and drank. Amen."

Hurrying from the table, we took our dishes with us to the wooden trough that served as a sink.

"When do we fix the salsify?" We could think of nothing else.

"As soon as the dishes are done."

At last she said—"Now, we are ready."

First, she brought out a bowl of buttermilk. Just how she had wangled it from *Baas* Mina, I never knew. She explained that you had to have buttermilk, or vinegar, for if you did not keep the salsify out of the air in this way, it turned brown immediately. She took the precious, stumpy, dark brown roots from the water and scraped the skin from them. Then she immersed them in the buttermilk. Mother talked as she worked.

"Uncle Albert was jolly when he was young. He always liked to laugh," she told us.

"Does he know any jokes?" Henry had heard a few from the handy men who worked around the kitchens and were "outsiders."

"I don't think he knows jokes. Besides, we are not supposed to tell jokes in Amana," mother answered as she worked. "I'll leave the salsify in the buttermilk until time to put it on the stove. And remember, we mustn't open the kettle while the salsify cooks."

"It has a funny smell." I still could not get excited about these horrible looking greyish hunks.

"Quick, children, help me with the table. I have everything ready." Mother pulled the table from the wall and raised the second leaf, then she spread a beautiful snowy linen cloth, patterned with large tulips and scrolls, over the blue-checked oilcloth we used every day.

"Mama, where did you get it?" I asked admiringly.

"It was a wedding gift to your father and me—from *Tante* Maria." Mother's face reflected her unabashed pride in her lovely possessions. "So was this set of white and gold china. It comes from France."

"Anna, I have washed the dishes and you may put the plates around. Take only one at a time," she cautioned.

I was thrilled to touch these precious pieces. The exquisite translucent cups reminded me of large egg shells. Mother unwrapped a towel and brought out the brightly polished silver knives and forks to be used instead of our black-handled steel ones.

"Was this a wedding present too?" Even Henry was impressed.

"Yes, Henry. Don't ask me any more questions. I must hurry, for Mina will be angry if I am late for my work at the kitchen house this morning. She thinks we are making too much fuss about Uncle Albert."

We stood back, surveying the elegantly set table and thought it the most beautiful one in the world. The big clock on the wall chimed eight times. Mother reached for her sunbonnet and hurried to leave for the kitchen house.

"Children, listen carefully. When the clock strikes ten, pour off most of the buttermilk from the salsify but leave a little and add water to cover it well. Put it on the end flame. I will leave the fire burning low so you will not need to touch a match. Do you understand?" She addressed the question to Henry.

"Yes, Mama," he answered.

"Anna, you may put on the new gingham dress I made for you, and both of you sit in the swing until I come back. I will be home early today. There are no vegetables to peel on *Mehlspeise* day." She had tied the strings of her bonnet under her chin and the doorknob turned in her hand.

"Be good children!" This was her usual "goodbye" to us.

That morning was one of the longest I can remember. Henry and I sat in the old wooden swing with its facing seats and played all the quiet games we could think of. We waited and waited. At last, when mother came back from the kitchen house, we dashed to meet her.

"You children watch at the little window and tell me when you see Aunt Ella and Uncle Albert coming up the street. I have many things to do." We ran to keep up with her.

Mother checked the flame under the salsify pot, but she did not remove the lid to peek in the pot. While we helped mother arrange chairs, we heard the door open downstairs. Henry and I ran for hiding places; mine behind the open door of the parlor and Henry's behind the door of the dining room.

So this pretty lady with the pink hat and fancy grey suit was Aunt Ella and this tall, good-looking, jolly fellow with the handsome gold watch chain was Uncle Albert!

"Hello, Sophie, it is good to see you." He smacked a big kiss on mother's cheek and she drew back with embarrassment.

"Come, we have opened the parlor for you," said mother graciously.

"The parlor! Oh, no, not for me. What do you want to do, make me feel like company? I won't be treated that way." He gave her a gentle pat on the arm.

Mother's face showed some disappointment. Aunt Ella came to the rescue.

"Since Sophie has it open, let's sit there until dinner. Maybe we would be in her way in the dining room?"

"All right, all right." Uncle Albert was a wonderful

person. I thrilled just to be near him and his booming, deep musical voice.

"Where are the children?" he inquired.

"Anna, Henry, come, Uncle Albert and Aunt Ella are here," mother called us very properly. Shyly we came forth.

"Anna, Anna, I had no idea you would be such a big girl." I could not bear to look at him while he shook my hand.

"Can't you say something to Uncle Albert?" mother prompted me.

"Yes," I finally answered, "I grow a little every afternoon."

Uncle Albert roared with laughter and turned to Aunt Ella.

"What do you think of that, Ella? She grows a little every afternoon!"

Aunt Ella put her arm around my shoulder as no one had ever done before. There was a delightful fragrance about her and she was adorned with lots of lace and ribbons. Perfume and fancy ornaments were unknown to us. She was saying—

"Never mind, Anna, it is good that you grow. Who wants to be a little girl all her life?" I sensed her sympathy and liking for me.

"I think Uncle Albert has something for you." He had caught her signal and was fishing a couple of small packages from his pocket.

"Of course, here is a little present for you, Anna, and one for Henry too."

We stammered our "thank-yous" and held the packages.

"Go ahead, children," encouraged Aunt Ella. "You may open them."

Henry began tearing at the wrappings. "I hope mine's candy."

"Henry!" Mother was embarrassed.

"I am glad if you wanted candy," said Aunt Ella beaming.

"And I wanted candy, too." I could smell the wonderful chocolate bar. "We almost never have candy," I added.

"Put it away for now, children. Dinner is ready," said mother.

I looked at Henry and he looked at me. We would have given most anything to have eaten all that candy right then and there. We carried it with us to the table but mother made us put it out of sight.

At the table, Henry and I stammered through the opening prayer. Uncle Albert said, "Amen."

"I am sorry this is *Mehlspeise* day," began mother, after we had finished our soup. She passed the fat, raised doughnuts. By each plate was a large side dish of applesauce.

"As I remember, *Mehlspeise* day was always my favorite," said Uncle Albert obligingly.

"But I have something extra today," said mother proudly. "Here is some ham. Please do have the ham." We had been told not to mention saving it from our Sunday supper.

"Oh, thank you, Sophie. You should not have bothered about us this way," said Uncle Albert.

"It was no bother." I had never seen mother so pleased. "And I have another little surprise for you. Please excuse me a minute." We waited eagerly to see Uncle Albert's pleasure when she brought the salsify to him.

"Now, what can it be?" he said. "Maybe that tempting, delicious-looking chocolate pie?" He could see the pie on the side table.

"No, this is just for you." Proudly mother set the bowl of rather sad-looking creamed salsify before him. "Your favorite dish!"

"Not salsify?" He sniffed delicately. "No, it can't be salsify!"

"Taste it and see," mother prompted.

"Sophie, this is a wonderful thing for you to do. But I cannot be selfish and eat it all by myself." Generously he offered the bowl around the table.

"But we don't like salsify," I explained.

"Sooooo," laughed Uncle Albert, his voice booming around the room. "You don't like it?" We all joined in his infectious laughter though we did not know what was so funny.

"Now I will tell you a little secret—I don't like it either."

"You don't like it?" Mother was almost speechless with surprise.

"No, Sophie, I don't like it. But—I must have liked it once upon a time, because everyone serves it to me now. Do you know how many times I have had salsify this week?" He held up four fingers of his right hand.

"Four times! Four times in four days I have had a big bowl of creamed salsify all to myself." He was laughing so hard he could hardly talk. Mother looked as though she might cry.

Then he turned to her.

"Sophie! Thank you, my dear Sophie, for all your thought and trouble. Would you mind terribly if I eat doughnuts and applesauce instead? I'm starved for some of these wonderful Amana doughnuts."

65

Never had we heard such laughter at our house and never again did we eat salsify without remembering Uncle Albert.

schooldays

THE TRUE INSPIRATIONISTS had simple but definite no-
tions about the education of their children. The village
school served several purposes: it satisfied the state law
by preparing students for the seventh and eighth grade
county examinations; it was a place to keep children
while parents worked; it taught children how to read
German so that they could participate in the church
services; and finally, it disciplined them in the catechism.
Formal education consisted of attending a one-roomed,
eight-grade school, six days a week, winter and summer.
Actually, we had to remain in school until we were fourteen, regardless of whether we had completed the eight
grades or not; at fourteen we were considered adults and
assigned to regular jobs. All of us, including the elders,
received this standardized instruction. The same text-

books, catechisms, and for years even the same teachers, were the lot of all students, from generation to generation. The elders made a few exceptions. In order to have doctors, dentists, teachers, and pharmacists for each community, a few students were sent outside for professional training, but only as vacancies seemed likely to occur. The society paid their expenses but made it clear that they were to return and serve in the communal way, without pay, when they were graduated.

Most of us remember a certain teacher above all others who taught us during our early years. For me there was Brother Schlegel, my first teacher, a plump, red-faced little old man with a fringe of white hair. I have vivid recollections of him and my Amana School. . . .

There was one thing you could count on and that was excitement. Each morning I trotted off with Henry to the schoolhouse at the other end of our village. We started early so we could play with other children before the bell rang, and so that I could meet my chum, Elsie.

"I wonder how old Brother Schlegel is feeling today? He surely had a bad time yesterday." Henry was apt to grumble about school.

"I think you big boys are real mean to him. Mama would be very much ashamed if she knew how you tease him."

"*Ach,* he's too old to teach school. Why, he's probably seventy years old. Just think he even taught our grandmas and grandpas."

"Mama says he was a brilliant scholar when the elders brought him over from Germany."

"Sure," said Henry, "but that was fifty years ago."

"I don't think he's so bad," said Elsie.

"Look at the way he can't make the boys behave."

"Well, look at how many there are," Elsie defended. "Twenty-two altogether, counting boys and girls, and that includes all eight grades."

Now we were in the schoolyard and Brother Schlegel was standing on the step, ready to ring the bell. November morning air was crisp and snow flurries began to blow around us.

"Good morning, Henry," beamed Brother Schlegel. "And Anna," he touched my tow-headed pigtails, "your hair is getting almost as white as mine." He laughed at his little joke but I was embarrassed and sidled off to be with Elsie.

Just then Michael Kramer came toward us leading little Adolph Klotz to Brother Schlegel. Adolph was crying and his clothes were all wet in front.

"*Ach,* what happened?" asked Brother Schlegel.

"Martin threw a dipper of water at him."

"*Junge, Junge,*" Brother Schlegel scolded, shaking his finger at Martin. Martin came running from the pump to defend himself.

"I didn't mean to. I never knew he was there." Martin did not want to be sent home, for his father would punish him.

"Well, Adolph, you go home and get some dry clothes on—and hurry back. Martin, you be more careful next time."

Someone was always getting soaked at the pump. And sometimes, one of the boys would hide the granite dipper. Then no one could have a drink.

The bell rang and we found our places in line. We came to attention, hands to foreheads and recited in German-accented English with singsong voices: "I 'bledge' allegience to the flag of the United States of America. . . ."

I never looked up at the flag, waving high on the pole, without remembering the Sunday morning after one Halloween when a bicycle was strung way up at the top. No one knew who managed to do it, or how. But Brother Schlegel was furious because he had to take it down before church. Besides being made conspicuous, he had had to carry out a very worldly assignment on the Sabbath.

When we finished pledging allegiance, Brother Schlegel said, "Now, march."

The big boys at the end of the line were tripping each other as usual. There was a noisy tromping of hard-soled shoes on the bare pine floors and each of us tried to be first at his desk. Mine fairly swallowed me up; only my head appeared above it while tall John could barely fold his long legs and arms in and around his.

"Now everyone get busy. I will start with sixth grade spelling today. First graders, draw pictures on your slates; second graders, do your arithmetic; third graders, study geography; and fourth graders, study agriculture. You must learn the agriculture well so you can help with the farm crews when you grow up. Fifth graders, study your history."

That same old history book! It was the one Brother Schlegel had given me for a reader when I was in the first grade. I don't know whether our school was too poor to buy readers or whether Brother Schlegel was too confused to know the difference. Mother tried to help me with my reading and was shocked when I came home with the history text.

"Brother Schlegel is getting too old to teach!" she exclaimed, but parents did not interfere with school affairs. We did not have a P.T.A. where problems of the school might be voiced.

Brother Schlegel was still giving directions in broken English.

"Seventh and eighth graders will have art as usual."

There was a mad scramble as books were taken from desks, the sixth graders rushed to the front of the room for recitation, and the seventh and eighth graders sauntered to the table in the back of the room where the "art collection" was kept. This series of pencil sketches for copying was our only source of knowledge about any form of art. The business of getting a sketch to work with created an appealing opportunity for wasting time and indulging in foolish antics. The changing of classes took place every fifteen minutes, so we had bedlam at least that often.

"Let's have it quiet, blease," shouted Brother Schlegel but no one paid any attention. He could not hear very well so the noise did not bother him too much. He continued in his unruffled way.

"John, you help with the recitation of the second graders."

John really had nothing to do. He was thirteen and had finished the required eight grades a year before. I felt sorry for him. He had to keep coming because of "the law," until he was fourteen. Then he could work with the men. He told us that he thought the elders were going to assign him to the farm department and he could hardly wait for the time to come.

Now the big boys began to giggle and I guessed what would happen next.

"*Ach,* where is that spelling book?" Brother Schlegel

71

peered through the lower part of his funny little glasses. He searched the row of books on the shelf high on the wall in the front of the room, mumbling to himself.

"I put it chust here yesterday, myself." Then he turned around. "Has anyone seen the spelling book, maybe?"

"No, Brother Schlegel," we chorused.

We all knew it was right there on the shelf where it belonged but it had been turned about so the labeled binding did not show. Someone did this on the sly just about every other day.

"Well, I guess we can't have spelling today. We will have to start with the reading," he said cheerfully.

Everyone in the class was delighted. Teacher could not find the book, so no spelling today!

Suddenly the room was quiet—too quiet. You could hear the wood in the potbellied stove crackling briskly as it caught fire. Then came a series of loud banging noises, as if the stove were exploding. *"Ach,* what is the matter now?" He rushed to the stove and looked through the isinglass windows.

"Soo—someone put some chestnuts in the fire again. You boys will get the best of me yet! I think you all will have to stay after school today. If you chop a little wood for me you won't have so much energy to fool around, maybe?"

But it was Saturday school that we disliked most, for then we were given special drill in German and the catechism. No religious or Bible instruction was given during the week, but on Saturdays we learned the catechism. We had no Sunday school and this took its place.

We entered school speaking only German, and learned English (Brother Schlegel's variety) in school. At least the books were in English. During my mother's school days, English was discredited and considered worldly. The elders wanted to make sure that the German language did not die out. Our daily use of German did much to keep us isolated. It prevented our communicating freely with outsiders and thus insulated us somewhat from outside influences. As long as Brother Schlegel taught, we had Saturday school.

"Anna, what did you learn from your catechism this week?" Brother Schlegel leaned on his elbows and peered over his glasses at me. The catechism awed me because I didn't understand it. I looked up at Brother Schlegel's stern face. It was as though I were reciting directly to God.

"Mama taught me part of the Apostolic Belief," I ventured.

"What part did you learn?"

"The part about God."

"Can you recite it to me?"

"Yes, Brother Schlegel:

'1. Is there more than one God?
   No, there is only one God.—Hear, ye children of Israel, the Lord, our God, is a jealous God.

2. What is God?
   God is a spirit, and those who pray to Him, have to pray in spirit and in truth.

3. How many persons are there in God?
   There are three, that are shown in Heaven: The Father, the Word (the Son) and the Holy Ghost, and all these three are one.

4. What are His characteristics?
   God is eternal, omnipresent, all-knowing, infinitely good, all-wise and almighty.

73

5. What is the meaning of eternal?
   Without beginning and without end. Before the mountains were brought forth, or even Thou hadst formed the earth and the world, even from everlasting to everlasting, Thou art God.' "

The catechism we learned did not vary greatly from those of other Protestant churches. The creed was made up almost entirely of quotations from the Bible. We were required to memorize the entire catechism in time and be able to recite it precisely, both the questions and the answers. We never had a discussion about the beliefs; whether we understood them or not was beside the point.

The catechism included more than a discussion of our creed; it was a guide for daily living. In fact, it set the pattern for our every thought and action, in school, at home, and in church. It formed the pattern for child training and was quoted whenever authority was needed, by parents, teachers, and elders. A translation of some of these rules follows:

1. Dear Child: As soon as you are awakened in the morning, get up. In fact, regulate yourself to awaken without being called and do not dawdle in getting up out of your bed.

2. Let your first thoughts be of God after the example of David—Psalm 139:18, "When I wake up I go with You," and Psalm 63:7, "When I wake up I immediately speak of You."

3. Next, greet your parents and brothers and sisters and others in the house with "good morning" not only out of habit but in true feeling.

7. The morning prayer should not be out of cold memory or habit but through hearty thanksgiving towards God who has protected you in the night; and call on Him meekly that He might bless your activities all day.

74

9. When you say grace at the table, don't let your hands hang to the floor. Don't lean on the table. Don't gawk around but be reverent before the holy majesty of God.

12. Don't be greedy over your food, don't be the first one to take out of the bowl, and especially don't show with words or nodding of your head if you did not like a certain food or ask for something that is not given you.

14. Cut your food into small pieces. Grasp the knife and spoon daintily and be careful not to soil your clothes or the tablecloth. Don't slurp your soup, etc., or make any other noise with your mouth.

19. Don't throw the bones, or whatever is left over, under the table. Don't dump them on the table-cloth but leave them on the edge of the plate.

22. Make no distinction between foods (for that is a sin) but eat everything that is given to you.

30. After the meal is over wipe your mouth, get up quietly, pray reverently, and then start your duties. Do not reach for the leftover foods or lick them greedily, for you must finish eating while you are at the table.

The elders must have had good reason for enforcing strict training in manners. The rules of conduct originated during the days when some thirty or forty men, women, and children ate their meals in the common dining room, the men at one set of tables, the women and very small children at another, and the older children at still another. Since not all members came from refined social backgrounds, emphasis on the more essential amenities became necessary. In the common dining rooms where people ate together regularly, obnoxious manners could have been most offensive, even to the point of causing serious discontent.

Saturday school with its catechism and German instruction was destined to end with the declining fortunes of Brother Schlegel. Eventually, the school discipline deteriorated so that the elders could ignore it no longer. Poor Brother Schlegel became childish and created disturbance by ringing the school bell at odd hours. His mind failed rapidly and, after he ran out in the street one day, only partially clothed, the elders had him taken away to a state institution.

Unfortunately, the young man who had been sent to the State Teachers College to become our next teacher had not yet finished his degree. Therefore, outsiders had to be hired to teach the school. Since they were only required to teach five days a week, the Saturday school was discontinued. The elders worried about not being able to offer training in catechism and German, but nothing was done about it.

One evening after school my cousin William came over to our house, boasting,

"I'm going to be leaving soon for high school at Marengo. The elders have decided that I'm to be a teacher." William swaggered a bit for you had to be an outstanding student to be selected. He was lucky to have finished school just as the elders needed a candidate.

"You?" scoffed Henry. "You'll make a fine teacher!"

"Well, it might be more fun to go to school than to work in the Amana woolen department." William was needling Henry who was already assigned to work there.

"Wait until you have to study every night. You'll find out."

"I might even go to college," William continued.

"Go ahead. I'm glad it's not me they picked." Henry was speaking only half the truth. He did not envy William, for Henry did not care to be conspicuous. He preferred taking his place wherever the elders assigned him, rather than to go outside and be considered "different." Yet he was well endowed for taking advantage of higher education and would have liked to have had a chance at it.

By the time I was twelve, I had been through or "listened in" on all the work given in our Amana School and I had passed my eighth grade examination for the county superintendent. Since I was not yet fourteen, the law required that I continue school. The teacher used me to "hear" the lessons of a lower grade, and how boring that was! During those two years, only one child entered school; I was his teacher and he was my only pupil. I still wonder if he ever learned to read!

A lifesaver for me was the correspondence course in algebra and history that I inherited. It had been bought for my cousin William and it was left at the school. Since William had been chosen for outside education, he had been allowed to take the first year of high school as offered by the University of Chicago. The elders were wary about sending their unsophisticated teenagers directly to worldly high schools, so they put it off as long as possible, using the correspondence method. I did the whole algebra course, with very little help from the teacher, though not for credit. It was already understood that I would be assigned to the kitchen house crew in two more years and so, according to Amana standards, there was no reason why I should have any more education.

"give us this day our daily bread"

JUST AS THE ELDERS of Old Amana were symbols of our religious beliefs, even so were the kitchen houses symbols of our communal living. They became the dynamic centers of the villages. They supplied us with food and demanded our allegiance three times a day. Our familiarity with them made us feel that they belonged to us individually as well as to the whole neighborhood. We also depended upon them for the only social life we knew, for snatches of gossip and legitimate news, and just ordinary companionship. For women, they were the countinghouse where one's debt to the Society was paid by one's labor, for most of the work required from the women by the elders was associated with the kitchen houses.

A typical neighborhood kitchen house could be recognized by the length of the building, enlarged and extended by an odd assortment of lean-tos, porches, and sheds. Here the food was dispensed to some thirty or forty people. Compared with modern kitchens they were indeed primitive. The long, flat-topped, wood-burning hearths, handmade of brick, looked more like tables than stoves, except for the eight kettle holes with their removable lids. There was a "store-bought" oven in one end of the kitchen and a long black pipe that disappeared into the chimney near the ceiling. We had cold running water, and a long wooden trough along one side of the room for a sink.

As a small child, I found the kitchen house the most interesting and pleasant of all places. Mother joined the women while I played with other children and this was our routine each morning and afternoon. In the winter, the women sat in a circle in the dining room and prepared vegetables on handmade wooden trays which they held on their laps. In summer you would find them working on the long porches or under shady arbors. Mother enjoyed being with the other women and I liked having children to play with.

Later, when I became fourteen, the elders assigned me to the kitchen house and I learned to work as a member of a group. To this day I prefer not to work alone.

I have never been a part of a more efficient organization than that of the Amana kitchen. The elders had learned long ago that single women, with no family responsibilities, could be most easily available for the meal duties, so most of the cooks and maids were single. Perhaps this was one reason women were encouraged to remain single, the better to serve the community. A kitchen boss (Baas), assisted by a "vice boss," was in charge of all operations. Three more women took turns in the three main jobs. For instance, one of them did the cooking one week; the next week, she would be responsible for cooling the milk, churning the butter, and washing the dishes; the third week, her job would be to set tables, clear away and wipe dishes. We worked cheerfully and cooperatively, each of us helping the others as we could. No job became too unpleasant or monotonous for it lasted only one week. Also, this turn-about system required that we take the dreaded early shift only every third week.

During my first few weeks on the kitchen crew, the "vice boss" helped me get started with my duties. After that, I was expected to carry on alone.

In addition to the two cooks, the three kitchen maids, and the neighborhood women who prepared the vegetables, there was a garden boss—a husky, robust woman who loved plants. The vegetables in her garden would have compared favorably with those pictured in seed catalogues.

There was always some excitement brewing around the kitchen houses. Along the road in front of each one was a bench-like landing platform, where various deliveries were made daily. As children we would climb upon the platform and sit, legs dangling, waiting for the horse-drawn vehicle of each delivery man. Meat was delivered by the butcher's wagon. It was brought fresh from the slaughter house, for we had no means of storing it. Milk was delivered twice daily in large galvanized cans directly from the dairy barns, still warm and unpasteurized. It had to be cooled by placing the cans in a trench of cold water in the kitchen house cellar, since the ice boxes were not big enough. No wonder I never learned to like it! The bread was brought by the baker's son, in his special bread wagon. As we chatted with the delivery men we helped unload their wares. Sometimes we would get to ride along to the next kitchen house.

Everything, including the menus, was done according to a set pattern, day in and day out, the year around, the only concessions being those made for differing winter and summer conditions.

The first breakfast, served at 6:30, was generous, for Amana people worked hard and had hearty appetites. The kitchen helpers often ate a second breakfast and those who went off to work in the fields and shops usually carried lunches for midmorning and midafternoon snacks. The Amanas had the reputation for serving five meals a day, although "snack time" was no more than the coffee break that has become so popular today.

At eleven o'clock, we had our main meal with a menu so routine that you could tell the day of the week by the food you were served. You could even tell what you would have to eat on a certain day ten years hence, should you live so long! I can still remember my personal reactions to the days of the week as characterized by the food served.

The menus for the day set the pattern of activity around the kitchen. Using mass production methods, the crew operated as a team, each woman doing a specific part of the job. Making doughnuts from great pans of dough was typical. My own contribution as a child was punching the holes with my thumb, this method being preferred—it avoided reworking dough which would be left by cutters. Boards covered with rising doughnuts were laid out on every surface, making an impressive sight. Noodles, too, a dozen "batches" at a time, were spread out to dry all over the dining room—literally miles of them. A little competition entered here, for making good noodles was considered a rare accomplishment. Each cook tried to excel by rolling the noodles tissue thin and cutting them into extra fine slivers for soup.

To me, the Amana-made bean shredder was the most entertaining of all machines. Operated with a crank, it forced beans past the edges of a cleverly set series of knives. As you cranked, the beans came out, "French cut." Many bushels were processed at a time, filling bucket after bucket with shreds of juicy beans. These were finally carried to barrels in the basement and salted down for preservation. As a hot dish, seasoned with bacon and onion, beans were one of the main winter vegetables.

All children were fascinated by the giant ricer. It was merely a large perforated tube with a wooden plunger which stood on the floor in a big pan. Cooked potatoes were placed in it and the plunger squished them out in worm-like strings in all directions. Riced potato concoctions such as potato dumplings, or croquettes, or similar dishes were served frequently, probably just because we had such an efficient ricer and lots of potatoes.

There was a time and a season for all things at the kitchen house. Tedious but thrifty methods of harvesting and preserving foods for winter consumption became a major occupation for all the women and some of the men. However, the time-consuming, inefficient ways of processing the products of the fields served a twofold purpose; they furnished group occupation for the

83

women, thereby keeping them busy in the harvest seasons, and they provided food for the colonies at a negligible cost. Since there was an air of gaiety about the group endeavors, people worked cheerfully and even looked forward to the changing seasons with their accompanying "festivals" such as the onion harvest.

During two or three weeks in the summertime, everybody gathered for this harvest. Wagon loads of onions were spread out on racks, under the arbors, on the porches, and in the yards, waiting to be cleaned. Men pulled the onions, women trimmed them, the children helped sort, and the garden bosses had a heyday, directing the whole enterprise. Sorting was done under the grape arbors or in some other shady place, where from twelve to twenty women and children would sit, working with their wooden trays of onions on their laps. The onions were sorted as to condition and size. The choicest ones were saved for seed. The next best were sacked for sale. Finally the poorest ones were held back for kitchen use. Amana onions had become quite famous in the surrounding towns and had a ready market. They were raised from seed which the early settlers had brought from Germany. They were milder and less perishable than other onions and hence were in great demand. The money derived from this enterprise was kept by the kitchen house to pay for such staple items as sugar, flour, coffee, and so forth.

As a special treat during the onion season, we were given afternoon refreshment breaks. Among the dusty piles of onions, we ate "store-bought" cookies with dirty, grimy hands and drank lemonade. And at the close of the onion session each of us received a small gift, a handkerchief perhaps, as a sort of bonus, and we were happy indeed.

Another process requiring hours and hours of women's time involved the drying of kale and green beans for winter use. The large crinkly kale leaves were picked, cleaned, and parboiled. Then, paper thin and nearly black, they were taken out of the water, unfolded individually, spread out on racks, and placed in specially constructed, slow-burning ovens. Beans were processed the same way, with each bean laid out separately on the trays after the boiling, to be dried in the oven houses. Then they were stored in tightly covered tin cans.

Turning piles of cabbages into sauerkraut was another community affair. Machines used for cutting the large heads are now exhibited among the Amana antique displays. Many women spent endless hours cutting up cabbage and feeding it through these voracious shredders. Several barrels were filled in each kitchen, for in the days before freezers and easily available commercially processed foods, sauerkraut was a dependable winter standby.

It was known generally that the colonies were well supplied with quantities of good food, and travelers looking for handouts were attracted to them. Now and then gypsies would come. I remember one summer day when Henry and I saw some of them. . . .

"Anna, the gypsies have come!" Henry yelled as he ran up the stairs and opened the door.

"The gypsies!" was all I could say, trying to decide whether to be scared or just thrilled with unusual, awful excitement.

"They're camping down by the river and they have a a big fire."

"How many wagons?"

"I counted eight, and lots of horses."

"I wish I could see them."

"You will—and soon. They always come to the kitchen house to beg for food."

"Let's go to the kitchen house."

Henry hesitated because we were not supposed to go there while the women were busy getting meals ready.

"Mama's there helping—and everybody knows gypsies steal children." That thought always made me want to be close to mother.

"All right," said Henry, "but hurry, we don't want to be kidnapped on the way." Already I was halfway down the stairs. We ran as fast as we could and rushed in the back door of the kitchen house.

"You children get in here and be quiet or the gypsies will take you." That was Mina, the kitchen *Baas*. The other women were looking out the windows, peering around the curtains so as not to be seen from outside. Mother seemed glad to see us. All she said was, "Anna, you stay close to me."

"*Ach*—all those nice chickens they took last time," grumbled Mina. "Tell Frederick to stay near the chickens. I hope he's around; he's about the most no-account handyman we ever had."

"Even if he stays it won't help," reminded Marie. "Last time they stole the chickens at night."

"There they come," someone whispered. "Everyone get busy—put all the food out of sight."

There was a scramble as jars, bags, and dishes of food were shoved, tossed, and thrown into various hiding places. Then the women returned to their jobs, picking up their vegetable paring trays, rolling dough, or washing dishes. When the knock came at the door every-

86

one was busy and Henry and I were sitting on the floor in the corner behind the work tables. Perhaps if we were very still, the gypsies would not see us.

Baas Mina went to the door, opening it only slightly in an effort to keep the gypsies on the front step. There stood two gypsy women, black-haired and insolent. They were small, like mother. Their bright, full skirts swayed gently as they moved about; the full sleeves of their blouses made colorful circles as they talked and waved their arms. They wore many strings of beads around their necks, gold rings swung from their ears, and their wrists were covered with gold and silver ornaments such as I had never seen before. Bright red triangular scarfs were tied about their heads.

Their searching black eyes peered around Mina into the room. Their brilliant, exciting appearance contrasted sharply with that of the unadorned, calico-clad Amana women.

The older, ugly one spoke. "Cross my palm with silver, madam, and I foretell your future."

"I know my future." Mina seemed inches taller than usual and tried to block the door while showing her distaste for this gaudy, dirty creature.

"Then give us food. We have no money, no food. Children sick." The gypsy held out her hand, speaking in a wheedling tone of voice suggestive of tears, and pushed her way in around the door jamb. While Mina was looking at her as though she might pick her up and throw her out, the younger gypsy also wedged herself into the room. Several open jars of jam stood on the table, covered with a white cloth. Quick as a flash, the cloth was swished aside and the young gypsy stuck her dirty finger into first one jar, then another, each time licking her fingers.

"Good, good," she said. "Give, madam, for the sick children." I thought she was going to cry about the poor, sick children as she picked up the large jar of strawberry jam. The two women seemed to be all over the kitchen at once, exploring the pots on the stove, searching the shelves, finding all the hidden food and smelling or tasting what appealed to them.

"Meat, meat, give us meat," said the older one.

"No," said Mina defiantly. "Soon our men will be coming in for supper. It is for them."

"Chickens, then." She seemed to know that the women were afraid. Mina hesitated. She hated to give up any of her precious chickens but she wanted most to get rid of these robbers.

"Give us *six* chickens and we go." The older gypsy smiled insolently as though she were accustomed to giving orders.

"No, two," said Mina holding up two fingers.

"Six—or I place a curse on this house."

"I don't believe in curses."

"I can harm you." The gypsy threatened and sidled up to Mina, her eyes staring like smoky lights.

"If I give you six chickens, will you promise to leave and not come back?" Mina was very serious and all the women had forgotten about working. They stared at the gypsies as if hypnotized.

"I go and not come back. Six chickens and a dozen eggs."

"No, just six chickens."

The gypsy swung around the room looking at each woman in a leering sort of way, her earrings jangling all the while. I admired the beautiful golden circles and wondered how she kept them on her ears. The women began working again as the two gypsies swayed around the room, gliding with easy steps, their skirts of yellow, green, and red showing in colored streaks as they swung first in one direction, then in another. They filled the room. The old one stopped abruptly before Mina.

"Six chickens and a dozen eggs and I go." She snapped her fingers under Mina's nose. Mina moved to the back door and called.

"Frederick." He was right there in his woodshed room.

"Catch six chickens and give them to these—these robbers!" Mina's face was red with anger.

Marie disappeared into the pantry and came out, a small bagful of eggs held gingerly in her hands. The young gypsy took it, shifting her two jars of jam.

"Now remember," said Mina. "You are not to come back." She meant, "Don't steal some more chickens tonight."

The gypsy stood straight and spoke as if she had been rudely insulted. "I not come back."

Henry and I slipped to the window for a better view of what was happening outside. Two more gypsies had appeared and were watching Frederick as he tried to catch the squawking hens. You could see him now and then in the flying dust and feathers. One of the gypsies reached down into the depths of her skirts and brought out several lengths of heavy twine. Frederick handed her one chicken at a time and she tied their feet together, then passed the struggling bird on to a companion. Soon the four of them were off, walking single file down the board walk, each well loaded. In the kitchen house we looked out the windows after them, and then at the disorder around us.

"I hope Frederick gave them the toughest, oldest hens on the place." Mina was rubbing her hands on her apron. The other women were beginning to inspect the damage, for anything that had been touched by the gypsies' dirty fingers would be thrown away.

"They'll probably be back tonight. Last time they also promised not to steal if we gave them food," Marie reminded us.

"How many days will they camp here?" I wanted to know.

"Oh, a week or two, maybe," Henry told me.

"Then they'll need more food."

"They'll go to a different kitchen house next time."

"Now, we are late," Mina was herself again. "Hurry, so we can be ready with supper when the men come in."

I wished I could go down by the river and see the gypsies around their campfire by night, and look in the covered wagons, and see what the children were like. Uncle Jacob said they were dirty and in summer wore no clothes at all. Gypsies must come from far, far away to be so different and so wicked.

hobo helpers

FREDERICK, *Baas Mina's* "no-account handy man" was one of the men hired by the elders as a concession to the women in the kitchen houses. Each kitchen house had one handy man whose duty it was to help the kitchen boss, assist with the kitchen garden, do heavy lifting, and take care of unpleasant jobs such as cleaning out the chicken houses and outside toilets. Most of these handy men were tramps who simply turned up and were invited to stay on. Some might stay a few days or a season, perhaps. Others stayed for years.

The handy men intrigued us because they were eccentric and different. Life in Amana was so routine that there was something strangely appealing about these vagrants from the "outside world." We longed to know about their past and what they did when they suddenly vanished for months at a time.

Henry and I had a chance to become acquainted with several of these characters. Their living quarters were in a lean-to attached to the community washhouse, which was near the garden house where we played all summer long. Sometimes they would come out and share the shade of the huge linden tree that spread its branches from our playhouse to the washroom, or give us a push on the tire swing that hung from its branches.

Such a one was John Loercher who was younger and nicer than most of them. He took a special liking to me and called me "Annie." No one had ever called me by a nickname before and I thought he was being fresh. He said I was his "girl friend" and brought me an occasional piece of candy, or offered me a ride on his horse-drawn wagon whenever he had errands to run. All this attention embarrassed me, at age nine, and I avoided him as much as possible, especially after my friends started teasing me about my "boy friend."

But not all handy men were pleasant. Frank Leibel, for example, had shaggy hair like a lion, and growled like one, too. He often talked to himself. I was afraid of him, but Henry liked to tease him to see what he might do. He'd run past Frank's window, giggling, making him think he was laughing at him. Usually his head popped out and he shouted, "Get away from here, you good-for-nothing brats." Or he would come running out with a big blast, shaking his fist, his long shaggy hair waving wildly. Then Henry would think up something new to make him roar. Once he hid Frank's pipe in his bed. Another time when Frank had his wash on the line, we tied his underwear and trousers into knots. I shudder to think what would have happened had we been discovered.

One particular morning Henry ran by Frank's window to see what kind of explosion he would arouse. We could hear the usual bellowing. Then suddenly Frank came dashing out the door waving a butcher knife, and chased after Henry. By now Henry was well off up the road and I ran to hide with the kitchen helpers, who were crowding to the windows to see what the commotion was about.

Henry and I had a few anxious moments. We thought we would be severely punished for teasing Frank. On the contrary it was Frank that took the blame. It seemed that he had had many violent fits of temper lately and was showing other signs of becoming mentally deranged.

That noon, Grandpa, who was the head elder of our neighborhood, asked Frank to leave. Rumor had it that Frank went to live as a hermit in the Amana woods. He came out once in a while, all tattered and dirty, to beg for food, and once he came to the doctor for some medical help. Many years later, while Henry and Fritz were out hunting mushrooms, they came across Frank's body. Apparently he had died during the winter.

Then there was "Gentle Henry." He lived in the same room where Frank had lived, but he was as quiet as Frank was noisy. Like Frank, he, too, was old. He must have acquired his nickname years ago, for there was nothing pleasant or attractive about him that I could see. I never liked to be near him because he would wear his clothes until the women would make him change. Sometimes they would refuse to let him come to the kitchen until he had taken a bath. In the winter little icicles would freeze in his bushy mustache from a dripping nose. One morning he did not come to help with the morning chores, and the kitchen boss who had gone to see what was the matter found Old Henry dead in his bed.

The garden boss who was truly sympathetic towards everyone was the only one who went to his funeral. She felt that everybody should have someone mourn their passing. Later I went to see his grave in that part of the cemetery set aside for outsiders.

The kitchen crew scrubbed the room where Gentle Henry had died, with strong soap and hot water. Mother said we had to remove the curse of death from it.

As the society prospered, the Inspirationists began to hire more outsiders. Maybe the elders noted an undercurrent of resentment among members assigned to cleaning out stables, doing the heavy drudgery about the barns, or cleaning the outdoor toilets, even on a rotational system. At any rate, the hiring of tramps for such jobs became customary.

Some of these wanderers who traveled about for seasonal employment were not a bad sort. They were generally younger than the kitchen helpers. They brought with them intriguing suggestions of the world outside Amana—one of them introduced the first car to us, and he was popular indeed. He became our friend and was admitted to our homes. In fact, he visited frequently at Uncle John's house and taught us card games and tricks. I am sure the elders would not have approved of this, but we were careful not to mention it when Grandpa was around.

The hired hands lived in the "Day Laborers' House" on the edge of town. It was furnished with beds and a stove; no luxuries! The hands swept it out occasionally and women from Amana cleaned and fumigated it every fall and spring.

Another one-roomed shack, equipped only with a stove and straw, was set aside for the use of hobos— tramps looking not for work, but only for a place to spend the night. Although the tramps were supposed to take care of it, they did not bother. I had often heard stories about how dirty it was but was not allowed to go near it by myself.

One early fall morning I went with Grandma Schneider to the kitchen house where she worked. It was here most of the farm hands ate their meals. Uncle John came and spoke to the kitchen boss.

"Has anyone seen Onion Frank?"

"No," said the boss and all the women paused in their work to listen. "Is he gone again?"

Uncle John pressed his lips together and nodded 'yes.' "We are taking the farm crew to cut wood over by the river today and we need him. I looked in at the day laborer's house for him but he had not slept there last night."

"He came in for breakfast yesterday, but he has not been here since," said the boss.

Onion Frank seemed always to be sad and alone. Once he gave me a lump of sugar from his pocket. It was all brown and I thought it was made of chocolate but it was really only stained with tobacco. Grandma quickly took it from me so I wouldn't eat it. Everyone called him "Onion Frank" because like some of the others, he never seemed to be clean enough. When he combed and washed at the bench outside the kitchen door, his copper colored hair seemed to match his red face. His ragged blue denim coat and overalls were so dirty that the cooks said they would "stand alone" if he took them off.

"I'll go and see if he is at the tramp house. Maybe he's sleeping it off again," said Uncle John.

The tramp house! I had always wanted so much to see the tramp house.

"Take me, Uncle John, please take me."

"No, Anna, Uncle John is in a hurry. The men are waiting." It was Grandma who spoke up. I just looked at Uncle John in a way he liked and so he said—

"You'll have to come back alone, you know."

Already I was putting on my coat and reaching for Uncle John's hand. I loved to do things with Uncle John. If my father had lived, he would have let me go with him, I knew.

"Be back in time for school," I heard Grandma's voice saying. But school seemed far away as Uncle John and I stepped out into the crisp bright blue morning. Over the hills, fields lay golden and ripe, and the trees around us were showing brilliant yellow and many shades of lovely red. But my thoughts were on the tramp house.

"Who takes care of the tramp house?" I knew that no women ever went near it.

"The tramps, but they don't seem to work at it much. You'll see how it is taken care of."

I was almost running to keep up with Uncle John, his steps making slow heavy beats on the wooden sidewalk and mine making fast light ones. The frost was disappearing from sunny places and the flowers in the gardens were black and drooping from it. But I felt gay and like running. Everyone along the way moved quickly, too—not slow at all as on hot summer mornings.

"Hello, George," Uncle John called to George

Schreiber, the whitewasher. He was moving his pails and brushes and ladders into Frieda Gruber's house. I wondered which room they were having done this season.

"Hello, John," George answered. "Heinrich Schuler was asking for you. He wanted to know where you were going to cut wood today."

"*Ach,* I know. I'm still trying to find that Onion Frank."

"Ho! Ho! Onion Frank. He maybe went out of town last night to find a tavern?" George winked at Uncle John thinking I did not know about the sprees of Onion Frank. Several days at a time he would be gone and this, I knew, was because he was sick from drinking.

Now we were near the little one-roomed house in the clearing. A slim stream of smoke came from the chimney and looked like a white ribbon in the clear blue sky. Uncle John knocked at the door, but no one answered. He opened it and looked in. I peeked around him and saw a bare room with no furniture or curtains or paint on the walls. It looked more like a workshed or a barn than like a home for the tramps. The heat from the potbellied stove made shimmers of light across the dirt-filmed window. Old blue denim coats, overalls, and once-white long underwear hung from nails around the walls, the bulgy, wrinkled legs of the garments making me think of bodies hanging there.

"Umm!" Uncle John grunted and bent over to investigate a pile of rags in the corner. Sure enough. Here was Onion Frank, sleeping the unconscious slumber of saturated intoxication.

"Well, I guess we work without Onion Frank today," said Uncle John as he turned to check the draft in the stove. The warm, stale air was making me sick

97

and I held my nose to avoid the smell. Uncle John looked down at me.

"Now you've seen the tramp house, *Kleinchen*. You'd better run back to the kitchen and I'll be off to the woods, one hand short."

"Uncle John, why do the tramps live out here alone?"

"Well, they don't belong to the society. They are outsiders and only stop here for handouts and a place to sleep. Don't you worry about the tramps, or Onion Frank either."

"But Uncle John, where do they go when they are not here?"

"Oh south, or somewhere, usually to a warm climate."

He was already moving away and I remembered about school. This was the only time I ever saw the tramp house, but soon after that everyone was talking about it. . . .

On a night soon after my trip to the tramp house, we were all awakened by the frantic ringing of bells. There were two bells in our village—one in the Post Office near our home and one in the other end of the village at the school house—so situated that all could hear them.

The ringing of the bells communicated messages to us. Our neighborhood bells rang at mealtime, announcing that food was ready to be taken to the homes, they also rang to tell us that church time had come again, and each Sunday morning they rang at eight o'clock sharp so that all clocks and watches could be set with correct time. But when the bells rang at odd hours and kept on ringing, they meant fire!

Fire! This was the most horrible fear that we knew. Mother had told us what to do if fire broke out in our building. Since we lived upstairs, there was only one way down—by the stairway in the middle of the house. On this night, I jumped out of bed and dressed as fast as I could. Mother and Henry were already downstairs on the front steps with Grandpa, and someone yelled in the night—

"The tramps' house!"

Unlike most fires, no one seemed to be going to this one. Then Grandpa said, "I'd better go see about it."

"Don't you go. Let the younger men go." Mother spoke quickly and anxiously.

"I don't see any of them going. These days, no one cares about the tramps' house." Grandpa spoke impatiently.

So Grandpa went in to his room and came out with a lighted lantern. As he trudged off alone, buttoning his long winter coat, mother sent us back to bed.

Next day I asked her what had happened about the fire and she said the tramps' house had burned down. Grandpa had tried to save it but no one came to help him. Later I asked him why. He said it was only put there as a favor for tramps and none of our people had been asked to look out for it. Grandpa shook his head and I knew he was displeased.

The tramps' house was never rebuilt. Years later an old boxcar was moved in to take its place.

For some reason, the tramps who came to the Amanas after the fire were not nearly as interesting as the old timers: John Loercher, Frank Leibel, Gentle

Henry, and Onion Frank. Or perhaps we had occasion to see more glamorous "outsiders" as cars became more plentiful and visitors came more frequently to the hotels, bakeries, and meat shops.

the pleasant hours

WE IN AMANA knew very little of recreation, as such. Since the early rules of the Inspirationists emphasized that idleness in all forms was sinful, even recreational activities were supposed to turn time to producing or creating something useful. The work assigned by the elders, and attendance at all the church services kept people busy most of their waking hours. For the small fringes of time remaining, everyone developed some particular hobby or craft.

Men created beautiful furniture, the kind that took endless hours of patient, painstaking labor. Some made intricate clocks. Others made toys for the children; my grandfather Guyer built a handsome wheelbarrow for Henry and doll furniture for me. A few young men had a pool table of their own, but playing pool was not approved by the elders because everything was supposed to be done for some purpose other than just entertainment. Fishing was a popular sport with the men though Grandpa never thought of going fishing. Men often went out for mushrooms in the evening, and there was some hunting. These sports were allowed, for they brought in food.

The men read more than the women, though reading material was scarce. The most important literature in the early days was the recorded testimonies of the various *Werkzeuge.* These had been printed and bound into volumes by the Amana printing shop and all elders were given a complete set. I now have the books that belonged to my Grandpa Guyer, the same ones he read during the leisure hours.

The colonies had no library and only a limited collection of odd books was accessible to us through the school. I recall only *The Swiss Family Robinson, Heidi,* and *Black Beauty.* A few books could be found in our homes, usually acquired as Christmas gifts when we were children. Thus I came to know and love *Elsie Dinsmore,* and *The Bobbsey Twins.* We owned a few bound almanacs called *Germania Kalender,* published annually in Milwaukee, Wisconsin. The cartoons and stories must have impressed mother as valuable information for some were ten or twenty years old. They were in German, of course, and Henry and I looked through them occasionally. Books like *Töchter Album,* a yearbook for young girls, drifted into Amana from Germany.

A few periodicals arrived by subscription through the society. *Die Hausfrau,* a woman's magazine published in German, offered a few stories, some recipes (for which we had no use) and ideas for fancy work. *Needlecraft* was a favorite of the women and *Successful Farm-*

ing interested the men. The *Chicago Tribune* was relied upon for news of the world but only a few elders read it.

The people knew how to read, but were so accustomed to making the hours "count" that they preferred creative pastimes; reading seemed a waste of time.

Amana women were never idle. At certain seasons of the year great demands were made on them by the society for harvesting and processing food, but in winter they often had long hours of "free" time when the main recreation was handiwork. It took a variety of forms and was often intricate and most artistically done.

All women crocheted and since it was a form of entertainment, only complicated designs were interesting. No satisfaction came from doing simple patterns. Mother liked to make up her own designs, sometimes using parts of several different patterns. The finished pieces were used in the homes, or sold to outsiders as a means of earning a little cash.

Knitting and crocheting woolen garments like stockings or mittens was not enjoyed as much as were the other crafts, probably because in the old days, every child had to learn to make these in school and later for the society to sell. This custom had been discontinued before my time. However, I learned to knit when I was seven. My first project was a washrag for my Grandpa. After mastering the plain knitting, mother showed me how to make inch-wide lace, with a pattern, to be used on a handkerchief. My grandmother gave me careful instruction in the art of embroidery and cross-stitch and when I was ten, I embroidered a tablecloth, with crocheting all around it, as a surprise for my mother at Christmas. A complete set of crocheted place mats means most to me for I started this set while bedfast with poison ivy—to keep from scratching!

Perhaps the most beautiful work done by the women of Amana was the filet work. Mother made many large tablecloths, using handmade net. She started with one tiny square, and using a bone tool, tied regular fisherman's knots to make the quarter-inch squares of the filet. After spending months of her spare time making the net, the design was darned in. A filet could keep her busy all winter, and often did. The cloths were impressively lovely and it hurts me to think that mother sold many of them for spending money.

Of course women made their own clothes, as well as those for all their family. But clothes were very plain and called for no ingenuity. I cannot remember that mother ever owned a ready-made dress, nor did I.

Rug making was another favorite occupation. Rags were dyed and torn into strips which the women sewed together for the Amana weavers. It was from these strips that our carpets were made. People would dye their own rags and work out their own striped patterns. Standard colors like brown were dyed in the mill. A man worked the loom and made the carpeting. This method explains why our carpets were similar from house to house. Other rugs were hooked, or braided, and again, intricacy of design added zest to the creation. Some women knit squares out of rags and sewed them together in a pattern. My grandmother knit four room-sized rugs in this fashion. Many outsiders wanted to see the handmade rugs and once a rug exhibit was held. Showcards were sent to neighboring towns and people came from miles around to see the exhibit.

Another important handicraft was quilt making. Sometimes quilting was a private enterprise, but usually it served as an excuse for the only form of social life known to the women of Amana. Every woman had a quilting frame. When a party was planned, the frame was set up in one of the family rooms and friends came to help with the fine sewing. They even had something special to eat, like rich chocolate pie or cake, compounded of ingredients hoarded carefully from the family rations. Yet not all women enjoyed the group quiltings. My mother preferred to work for weeks all by herself, thus making sure of an even quality. When several women sewed on a quilt, some stitches would be fine and even while others would be coarse and ugly. With mother's long-term project, we often had the quilting frame up at home for weeks at a time.

In quilting, as in crotcheting and knitting, women delighted to originate patterns, for this was their only means of self-expression and the only recreation they knew. They had no opportunity to sample the joys of painting or any other form of "useless" art work. Some women were considered more artistic than others and their patterns were borrowed from house to house.

Little provision was made for the amusement of children. Youngsters were supposed to help around the homes by keeping the woodboxes filled, carrying out ashes, and by doing other small chores. There was little time left for play, especially since Sundays were to be spent in quiet contemplation. We did have sandboxes in the home and school yards where we spent hours and days at a time laying out roads and villages. In the winter girls played with dolls and doll houses full of beautiful handmade furniture. Boys were allowed to trap in the fields and streams. We played many Old World games of the parlor type, such as might be handed down from generation to generation. I liked the ones calling for little German rhymes, some of which were variations of the well-known "Ring around the Rosie" *(Ringel, Ringel, Rosenkranz)* and "Button, button, who's got the button?" As we slipped the button through the children's hands we said:

> *Leg ein, leg ein, ins Gräbelein*
> *Süsz und sauer und allerlei Wein.*

> (Fill the crevices with
> Sweet, sour, and all kinds of wine.)

We were entertained by German fairy stories and lore, also learned further by word of mouth.

All during the life of the colonies, boys had been allowed to play ball, so it was not surprising that baseball caught on as a natural outcome. Teams began to organize informally and soon Saturday afternoon games were the rage with the young people—and with many of the men. Regular tournaments were held, the different villages competing with each other. Middle Amana had a particularly good team and an outstanding player named Bill Zuber. As is generally known in Iowa, Bill was eventually to leave the colonies to become a national figure in big league baseball.

But in the days when Bill played baseball in Amana, women and children joined the ranks of cheering game watchers on Saturday afternoons. The ball "field" was at the edge of town in a former pasture. I was a kitchen helper at the time and could hardly wait for Saturday afternoons when we would all go to the highly exciting ball game. The elders soon realized that work in the Amanas was not being done while the games were going on; a large part of the population was wasting time at the ball games. Official action forbade the ball games and caused more dissatisfaction than any order ever before given by the elders. Actually the ball games continued on the sly, and people managed to sneak out to see them. The general idea seemed to be that you could take almost any liberty you might wish, provided the elders did not find out about it.

Teenagers were regarded as adults at fourteen and enjoyed almost unlimited freedom. They were supposed to be responsible for themselves and to behave like grownups. They knew that their self-respect was at stake if they got into trouble. In the old days, young people had been subject to a nine o'clock curfew but this was no longer enforced in my time. Getting together was a natural thing for us to do and we gathered practically every evening at one home or another, or at the orchard, which served as a sort of park. We all knew each other so we had no problem of getting acquainted. Activities, such as they were, involved groups rather than "dates," and we were never chaperoned.

In the years before the reorganization, along about 1920, a club known as "The Homestead Welfare Club" was started. The village doctor, who had been outside to study medicine, was one of the leaders of this unusual innovation. Outside contacts were casual and frequent for the doctor. He was one of the few people for whom the society furnished a car. He went to medical meetings and conventions and was permitted to treat patients in the farming communities near Homestead. He noticed that there was nothing particularly wrong about seeing movies and about social gatherings and he was convinced that the people of Amana should enjoy some of the privileges known to people on the outside.

The Welfare Club, with a president, secretary, and other officers, ushered in a new era to Amana. The doctor himself served as president. Now, events other than strictly religious ones brought the young people together and introduced new and "worldly" ideas. Originally, the club sponsored two big celebrations each year, a Christmas party and a Fourth of July picnic.

We practiced hard in school preparing a "program" of verses and recitations for the Christmas party. The teacher was also a leader of the club. I can remember well my first assignment, the memorization of one stanza of the song "Oh Come All Ye Children." I was so thrilled about the program that I learned all the stanzas and then became ill from excitement and missed it all.

At the Christmas party the children of Amana were visited by a real Santa Claus. He handed out little presents and later made calls at the homes, going from door to door. But parents never dressed up like Santa Claus.

The club took up headquarters in the basement of the church, where once the village wine had been stored. Here we saw our first movies; pictures such as "Heidi" thrilled the younger members. Older members, like my grandfather, were more and more disturbed by the new developments in Amana and would have no part in them. The elders, however, did not interfere with the club's events, sensing that changes had already taken place. To them, this was a sign that Amana was crumbling. Younger members had begun to know about things on the outside and they wanted them for themselves and for their children.

As I grew up, the club began presenting plays having nothing to do with religion. At first the plays were given only for our own entertainment but gradually we invited outsiders and charged admission as a means of raising money. Once we were even invited to present our play in a neighboring community. Every summer the club held outdoor movies several times—long before drive-ins were invented!

The innovation causing the most excitement of all was the fireworks display put on by the club on the Fourth of July. Never before had the people of Amana seen fireworks and they were something to talk about for days and days. These were all part of the Fourth of July picnic. This was a family-type picnic with prizes for all sorts of races: women's races, dress-up races, peanut races, and stunt races. What's more, we had a meal of hot dogs, hamburgers, and ice cream, a real treat because this was never served by the kitchen house. The ice cream was a most special delight; only rarely had we tasted it before. We had a program too, similar to the Christmas program: the children memorized recitations and the young people put on plays.

The Welfare Club seemed very important to me for it represented all the social activity not associated with the church. We held regular meetings once a month. There was no dancing but we did have card parties, pinochle being the most popular game. No refreshments were served at any meeting, not even the Christmas party, since we had no provision for getting or handling food.

One of the significant contributions of the club to the community was a subscription to the National Geographic Magazine. It was handed from member to member, each one keeping it a day or two. New ideas were taking hold.

The good doctor, who gave us the club, loved Amana and believed in it. He did all he possibly could for it, appreciating that changes were bound to come. He understood that the Inspirationists had been secluded in their isolated community all too long. The world had turned fast and they had made no effort to keep in touch or to assume any responsibility beyond their own prison-like environment. He could see talent wasting away for want of cultivation, abilities undeveloped because there was no need, and most important of all, he could see the outside world bearing in on the colonies and finding them defenseless in the wake of modern living. Nor was there any means of holding it back.

Radios were bringing in music and ideas of music. The state of music in Amana was particularly pathetic. Singing, the only form of music permitted in the churches, was unaccompanied. In fact, there were no pianos or organs in any of the churches. A few homes had acquired old reed organs. No one could instruct in music for no one had been trained musically since the Inspirationists left Germany. The singing of the hymns had been learned in church, each new generation listening to the older people. No voices were cultivated; the loud ones were the leaders.

Some men had mandolins and in my father's time the young people gathered occasionally for a "sing." If the teacher happened to be able to sing, we learned little songs in school. I tried to play on a reed organ. Someone at an earlier time had taken a correspondence course for playing the organ and the instruction sheets were sold from family to family. I never learned to play very well! Henry picked out a few songs from charts that came with the mandolin he had purchased from a mail order house. I knew of no violins or other orchestral instruments in Amana.

We had holidays in Amana but they belonged in a far different category than holidays on the outside, for they were merely extra church days. Not only did we have church on the day itself, but there were double holidays on Christmas, New Year's, Easter, Pentecost, and others, and if a Sunday preceded or followed the two holidays, we had church, three times a day, three days in a row, when children were not supposed to play or have any fun and grownups were likewise restricted.

The double holiday of Easter was particularly boring because during Holy Week we had services every noon and evening. Good Friday was a holiday, too, with three church services. This was a day of fasting. We had a piece of dry bread and some coffee in the morning, and nothing more to eat until the early evening supper.

By this time we were ready for the Easter bunny! On Saturday afternoon children were invited to several kitchen houses to hunt Easter eggs. We hunted around the sheds and wood piles and bushes in the yard until each of us found a nest containing six beautiful, glossy, painted eggs, a life-sized bunny "cookie" with a raisin for his eye, and a cluster of candy eggs. Once I found my name on a nest with a note from the bunny saying,

> "You must eat the egg whites, too,
> Or next year, I will forget you."

I wondered how the bunny knew I did not like egg whites! After visiting three kitchen houses Henry and I came home with three dozen hard-boiled eggs. Nobody cared for hard-boiled eggs at our house. We kept them on display for a day or so and wished they were all candy eggs. Finally mother would pickle them or give them away.

Thanksgiving, instead of being a day of feasting, was

111

another day for special church services. As mentioned before, it was the day when the Inspirationists repledged their loyalty to the society and to the elders. So great was the importance attached to it that the women were excused from kitchen duties. All women were given the morning off and expected to attend. At the morning service, they walked past the elders, shaking hands with them as a sign of reaffirmation of faithfulness. Young girls who were not yet of age stayed in the kitchens and made soup for the noon meal. After the noon meal everyone went back to church; it was the men's turn to walk around and shake hands with the elders. Such was Thanksgiving in Amana.

We looked forward to Christmas also with limited enthusiasm. Fortunately we received the benefits before the church going. Early in December we started hanging our long wool stockings on the bed post several nights a week. The next morning we might find a piece of candy or a nut or a tiny toy. On the Sunday before Christmas we had our celebration at Grandma Schneider's house, with great-grandmother Schnoebele and her sister, as well as Uncle John and his family. It was here that we received special toys and games. Once I had a life-sized doll from great-grandmother Schnoebele. On Christmas Eve we had our tree at home with gifts, mainly of clothes, from mother and always a pair of shoes and some oranges from Grandpa. On Christmas Day and the day after, we went to church, church, church. . . .

There was always much secrecy about the preparation for Christmas. We never helped decorate the tree, nor did we find any suspicious-looking packages to pry into. Santa Claus brought everything already decorated on Christmas Eve, and that was that. One year we were having the table in our living-sitting room repaired. A few days before Christmas mother told us very seriously, "I don't know what we'll do if we don't get our table back. Santa won't have any place to put the tree and the presents. I'm afraid we won't have any Christmas this year."

We were sad children indeed, but we never doubted her word. Christmas Eve came and we barely nibbled at our supper. The next day would be worse. All the children would compare notes after church and visit each other's houses, to admire all the splendor. We would have nothing to show. They would even think we had been bad children, for Santa Claus only neglected the ones who had misbehaved.

Mother washed the supper dishes. We heard Grandpa come back from the kitchen house where he had had his supper. He went directly to his room and did not even stop to visit with us. Glumly Henry and I looked over our last year's toys. Could we make them look new so we would have something to show, at least? But no, everybody knew our toys as well as we did.

Suddenly we heard a funny noise, like the tinkling of a bell. There was tramping of heavy footsteps coming down the stairs. The back door slammed. (Santa had to use doors in Amana because we had no fireplaces.)

Henry led the way upstairs, leaping three steps at a time. Could it have been Santa Claus? But no, the room was bare. He must have been here and left because there was no table. Now we felt worse than ever.

It was mother who saw a faint crack of light underneath the parlor door. She suggested we investigate. Gingerly we opened the door, afraid to get our hopes up again.

There in the center of the parlor stood a table we had forgotten about. On it was the most beautiful tree we had ever seen, all heavy with tinsel and burning candles. And there were shirts for Henry and a new dress for me, the usual shoes and the oranges from Grandpa, and best of all a pair of skates for each of us.

We danced around the tree, unbelievingly. With a twinkle in her eye mother reminded us that Santa Claus was a pretty clever man to have found a new place for our Christmas tree.

It turned out to be our best Christmas ever.

George, the whitewasher

WE OF AMANA spent many hours keeping our homes clean and maintaining the common buildings. The elders assigned major tasks of maintenance and cleaning to specific groups of workers but each family took care of its own rooms.

Though I live to be a hundred years old, I shall remember those back-breaking, bone-wearying upheavals—the spring and fall housecleanings! We began by carrying every movable object out of the room to be cleaned. We steamed and puffed as we lugged all the bedding into the sunny yard for "airing." The heavy, solid horsehair mattresses, made by the harness man, came in three sections, for "easy" handling. Then carefully we removed the hundreds of little, black-headed tacks which held the wall-to-wall strip carpeting in place, and hung the carpets on the line in the yard for a vigorous hand-beating.

With money a scarce article and paint expensive, whitewash tinted with a characteristic bright blue pigment, gave us our only touch of decoration. Each cleaning season, certain rooms in the various buildings received a new coat of the comparatively inexpensive blue "whitewash." Whitewashing, the only pleasant part of the housecleaning routine, brought us color, gave the rooms a fragrant, wet freshness and made them clean. Best of all, it brought us jolly George, the whitewasher.

We could see George's plump, robust figure come swaggering up the walk, his large blue-smeared pail in one hand and his long-handled brush balanced on his shoulder with the other. His hat was tipped at a rakish angle and his overalls were a study in splatter painting. Henry and I held the door open for him and he set down his equipment to salute us effusively.

"*Guten Morgen, guten Morgen,* my good friends." He glanced about the room professionally. "Well, well, where are we to throw whitewash around today?"

No one ever talked like that in Amana except George. He struck us as frivolous and daring and exciting.

"You are to do the dining room," I volunteered.

Mother had been standing by, trying not to show her disapproval of this rowdy, carefree character. She said—

"Brother Schreiber, I would like to have a nice neat job."

"Of course," said George as if to say, "How can you mention such a thing?" "I have been working hard today. I think a little drink of something, maybe a little wine, might help me?" He hinted broadly.

"I do happen to have a little of our wine ration on

118

hand. Let me see a sample of your work and I may let you have some," said mother. This repartee went on each time George came to whitewash at our house.

"*Jawohl,* Sister Schneider." He swept the hat from his head and gave a mocking bow. "I shall be glad to accept—at any time." Mother produced a large bottle of wine. He watched with obvious pleasure, rubbing his hands on his already blue-washed overalls. I had never seen a clown, so had no way of knowing he closely resembled one.

"Sophie, you are a good woman—and a beautiful woman, to save your wine ration for me. You will not be sorry!" Even though he was much older than mother, when he called her "Sophie" he seemed a bit familiar. He gave her a sly and flirtatious look and I knew we would get a good job on the dining room—and maybe the hall as well.

Mother blushed. She knew George was playing up to her and he knew he had an advantage over her. We wondered why mother did not scold George. He tasted the sparkling wine, sniffed its bouquet and held the glass to the light, admiring the ruby red color.

"It's good—yes, it's wonderful—to taste real vintage wine, my fair lady," he beamed at mother. "Most of my 'customers' give me only raw *Peistengel,* and sometimes diluted at that!" He made a wry face and shrugged his shoulders. "What can I do? It burns the throat like fire, but I have to drink it or hurt their feelings. But this, this is what wine should be." He helped himself to another glass. As soon as mother could manage without being too obvious, she quietly disappeared—with the bottle.

George had been working on several jobs at different homes that day before coming to our house, and ac-

119

cumulated refreshment had taken the drudgery out of his work. He talked continuously as he swung the long-handled brush, the whitewash dripping and spattering as he went.

"I wish this were not Saturday," he remarked with a sudden switch of topic.

"Why, what's wrong with Saturday?" Henry asked.

"I'm starved, and you know what we get to eat on Saturday night."

Indeed we did know. Potatoes boiled with their skins on and creamy cottage cheese.

He paused with his brush in mid air. "I just can't stand cottage cheese—and never could."

"I don't like it either," I chimed in with feeling.

George balanced uncertainly on one foot and reached for an out-of-the-way corner. "Guess what I used to do with it when I was a boy." We had heard the story many times but feigned great interest.

"What did you do, Brother Schreiber?" I asked. He needed little encouragement.

"We all ate in the kitchen house in those days—the men and women at separate tables and the children by themselves. Everyone watched us to make sure we cleaned our plates. Well, I could not eat that smelly, soggy cheese, so while some other boy attracted attention, I dumped my cheese into my pocket." He laughed uproariously at his own comedy and Henry and I joined in.

Mother returned with the wine bottle when the room was nearly finished, and George stopped at once for another drink. Mother remarked—

"The dining room is beautiful. It's too bad the hall is so dingy." She began eyeing the unused "wash" in the pail. "Maybe there is just enough here for the hall?"

Then, as if struck with a sudden idea, she continued—"If you want to do the hall while you are here, maybe I can find another bottle of wine."

"*Ach ja,* Sister Schneider," said George thickly, "I think there ish chust enough wash to do the hall." Watching him as he moved unsteadily about the room, I wondered how he would manage it. He dipped his large brush in the bucket and sang a lusty song—I couldn't understand it but it had something to do with a sailor and a lady.

Then came a crash as of a house falling to the ground. There sat George, his face and hair and clothes splashed with blue whitewash. He had bumped into the bucket and had rolled down the stairs, bucket and all. He picked himself up, dripping from head to toe and began wiping his face with an old rag.

"Maybe it is best you keep that bottle until next time?" he told mother. And away went our favorite, jolly George, drifting along with the falling leaves, to grace our home no more until the coming spring. It took mother and Henry and me hours and hours to clean up the mess. "Throwing" the whitewash was a fairly accurate term. Mother made us scrub the woodwork and bare pine floors with strong soap and water until they shone bleached and spotlessly clean.

Though it had seemed like hard work to remove the furnishings from the rooms to houseclean, the real work came with putting them back. First, of course, everything had to be thoroughly beaten, scrubbed or dusted, according to its nature. Replacing the carpets required the hard labor of two or three men. The man of the family might leave his work to come home for the carpet laying. Newspapers, spread out underneath as a pad, kept slithering out of place but with the aid of an ingenious "stretcher," the men pulled the carpet to a hard smoothness and tacked it down for another season.

All the bedding, which included white hand-woven linen coverlets for the three sections of each mattress, had to be laundered. This was done in the neighborhood washhouse, which we shared with several other families. The washhouse was equipped with a large open hearth, similar to those in the kitchens. Huge iron kettles were set into round openings in the top of the hearth, and heated by flames from burning wood. Water was carried in from the cistern in the back yard.

Curtains, too, received a rigorous laundering. We were proud of our pretty white marquisettes for they were store bought—not just handmade in Amana.

Next the bedsteads had to be cleaned and dusted; the bedboards and coiled springs were scrubbed and aired. When they were dry the beds were ready to be made. Mother gave special supervision to the mattresses, because the sections had to be rotated according to a system known only to her. The rotation went on with each weekly cleaning as well as in the spring and fall. Also, the mattresses had to be matched to the beds, which differed in size, according to the size of the individuals.

How wonderful it was to sink into bed that night, utterly exhausted, yet smug with satisfaction over the freshness of our bed and our newly housecleaned Amana room.

*   *   *

Nor did the housecleaning ordeal end when our home was finally cleaned. The kitchen, churches, the warehouse where Grandpa worked, and other public buildings were given the same order of renovation. Cleaning the kitchen houses was looked upon almost as a social occasion, for it was one of the few times we were treated to refreshments of lemonade and bought cookies. Groups of women worked together as a willing team, carrying out the directions of the kitchen boss. All the dishes were removed from the shelves, soaked in a lye solution and washed carefully before being replaced in the scrubbed cupboards. The great stone hearths of the stoves were scrubbed and cleaned and the iron tops blackened and polished. No board of the woodwork or floor escaped our strong soap and water treatment.

Mother and I took part in yet another housecleaning —that of the neighborhood *Sälchen*. Since we lived next to the church building, the elders made Grandpa a custodian of it. He kept the fire going in winter and lighted the lamp before the evening prayer meetings. Mother kept it clean. As a child, I went with her each day and played about the meeting hall while she dusted the benches and made sure everything was spotless. At housecleaning time, mother occasionally had the assistance of one of the kitchen helpers. The plain pine floors and the unfinished pine benches were bleached with much scrubbing. The walls, too, had their coat of "Amana Blue" refreshed by George the whitewasher every other year. When it was finished, the room had an airy, almost antiseptic, appearance. Even though there were no curtains at the large deepset windows, the classic simplicity and refined cleanliness of the room gave the "church" a charm and appeal all its own.

Faith of Our Fathers

the thunderstorm

As CHILDREN WE NEVER TIRED of hearing about the epic journeys of our people. Grandpa Guyer had a way of transforming many a dull moment into fascinating story time.

"Anna, wake up. We must go to the hall." It was mother waking me in the dead of night. Whenever a bad electrical storm blew up, night or day, mother herded us all into the hall—her idea of a place of safety.

"I'd rather stay here in bed." It was cold in the drafty hall and many times my back had nearly broken, sitting out there on the stairs, waiting for the lightning and thunder to stop.

"No, you must come, now hurry! Grandpa and Henry are already there. Here, put your clothes on so you will be dressed if we have to leave the house." It

127

was an early June night but the fast-falling rain and darkness seemed cold and uninviting. Occasional lightning flashes lighted the room bright as day. As I dressed sleepily, I could see mother standing there, fully clothed.

"Maybe Grandpa will tell a story," mother encouraged.

"I'm coming." Sleepy as I was, I did not want to miss Grandpa's story. Maybe he would tell us about the old days. Usually he talked about our ancestors who had lived in Germany, and how they came to America. Grandpa could list all the families and their children's children, right down to our friends and neighbors.

Out in the hall, Henry crouched on a low step facing Grandpa, who had brought a chair from his rooms. Now the lightning flashes at the windows showed the outlines of the hall, the stairs, and mother sitting on the step beside me. She folded her arms tightly across her chest and each time the thunder crashed, she cringed as though a shot had been fired in her direction. I was frightened, too, and I liked feeling her warm body next to mine.

"I don't see why we have to come out here every time it thunders," Henry objected.

"I have told you over and over that lightning often strikes chimneys. We must stay away from that big one in our bedroom. Besides, there are stoves in each room and lightning comes right to them. Remember how it struck the chimney at Grandma Schneider's one time and the fire came right into the room where they were?"

"I'm scared," I said, thinking how terrible it would be if fire came into our house.

"The Lord will watch over us," said Grandpa kindly. "Let's talk about something else."

"Will you tell us a story?" Henry asked.

"What would you like to hear?"

"Tell about the *Werkzeuge!*" This was the favorite for both Henry and me, and we knew Grandpa liked it too.

"*Ach ja,* the *Werkzeuge!*" He paused so long I thought he was not going to say more. Then he continued just as a mighty blast of thunder shook the house.

"The *Werkzeuge* were the men and women, chosen by God to speak His holy testimonies, as the prophets did in biblical times. They were pure in heart and mind and very pious. God used their voices for giving the people messages.

"How did the *Werkzeuge* know they had been chosen?" I wondered.

"The Lord gave them a sign. They felt His presence and heard His voice speaking to them. It is hard to say how they knew."

"I like to hear about Christian Metz and how he became a *Werkzeuge,*" I said, trying to have this be the story of the evening. Metz seemed quite real to me, for Henry had shown me his grave in our Amana cemetery.

"Oh, yes, that is a wonderful story." Grandpa shifted to a more comfortable position on his chair and began:

"*Ja,* Christian Metz was a great man—and a true apostle of Christ. His grandfather had been an old-time Inspirationist in the days of Rock and Gruber. When Christian was a boy, growing up in southern Germany, he heard many stories about the wonderful revelations the Lord gave to the people. He must have known about the old-time *Werkzeuge* and how they received messages directly from God." Grandpa was lost in the story and none of us remembered the storm out-

129

side. "Christian Metz' father was a carpenter, and he was a carpenter, too. If you want to see how good he was, look at the floor in the South Amana meeting house. He laid most of it all by himself." Grandpa boasted as if speaking of his own relative.

"When Christian Metz was a young man, he committed a very terrible sin. Remorse about it made him so unhappy he was sick and could not work. He wanted most of all to make atonement and he prayed to God for forgiveness, promising to dedicate his life to serving Him."

"What was his sin?" Henry asked.

"You would not understand. When you are older, you will know."*

"How did he become an Inspirationist?" This was the best part of the story. Grandpa's voice was vibrant with feeling.

"The Lord took pity on him and sent a *Werkzeug,* Michael Krausert, to preach in the village where Brother Metz was working. He listened devoutly. Christian Metz wanted most of all to be a follower of the true Word of God. He worked and prayed and one day the Lord found him worthy and called him to be a *Werkzeug.* He received the divine 'Gift of Inspiration.' "

"Christian Metz was the most important one of all, wasn't he?" Henry was partial to him.

"Yes, but he had lots of elders to help him," I remembered the stories about the elders.

"Yes, there were elders, but only Christian Metz received messages from God. He was the only *Werkzeug*

---

*Grandpa never told us what Metz had done but years later I learned he had loved a woman and his child was born to her—out of wedlock. The mother died in childbirth and Metz took the child; she was reared in Amana.

for twenty-five years. That was a time of trial and hardship and many, many problems. Brother Metz and the elders had to find ways to take care of all the people who had come together at their refuge near Ronneburg in Hessen, Germany, and later all had to be moved to America. If the Lord had not guided Christian Metz with many 'Inspirations,' it could not have been done." Grandpa spoke with feeling.

"Tell about how they came to Amana," I urged. I had no time for Old World history.

"Anna, there was no such place as Amana in those days. The believers first settled in Ebenezer, New York, but after a few years the outside world crowded in on them. The Lord wanted the colonists to move away from this worldliness, so Brother Metz had an Inspiration to send a committee to go west and look for a new home."

"Did Christian Metz find this place for them?" Henry asked.

"No, he was ill with cholera so other men had to go. They searched a long time and had many hardships before they found the beautiful fertile hills of Iowa, with the river to furnish water power. They went back to Ebenezer and told the elders about the wonderful land the Lord had shown them. That is how Amana was chosen to be the new, and the last home of the True Inspirationists."

"I wish I could have been here when they were building the villages," said Henry.

"*Ach,* that was a busy time. They had to plan the communities, clear forests, make bricks, and start sawmills. Some were building new homes in Amana, while others were moving from New York. It took ten years to move the communities from Ebenezer to Amana.

131

This could not have been done without Christian Metz and his revelations from God," said Grandpa with conviction.

"What did he look like?" I wondered, thinking of Metz, the man.

"He was small physically, but he was an inspired speaker with a powerful voice. His 'Inspirations' were like hearing God Himself. The Lord even spoke poetry and hymns through testimonies by Christian Metz. *Ja,* he was a holy man." Grandpa fell silent.

He seemed to have finished the story. We had forgotten about the storm, nor had we noticed that the lightning no longer flashed nor did the thunder roar. The story of Christian Metz had held us spellbound. Mother stood up.

"Now we can go back to our beds," she told us.

Stiffly, we rose to our feet and the cold air enveloped us, making our teeth chatter. I had felt no coldness while listening to Grandpa.

Henry said, "Can anybody be a *Werkzeug?*"

"*Ach,* no, no, my child," replied Grandpa. "Only a few of the most pious people have been chosen by God to be *Werkzeuge.*"

"Why don't we have a *Werkzeug* in Amana today?"

"Since Barbara Heinemann died back in 1883, the Lord has found no one worthy to be chosen."

"Will we ever have another?"

"I don't know," said Grandpa sadly, "I don't know."

religious tradition, the "law" of Amana

AMANA CUSTOMS AND RELIGIOUS TRADITIONS were based on the early practices of the True Inspirationists. Some originated with Rock and Gruber, others were added along the way in the Ebenezer Society, and a few newer ones were adopted in Amana. Christian Metz and Barbara Heinemann were keenly aware of the importance of keeping the religious traditions faithfully. No doubt this policy was largely responsible for the society's long survival.

The strict order of seating in church developed very early in the life of the society. It indicated recognition given an individual's spiritual standing in the community, based on degree of piety—that holy condition sought by all members. It divided or "graded" the population of each village into three distinct congrega-

135

tions, with each member assigned to a specific group, depending on his age and spiritual state.

The first *Versammlung* claimed the older, most pious members. They held their Sunday morning service in a small meeting room in the main church. This was the most distinguished congregation, and everyone looked forward to meriting a place in this group.

The second *Versammlung* was mainly for the middle-aged members and their Sunday morning service was held at the same time as the first but in a smaller assembly room or little meetinghouse.

Finally, the third *Versammlung* included children (past the age of seven) and the young married people. Children did not attend a Sunday school.

From time to time, members were promoted by the elders, from one congregation to a higher one, or moved toward the back of the room as a sign of advancement in general standing. But the elders could also demote members, moving them forward in their *Versammlung* or even to a lower church.

Another striking feature of the seating system was the separation of the men from the women. The Inspirationists were quite consistent in their efforts to keep men and women from getting "interested" in each other. And they wanted to avoid anything that might distract from the piety of the services. Hence the men sat in rows of benches on one side of the room, the women on the other. They even entered by separate entrances so there would be no flirting in the halls.

Seating position was such an important social index that it provided the only punishment, spiritual or civil, that was needed in these colonies. To be demoted in church was a form of severe disgrace and to be banned entirely was the worst punishment that could be given to anyone. The penalty lay in being made conspicuous before the group. We all tried to conduct ourselves so that we would not be demoted. However, if the worst did happen, and a member was banned from attendance entirely, he could be reinstated by appearing before the elders and the congregation and confessing his wrongdoing, with a request for reinstatement. So embarrassing was such a performance that many a sinner preferred to leave the colonies and fend for himself in the outside world. However, deserting the community was considered a sin in itself and persons who wished to return and be reinstated were usually banned from the church for a year.

Most misdemeanors were minor and the elders had only to move offenders forward in the congregation where they stayed until they proved themselves worthy to be moved back.

A common cause of demotion in church was marriage. It was customary to demote the newly married couple from the back of the church to the rows directly behind the children in the Third Church, or even from the Second Church back to the Third Church, as a sign that they had sinned (by giving in to the ways of the flesh rather than being willing to devote their lives to the glory of God). Again, with the birth of each child, parents were demoted, either within the Third Church or from the Second to the Third. During my childhood, some couples from the middle church spent most of their time in the Third Church, for children kept coming and kept them demoted.

The really important role of the church seating, however, was its remarkable influence on behavior of the members. So effective was the general fear of public disgrace encountered by being demoted in church, that the Amanas needed no civil law and no law enforcement officers. The far-reaching influence of the demotion system, in both temporal and spiritual matters, proved to be a most effective method of control. It was enforced by the *Werkzeuge* and later by the elders.

The result was that we lived in a community with no jails and no need for jails. No record exists of any serious crime having been committed. Occasionally, questionable situations came up but no investigation was made of them, other than the evaluation given by the elders. Never has there been a murder. Few members ever conducted themselves in such a manner that the elders had to ask them to leave. Divorce was practically unheard of. There was no thievery. Since no emphasis was placed on owning property, we were quite indifferent to it. We had no reason to steal from each other. Everybody was provided with necessities and nobody had any luxuries. We did have a night watchman who made the rounds during the night to inspect the warehouses and factories, but he was hired to protect us from outsiders who might come to steal.

In a community where we lived together so intimately, it was not easy to trespass without being detected. Occasional offenses of drunkenness were handled by individuals. In addition to the chance of being demoted in church, there was that pressure of "What will the neighbors say?"

Since we had no civil laws, we needed no courts. Legal matters were handled at Marengo, the county seat. County health officers would tack up the quarantine signs when they were needed.

We were citizens of Iowa although we had no polling places. In the old days, voting was considered worldly and not permitted. Occasionally, some of the members would go outside and vote secretly. If they were discovered, they were banned from church for several Sundays.

One day I came home from Elsie's house and found mother in a state of panic.

"What happened, Mama?"

"I have just done a terrible thing. If I tell you about it you must promise not to tell Grandpa," was her weeping reply.

"I won't." I felt flattered that mother would confide in me and secretly glad that she, too, resented having Grandpa dominate over us. I couldn't imagine mother "sinning," however.

"I was cleaning the schoolhouse with Katy Mueller and *Tante* Louise," she started hesitatingly, wondering whether she should go on and reveal her sin.

"What's so bad about that?"

"Mr. Wilson from Marengo drove by when we were out at the pump. He stopped and treated us to some candy. Then he asked us if we had voted yet. Of course, we said 'No.' He gave us some more candy and told us that it was really our duty to vote and that he would be glad to take us to the election place in his new Studebaker. We just couldn't turn him down. And it was so nice to get to ride in an automobile. He told us he was running for sheriff and would appreciate having us vote for him."

"Did you?" I asked.

"Of course; he was so nice I am sure he will make a good sheriff.

"And then the most horrifying thing happened. On the way home Mr. Wilson saw some more women out at Beck's kitchen. He stopped to talk to them, and there we were, sitting in his car. Frieda Klipfel was there. You know what a big gossip she is. I am sure the elders will find out and I will be banned from church. And since it is November I won't get to go to the Thanksgiving service and everybody in town will know I sinned, and worst of all, Grandpa will be furious!" By now she was really crying.

"Oh, Mama, don't worry; he might never find out." I tried to comfort her.

As it turned out, either the elders did not find out, or else they ignored the situation. Apparently Mr. Wilson was not the only solicitor for votes for that particular election and many men and women were "convinced" with cigars and candy that they should vote. People were beginning to take more interest in politics. Even the older people took sides. One old lady became so excited she scratched the eyes out of a certain candidate's picture whenever she saw it in the newspaper.

When the presidential election came around two years later, we were studying about the candidates in our "current events." I became a fervent Hoover fan and pleaded with mother to vote. Since she had gotten by once before, she decided to go, just to please me. However, this got her into more trouble. Three weeks later she was called for jury duty. Now she was sure she was being punished for her "sin" of voting. She was much too worried and shy to commit herself to participate in experiences so new and strange. It would have involved going to Marengo for days at a time, perhaps, and to associate with outsiders, as well as to talk in English in front of great audiences of people. She fussed and struggled with herself for days. Finally I helped her write a letter in which she asked to be excused from serving.

She did not vote again for many years.

* * *

The church seating tradition also served as a check on morals. One man fell into disgrace through an affair with an "outside woman." Of course, we all knew about it and the elders banned him for a year. By the end of the year he repented and was forgiven. Years later he even became an elder. It was a general practice in the colonies that when anyone committed a misdemeanor, was reproved or demoted, or banned from church, and then later repented, he was received back into his former position and no mention or reference was made to the trouble. It was erased from the books.

Rumor has it that such was the case with Emma. Like most other Amana girls, Emma found the attractions and charms of men from the outside much more desirable than those of "any old Amana boy." Emma met and fell in love with a man who had come to Amana to work. Her parents did their best to discourage her infatuation. But, as may be expected, this only made the girl more determined than ever to be with the man. In time, he left Amana and Emma found she was to have a child. Desperate and ashamed, she left the society and moved away.

Strangely enough, everyone felt sorry for her, not outraged or self-righteous. Her people, especially her father, begged her to come home with her baby. Actually, due to her Amana upbringing, she was utterly unprepared to cope with life outside. So she came back and was received as if she had never been away. True, she was punished by being banned from church attendance for a year and in time confessed her sin before the assembled congregation. Her child was then a year old and everyone had forgotten the unpleasant beginnings of the story. The confession was a matter of routine for she was again one of us. There was no comment or question about her position. She lived on in Amana as did her beautiful child, undistinguished in any way.

the elders

EVER SINCE THE DEATH of Christian Metz and Barbara
Heinemann, the elders had assumed the responsibility
for the "law" of Amana and its enforcement. At first
they had simply carried out the wishes of the *Werkzeuge,* after the pattern established over the years. As
time went on a "Council of the Brethren" was formed
as a governing body. It consisted of representative elders
from each village, who in turn ruled on all local problems: who should live where and with whom, where
members should work, who should take care of the
churches, who should run the mills and shops, who
should travel abroad as salesmen, and who should be
responsible for looking after old people, specifically the
unmarried members. They also gave permission for
marriage and could make effective objections, should

the case demand it. Hence they controlled the delicate problem of preventing too close intermarriage.

The members could do very little without consulting the elders. They even had to ask permission if they wished to visit in other villages, or outside.

There is a story about my Grandfather Schneider, who was the elder in charge of granting permission for the use of transportation facilities. A young man asked him for the use of the society horse and "top buggy" on a certain Sunday, so that he might go to East Amana, his former home. The man making the request was very shy about it and grandfather said—

"No, you can't use the buggy. You just had it last Sunday."

The young man accepted the decision without comment. There was only one "top buggy" that could be used to go calling and it was supposed to be shared. It turned out that he had received word of his mother's death and had needed to go home. When grandfather later heard about this he apologized and permitted the man to go.

The clerical duties of the elders included presiding, in turn, at all regular church services, as well as participating with "sermonettes" at every service. For this office they sat on a bench in the front of the church, facing the congregation. Also, the elders of a village conducted marriages and funeral ceremonies. They represented their respective communities at the various special church services that rotated from village to village, and presided over the important annual services such as the *Unterredung* and the *Liebesmahl*.

144

As secular members of the Society, the elders all had regular jobs, as farm hands, workers in the woolen mill, or in some other capacity.

New elders were appointed by the Great Council of the Brethren and usually children of former elders were chosen. Hence, elderships rather ran in certain families. In the old days, it was an honor to be chosen. As time went on, men tended to avoid serving. No one actively sought an appointment. There was no pay or other special advantage to be gained by serving, so it meant only more duties to perform and the chance to be criticized. We had no electioneering and no politics. If a man's habits were not good, or if he tended to be slovenly or crude or drunken, he would not be asked to serve. This informal system usually served to select the best men. Once a man accepted an appointment, he was an elder for life—unless suspended for "just" cause.

The records have it that several elders were suspended in Ebenezer for marrying, others for negligence of duty, and others for not believing. Once, an elder in one of the Amanas was suspended when he and his wife had a child—which indicated, of course, a lack of piety.

As I was growing up, all the elders were old men. Many years went by without the appointment of a new one and finally the number dwindled as the old men died. About the time I left the colonies, the Council of the Brethren was trying to appoint new elders. Most of the young men they asked refused to serve. Although an elder's position was still one of prestige and honor, it had many undesirable features. Younger elders, especially, were chided and viewed critically, much as are school teachers in some communities. They were expected to set fine examples of character and conduct.

The younger men did not relish being placed in

145

positions of self-righteousness. They felt foolish about sitting in front of the congregation and conducting church, for they had not been trained for it, and giving a sermon did not come easy. Many of them stammered through the service in a painfully labored way. Others preached excellent sermons, comparing favorably with many I have since heard by educated clergymen.

Another duty the new elders disliked was reprimanding backsliders. It had been customary for the *Werkzeuge* to reprimand persons who had sinned by preaching about them in church, and this the elders were now supposed to do. It was an embarrassing business. They became more and more lax about enforcing the old austerities of Metz and Heinemann. They handled reprimands by making a blanket statement in church, without mentioning any names, and that served as pointing a finger of shame at the sinner. Or complaints were woven into sermons and wrongdoings were "declared" as a part of the service. Eventually it became easier to ignore most of the old restrictions. Drinking was condoned. If a man became drunk, he was no longer considered sinful, just foolish. We knew who were drinkers and who were not, and that was all there was to that problem. Other relaxations of the rules included the privilege of purchasing merchandise on the outside, such as cars and radios. In time people even married without consulting the elders.

Although the elders were expected to keep the traditions from disappearing, conformity was now maintained largely by fear of being different. We all knew what conduct was acceptable and what was not, what would be all right and what would not. We consistently avoided being conspicuous, particularly in church. Being late to meeting was something which was *not* done.

146

Mother would have gone home rather than enter late and to her, being reprimanded in church would have been the worst disgrace that could happen. Fear of public criticism was so effective that members were kept law-abiding, with very few exceptions.

Actually the elders of Amana deserve much credit. They assumed responsibility for running a large business enterprise and received no compensation for their services. They worked under severe handicaps. Only a few of them had more than the required eighth grade education, so their educational qualifications for leadership were no different than those of the people they led and directed. However, they seemed to have had more "know-how" than the average citizen. They kept up with the news and a great deal of practical ability had been passed on to them from preceding generations.

As outside influences crept in, the elders felt more and more inadequate. They recognized their lack of training for making speeches, and even for reading aloud. Furthermore, they were known so intimately by their congregations that it was not easy for them to assume prior positions.

In about 1955, the lack of interest of younger men in elderships caused a crisis in one of the Amanas. There was only one elder left. It seemed inevitable that a Sunday should come when he might be sick or gone and there would be no elder to preside at the church service.

This actually happened one Sunday and naturally the older members in the congregation were desolate. The time for the opening prayer was a still moment. From force of habit, all members rose in their places and, after only a slight pause, one elderly lady started repeating the Lord's Prayer. The others followed in unison, and the service proceeded according to well-known routine.

This village was one where an elder had been deposed for the "sin" of becoming a father, and so it is not strange that younger men shied away from the position. Finally, elders from neighboring villages began conducting services for the "Amana without an Elder."

my first day in church

It always seemed to me that grownups went to church just about all of the time. Before I was old enough, I often imagined what it would be like to go and have a place assigned just for me. Of course, I knew that at first I would have to sit in the front row where the benches were small and for children. And, as I grew older and more pious, the elders would move me back, row by row, until finally I would have a place in the back and so be most honored in the church. Then, I fancied I would be so good that soon the elders would have to move me up to the Second Church where mother went. But never in my wildest dreams did I think of being moved to the First Church reserved for the oldest, most pious members in the village.

Mother told me about the service—how one of the

elders presided, how the congregation, following a leader, sang hymns together, how the elder read from the testimonies of the True Inspirationists and how each member of the congregation, in turn, said a prayer and read a verse from the Bible text. Although mother never said so, I knew that she was more self-conscious about reading and speaking in church than anything else. She would come home from church and tell us how some of the members had bumbled through their reading, or were unable to read at all. And she would say, "I hope that when your time comes you will read and speak without making mistakes or being tongue-tied."

So, I wondered and wondered how I would do when I went to church. I was anxious to prove to mother that I could make her proud of me but I was not at all sure that I would not turn out to be one of the pitied tongue-tied. There were many things to think about in those long weeks before I started to church.

I was most excited about my church costume, feeling that it would somehow be more outstanding than those of the other women, although, of course, it would be much the same. Mother explained the tradition. She said it started back in Germany in olden times when the True Inspirationists were rebelling against the "Worldliness" of the Lutheran Church. The women had said they would not dress up and be vain when they went to church for worship. So they wore their dark simple everyday clothes and no fancy hats. Since women's heads must be covered in church, they made little black caps with ribbons to tie under the chin. A shoulder shawl and apron completed the costume of German women in those days. In time, when Amana women wore more modern dress for everyday, the simple costume became the traditional church costume, all the women dressing in the same manner. Mother explained that one shows respect for God by one's dress. This is why the costumes of old Germany are still worn in Amana and this is why mother and all my aunts made a special outfit for me.

First, mother made my dress, a nicer one than I had ever had before. It was made of Amana flannel, a dark blue color, one of the famous flannels that John, the salesman, had sold in many far-off cities. *Tante* Lina made my shoulder shawl and this I loved most of all. It was triangular and of sheer black wool with tiny yellow figures woven in it. I could feel the long silken fringe sway gently as I walked. *Tante* Louise made the cap of fine black gauze, trimmed with a tiny black tatted edging and with satin ribbons. *Tante* Marie gave the heavy shawl to be worn instead of a coat in winter. I loved to try on my new costume and to admire it when no one was looking.

At last the day arrived when I was to start to church. Mother helped me dress although I wanted to do it alone now that I was big enough for church. We began early, for mother took no chances about being late. "No one comes late to church," she would say.

"What happens if they do?" I asked.

"They go home. No one comes late to church."

When the village bell rang for eight o'clock, and everyone checked their clocks for correct time, mother was arranging my shoulder shawl.

"Let me see; is the point exactly in the middle of the back?" I asked as she had so often asked me about her own.

"Yes, Anna. Here, you can stand on a chair and look in the mirror." I was quite satisfied and let her cross the points in the very middle of my waist in front.

"Now hold still while I tie on the apron. Such a pretty apron that *Tante* Alma made for you!"

"Make a big stand-outish bow. I'd like a real wide bow."

"That is as large as it can be, child. If I make it larger, it will droop."

Actually the bow was a beauty, almost as wide as my waist. I climbed down from the chair and faced about for the cap. It seemed to be a magic cap, as mother tied the ribbons under my chin. She left the room for something and I had a good chance to peek in the glass. I thought I looked quite pretty but kept reminding myself that being vain was a sin. Yet all the women were very proud of their shawls and were always on the lookout for pretty material to use for them. Mother had sixteen different ones, some for winter and some for summer.

I was sorry I could not wear my lovely "coat" shawl because one did not need a heavy shawl in September. I always liked to see the women walking along the sidewalks with their heavy black winter shawls, worn instead of coats in order not to wrinkle the shoulder shawls. Mother had talked to me about keeping my costume pressed and neat. It had to be just about perfect.

At eight-thirty, mother and I walked side by side on the narrow sidewalk to the *"Sälchen,"* the church for the young people where I would go. Before leaving me, mother said:

"Let me look at you, Anna." She pushed back my cap and let my blonde hair show a little more. I knew she was pleased that I was starting to church and that I looked well in my new costume. "Now you watch what the others do and if you can't find the chapter in your Bible right away, don't annoy people by thumbing through the pages. It is better you should look on with Elsie."

"I can find it myself, because I learned how to do it in Saturday school." I started to recite the names of the books of the Bible in rhyme from the catechism:

"Five books of Moses,* Joshua,
Judges, Ruth, two books of Samuel,
Two Kings and Two Chronicles.
After Ezra comes Nehemiah.
Esther and Job show us next
The wonderful works of God. . . ."

I was in a hurry to be off. Women were passing us in little groups going to the women's entrance.

"Be a good girl, Anna. Remember God is watching everything you do." Mother told us that so often that I felt God must be neglecting other people if he spent all his time watching me.

Mama left for her church and I walked as fast as I could to the entrance where my friend Elsie was waiting.

"Anna, you look real pretty. Turn around, let me see the bow."

I suddenly felt that not only God but everybody was watching me and I wanted only to find a corner to hide in. Lots of the women spoke to me but some were too busy visiting in the hall to notice. Elsie picked up her books from the long shelf where they were kept and opened the door to the church room. I followed her to a seat on the bench in the front row. I wanted to look around and see who sat in back of us but I was not sure that God would approve. So I admired the green felt cover on the elders' table and watched a lost fly flitting

---

*In the Lutheran Bible the first five books are grouped together and called the Five Books of Moses.

about. The six large windows with the small panes were like frames for the pictures of fields and trees. The martins in their house just outside were busy with housekeeping. The sky was my favorite bright blue. Best of all, I could see an apple tree full of fruit on a far off hill. And such quietness. Except when little groups of women came in with a rush of feet clomping on the bare pine floors it was utterly still. As soon as they sat down, there was dead silence again. I wanted so much to say something to Elsie but nobody talked in church, mama said. Suddenly, there was a burst of clomping feet on the men's side and the elders marched to their places in the front of the room. Elder Becker took his place at the table and laid his books out, opening them to marked places. He looked handsome in his Sunday suit, so unlike the clothes he wore to run the mill on weekdays. I had trouble recognizing him, so much dignity and authority did he assume today. I thought he gave me a special glance because he knew this was my first Sunday in church.

The other elders had taken seats on the long bench, facing the congregation. I knew them all; Brother Weber, the cabinet maker who also made the coffins; Brother Staab, the pharmacist; Brother Martin, the clockmaker; and my Uncle John, the farm manager. I wanted to laugh for they all looked so strange, as if their Sunday clothes did not belong to them. Elsie nudged me. I had not noticed that all heads were bowed for prayer. Already Brother Becker was announcing the number for the first hymn and there was quite a flurry as pages turned throughout the room. My own *Psalterspiel* was upside down and I was still looking for the number when Mina Jung started the hymn and a loud burst of singing rang out on all sides. Again, I wanted to laugh, for the strange sounds were like nothing I had ever heard. As they sang verse after verse I found myself joining in and trying to follow. On some parts Brother Martin sang out above everyone and I felt safe to try, too. The singing was good and I liked it.

Next, Brother Becker gave the Bible reference and again there was a rush of books, this time Bibles being taken from their cardboard containers. I noticed that the elders put the Bibles back after each use and had to get them out several times during the service. I was all fluttery and could not see the names, being so afraid that I might not be ready to read when my turn came. Men in the back row were reading verse by verse, then the boys read. Still I had not found The Acts. Elsie offered me her book and I looked on with her. When the reading started with the women in the back row, I was thinking of running away, and never stopping. I knew I could not make a sound. Reading in German was still difficult for me. The sound of the voices came nearer and nearer. Then it stopped. All verses had been read and there were none left for us in the front. My heart began beating again though my mouth was still dry. At least I was saved from the Bible reading but not before I had heard several men and women stumble with pronunciation. Nor could I understand what they read.

Elder Becker began to read from the Testimonies of Christian Metz, telling about his troubles when the True Inspirationists lived in Ebenezer, New York. I could not follow this too well, so I watched the elders. Brother Schultz was old and I had heard stories of how he slept in church. Sure enough, his head began to wobble around and his mouth hung open. I was fascinated, wondering how he could let his head roll around like that. Then he gave a quick jerk and looked around to see if anyone had seen him. Brother Martin had his legs stretched out in front of him and his hands clasped across his stomach. He looked comfortable but I had expected elders to sit up straight in church. Then I watched Brother Staab who had his hands folded so that he could twiddle his thumbs. He would whirl them in one direction until I was nearly asleep; then he would roll them in the other direction. Uncle John leaned first one way and then the other as though his back was not comfortable. I could understand that because my own back was ever so tired. The Inspirationists who had made our benches did not have comfort in mind. Those wide pine board seats with the four inch wide "backs" were about the most uncomfortable places to sit that I knew of. Brother Becker read on and on in a sort of monotone, the German words making no meaning for me. I was glad when prayer time came and we could turn and kneel on the floor, resting our arms on the seats of the benches. But the plain old pine floor was hard, too, and hurt my knees. By peeking a bit, I could see under the "back" board and admire the pretty shoulder shawls. I had to be quiet and wondered what to do about a mosquito biting my ankle. I concentrated on moving my foot over the itchy part but that did not seem to help much. Elsie whispered to me, telling me that Catherine Krumbolts was in our church. I was embarrassed, but the elders could not see us for they were facing their own bench and had their backs to us. Catherine must have sinned to be demoted to our church from the middle church. I wondered what she had done. Elsie would find out and tell me; Elsie was older and heard the women talk.

Suddenly I realized that the prayers were being said, one after another, along the rows, and already the girls in the row back of us were speaking. I listened to them, one by one, as they came closer to me. Some of them I recognized as the rhyming prayers I had learned from the catechism:

> Oh, my dearest Jesus,
> Make for Thyself a soft bed
> In the shrine of my heart
> That I may never forget Thee. Amen.

> Help me to grieve
> Whenever I sin,
> And make me truly repentant
> Over my wrongdoing. Amen.

> Jesus, I, Thy lamb, am calling
> To Thee with remorse.
> Search for me: I am lost,
> Oh, my dear Shepherd. Amen.

> Help me, that by constructive thoughts
> I may lead my heart to Thee, Oh, God.
> Knock at my heart
> Whenever I am on the wrong path. Amen.

I could not think about the meaning of the words, I was so busy reciting the one I had learned to say for myself. Mother had told me to say a simple, two-line prayer the first time. I took a deep breath and raced away:

> "Jesus, let my faltering voice please You,
> That I, Your unworthy child, may find grace. Amen."

After that the horrible rush of fear began to leave me. I liked the last hymn and was sorry when all the singing stopped and Elder Becker read the remaining verses. He said the closing words and everyone began picking up books to leave.

I was not at all sure that going to church was as much of a joy as I had expected. Now that I had started, I would have to go to all the services and, counting three on Sunday and one every evening, plus a Wednesday and a Saturday morning service, there were eleven each week. Dressing and undressing, eating and dressing again for church was to become a boring routine.

Out in the hall, the women were speaking to me and asking me how I liked going to church. I could only think of going home to tell mama all about it. I wanted to find out, too, why Catherine Krumbolts had to come to our church instead of going to the Second Church where she belonged.

"Mama, Mama, I said my prayer without any trouble." I met mother at the door when she came home from her church. Their services had lasted a little longer than ours.

"That is fine, my child. I am very proud of you." She took off her black cap and shoulder shawl and folded them neatly, then picked up mine which I had piled on a chair. "You must make room in a drawer for your church outfit and keep it neat," she reprimanded.

"Mama, how old is Sister Krumbolts?" I wanted to know.

"She is about my age. Why?"

"Then why didn't she go to the Second Church with you?"

"It doesn't matter how old a person is. We go to the church assigned to us by the elders. They determine who is pious enough to go to the Second or First Church."

"But did Sister Krumbolts sin?"

"No, my dear, she had a baby recently and that means that she has to devote more time and energy to

160

her family than to God. She will have to stay in the
Third Church for a year. Then she will come back to the
Second Church. Now run along and don't worry about
these matters."

a Sunday walk
with Grandpa

AS THE YEARS WENT BY, Sundays became the dullest days of all. When Christian Metz and the elders set up the Amana system, they made sure that Sundays would be used for True Inspirationist worship and meditation. Consequently, we who were accustomed to working hard during six days of the week, could scarcely endure the hopeless, boring inactivity Sundays imposed on us. The church services—one in the morning, one in the afternoon, and another in the evening—proceeded according to monotonous, standardized routine, week after week. Then on Sunday afternoon, when we were free of church for a few hours, we had a choice of reading the Bible or a religious book, or doing nothing at all!

Henry and I had one escape. During the spring and fall seasons, Grandpa Guyer might take us for a walk in the woods. We were always impatient for him to come. Mother would try to quiet us:

"Anna and Henry, do be quiet. You know Grandpa had an elders' meeting after church today."

"But Mama, it's three o'clock now and he promised to take us today," I wailed.

"He will take you, child. He likes to walk in the woods as much as you do. Just sit down and act as you should on Sunday. And you, Henry, put that hammer away. You know better than to pound on the Sabbath."

"See, I'm making a wagon and it's nearly finished." He held up a small box with two wooden wheels attached.

"Put it away, Henry."

Just as slowly as he could, Henry edged the hammer onto the window sill. I folded my hands and tried to sit on the low rocker. I rocked just a little and tested whether that, too, was forbidden. Mother opened her crochet book. She could "pick patterns" and study them on Sunday even if crocheting itself was not allowed.

"Mama, may I put on my roller skates?"

"No, Anna, of course, you may not. The neighbors might hear you."

"I'll probably find a lot of mushrooms in the woods," Henry mused. "I'm glad we can at least pick mushrooms on Sundays."

"I wish there was no such thing as a Sunday," I complained.

"Anna, you must learn to use the Sabbath for thinking about God and ... good thoughts," mother reminded me.

"I don't seem to have many good thoughts," I answered, "especially on Sunday when there is nothing to do."

164

I thought of my favorite pastimes—meeting Elsie in the orchard, playing games with Henry, or even knitting or making doll clothes. All were forbidden.

Henry stretched and groaned.

"All right, if you will be quiet, you may wait for Grandpa on the back porch."

Henry and I were up like a flash. Grandpa could not help hearing us tramp, not too lightly, as we dashed through the hall and down the stairs. Soon he came, a more friendly smile on his stern face than usual. I wished Grandpa would not *always* be an elder, especially when he was alone with us.

"Now, *meine Kinder,* are you ready?" He seemed happy about going and this promised to be a good day. He took his walking stick and the three of us started out, single file, on the narrow wooden sidewalk with Grandpa leading the way. Out in the country, we would walk together with Grandpa between us.

Along the way we saw rich black fields with rows of neatly set young corn; the river, angry and swirling high from recent rains; the woods thick with newly leaved trees and, over all, a wide, wide blue sky. We asked many questions and Grandpa seemed to have answers for them all. He taught us the names of the trees and flowers. He knew where to find the bluest violets, the tallest jacks-in-the-pulpit, and the most delicate May-apples. We picked great bunches of violets for mother, for they were her favorite flowers. He led us to the musty hollows where the mushrooms grew and taught us how to recognize the edible sponge. Grandpa knew so many things!

We had walked along the river for a few miles when Grandpa gave the signal for a rest. He selected an old log and sat down easily, resting his arms on his bony knees. Henry and I spread our coats on the ground and sat on them, facing Grandpa. We loved learning Grandpa's secrets of the woodlands but it was the stories he told about the Inspirationists that carried us away to an enchanted land. We always waited expectantly.

"Grandpa, will you tell about Barbara Heinemann today?"

"Aha, Anna. You like to hear about her because she was a woman *Werkzeug*, don't you?" He teased me.

"No, I like to hear about her because she was the last one of all and she lived in Amana a long time," I answered.

"*Ja*, that is a wonderful story." Grandpa nodded and began:

"Long ago in the old country, Barbara was an ignorant servant girl. Her parents were peasants—simple country people. Barbara yearned to be holy and good and she prayed, seeking the Lord. One day she heard a great preacher, Michael Krausert, who came to her village preaching about God's power to speak through his chosen 'instruments.' Soon after that she began hearing the voice of God speaking to her—just as if He were in the room with her." Grandpa looked at us directly to drive home this amazing idea. "Barbara knew that she had been chosen by God and she left being a servant girl and wandered all around central Europe preaching about the messages God gave to her. Many people believed and followed her."

"Did she write the messages down?" asked Henry.

"No, Henry—you forget that she was only a humble peasant girl. Only rich people could read and write in those days. She did try once to write a testimony but no one could decipher it. A learned scribe began making records for her and later she taught herself to read and write. She used the Bible for a textbook."

"Tell about how she lost her power."

"*Ach, Ja,*" Grandpa nodded knowingly. "You see Barbara Heinemann was a young, strong woman. She traveled alone about the country, telling people about True Inspiration and how the Lord spoke to her. Many times, she had no place to spend the night and had to sleep by the side of the road. Not everybody believed her. Often she had no shoes for her feet—yet she walked miles and miles. It was during her travels that she met George Landmann and yielded to the temptation of marriage. But it was sinful for her to prefer marriage when God had already chosen her for His service so she lost the power of revelation for twenty-five years. Not until after she came to America and was much older and more pious did God find her worthy again. The Gift was finally restored to her."

"Then we again had two *Werkzeuge,*" I prompted.

"Yes, the two *Werkzeuge* worked together until Brother Metz died. Then Barbara Heinemann carried on alone until she died—in 1883.

"What was Barbara Heinemann like?" I asked curiously.

"She was a large woman—as tall as I am. She spoke with a deep mighty voice when she gave testimonies in meetings."

"How did she know when she was having an 'Inspiration?' " Henry asked.

"She would 'fall into Inspiration,' often in the middle of church when all the people were together. Her body would shake and her voice got deep, and loud, and strange. She would speak in the manner of the Bible.

167

She said many wonderful things." Grandpa looked at us soberly over the top of his glasses.

"What were the revelations about?" Henry asked.

"Revelations were about most anything. The Lord would tell her when we should harvest our crops, how the elders should manage our affairs, and she even reprimanded sinners in the name of God."

"Mother says that people were afraid of what she might say about them in meetings and hated to be in church during her 'Inspiration,'" I interrupted.

"Only if they had sinned, Anna. If a man had been drinking too much wine and had become drunken in his habits, the Lord might warn him in the meeting, through a testimony of Barbara."

"Did that ever happen?"

"Once I saw it happen in church. The man fell on his knees and wept, promising to sin no more. The Lord sees everything, and the *Werkzeuge* spoke for Him, warning the sinners."

Grandpa took from his pocket his large gold watch with the heavy gold chain.

"Now, *meine Kinder,* it is time to think about going home."

"But Grandpa, I want to hear about how Great-grandma Guyer came to America." Henry tried to delay going home as long as possible.

"Another time, Henry. There will be another time. Now we must go. The sun is making long shadows and the supper bell will be ringing before we know it. Besides, we must change our clothes for supper."

"Yes, and after supper we must change for church," I added, taking hold of Grandpa's hard, strong hand. I wished that I might some day be a wonderful *Werkzeug.*

"it is better to be unmarried"

THE ONE PROBLEM that plagued the Inspirationists more than any other was marriage. In the history of religions, leaders have often believed that being unmarried made them better able to dedicate their lives to serving God. But the Inspirationists did not stop there; they extended the implication to all men and all women.

When Gruber and Rock organized the Society and published the Twenty-Four Rules, no mention was made of marriage but the question came up soon afterward, and Gruber, who was married and being assisted by a son, was put on the defensive. The argument referred to the Holy Scriptures:

I Cor. 7:32-34.

> *He that is unmarried careth for the things that belong to the Lord, how he may please the Lord;*

But he that is married careth for the things that are of the world, how he may please his wife.

There is a difference also between a wife and a virgin. The unmarried woman careth for the things of the Lord, that she may be holy both in body and in spirit; but she that is married careth for the things of the world, how she may please her husband.

As religious fervor intensified, the question of celibacy became more and more disturbing. Gruber, in his *Jahrbuch* for 1727, gives an account of a serious threat of the Lord (delivered as an Inspiration through Gruber) to a young physician and a lady of noble birth, should they marry. Already, a strong feeling existed among members of the Society that marriage was a worldly, and even a sinful, state. Young people were forever being urged to beware of "the temptations of the enemy" and to "withdraw their love entirely from the lusts of the flesh." Metz and Heinemann preached that marriage not only interfered with complete dedication but also was itself a spiritual fall. The negative attitude toward marriage persisted throughout the entire history of the Inspirationists.

Each of the important *Werkzeuge* had a crucial, personal decision to make about marriage. Gruber, whose position was already compromised, was inclined to preach that, under proper conditions, marriage should be sanctified; Metz' experience was different. Although he had loved a woman, and she became the mother of his daughter, he did not marry her. It was Metz' deep repentance over his sin, at the time Krausert was preaching the Reawakening, that moved him to dedicate himself to God. He therefore took a firm stand against marriage although he realized it had to be permitted under restricted conditions if the Society was to be perpetuated.

We have already told the story of Barbara Heinemann's struggle with her "natural impulses" and the marriage that caused her to lose her Gift for twenty-five years.

An important idea entered the thinking of the Inspirationists with the loss of the power by Barbara. It was that many pious and gifted young people might well be potential *Werkzeuge* but that the power could not be granted to them if they married. This seems to have been the reason why Brother Metz, and later Sister Heinemann, made such bold and brave efforts to keep likely young "prospects" from falling into the sinful trap of marriage. It also prompted them to point out repeatedly how God punished severely, even unto death, persons who might be suitable for the high calling but preferred marriage instead. A few quotations from the records leave no doubt about their positions. The following is a translation of the account by Gottlieb Scheuner, the Society's historian, about the tragic death of Louise P———. (*Inspirations-Historie,* p. 829, 1817-1867):

> Sister Louise T———, daughter of Martin T———, had been a most capable person, gifted in every way. According to her calling, she was included among the faithful group of single women who devoted themselves only to the Lord. But while she was traveling with the first group of members migrating to Iowa from Ebenezer in the summer of 1855, in order to help establish the new home there, she weakened in her calling. Her attention was divided and she let the flesh take the upper hand until finally she no longer heeded her warnings. She married Brother Fritz P——— after she received a forced permission from the Lord and from the elders. Her death followed a hard and excruciating childbirth.

171

She had sensed that she was going to die and had had a chance to recognize and repent her sin. She was in the fortieth year of her age.

Christian Metz fell into "Inspiration" at her funeral and gave advice in the form of a song for others like her, who have a similar calling for a better lot in life, but prefer not to assume their responsibilities:

"Alas, alas, for you a better lot was chosen. . . ."

Another story about a "struggle with the flesh" is related by Scheuner, *Inspirations-Historie* (1817-1867), pp. 357, 358:

In October 1844, Brother Wilhelm N____, who up to now had been one of the leaders in the purchasing of the land and the founding of the Society in Ebenezer, became an affliction to the Lord and the whole Society. All summer there came warnings to him because the Lord saw the threatening danger. But he could no longer be held. The burden and sorrow of the Society had become too much for him. He began to doubt whether the Society could sustain; he lost his sacrificial love for his people, and his heart became captured by thoughts of providing for himself and of love for the flesh. He finally came to the conclusion to forsake his calling and to get married. When he asked the Brothers to be relieved of his duties, he received a parting letter from the Lord in the form of an *Einsprach* by Christian Metz, asking him to leave the Society:

"There is a messenger sent out from the sanctuary of the Lord. He has the letter of farewell that you have asked for, Wilhelm N____. . . ."

Brother N____ had been so esteemed, however, that he was later again accepted by the society. On May 24, 1849, he returned to Ebenezer with his wife and three children.

Similarly, whenever a marriage was "sinful" because it was not sanctioned by the elders, it invited a direct curse from the Lord. The next account is taken from the *Tagebuch von Christian Metz*, p. 454:

> About fourteen days ago Christian S⎯⎯ and Margaretha B⎯⎯ secretly left the Society, were married on the outside and moved to Cedar Rapids. They had been going in secret, sinful ways for some time and did not heed their warnings. The Lord had sent out sharp admonitions to them (through Christian Metz) and had repeatedly spoken His curse and displeasure.

It continues on p. 472:

> I received a letter from Amana (Metz had gone back to Ebenezer). . . which brought the terrible death notice of young Christian S⎯⎯, who had secretly and disobediently married Margaretha B⎯⎯ last summer. They were both very young and were living in Cedar Rapids, until they both fell sick onto death, he with pneumonia and she with erysipelas. Her mother, (Sister B⎯⎯), was there and took care of them, but Christian died January 7, 1857. Margaretha recovered. . . .
> The following day, Sister B⎯⎯ and her daughter brought the casket to Amana on a sled. This was the end of the five month marriage, which had taken place against the wishes of their parents and the elders, and which had started even without the fear of the Lord in sinful and insolent lust and desire. . . .

Actually, celibacy has been a point of conflict for many religious sects, particularly those practicing communal living. Some, like the Shakers, went so far as to prohibit marriage entirely and even adopted children to keep the organization going. The Inspirationists never quite abolished marriage but they compromised with it grudgingly and put various discouraging obstacles in the way of it. Everyone understood—

"It is good to be married but it is better to be unmarried." To this day, according to the beliefs of the older Amana members, it is more honorable and more pleasing to God to be unmarried than to be married.

Sociologically, there are other reasons for controlling marriage (and consequently, population) in a communal society such as Amana; there is an optimum number of people who can be supported feasibly on a certain amount of land. If there are too many people for the land and the income, the economy is thrown out of balance. Also, under the communal plan, the community rather than the parents is responsible economically for supporting the children. Every new child is a common liability until he can earn his way. It is best not to encourage practices which could result in more mouths to feed, more housing requirements, more services, and in general more complications.

The practice of controlling marriage was also necessary as a barrier against too close intermarriage, since there was a natural tendency for men and women of similar backgrounds to marry, the Bavarians choosing Bavarians, the Saxons preferring Saxons, etc. In such a closed community the number of eligible mates was limited, and eventually many people were closely or distantly related to each other. There were no cousin marriages, however, because the people themselves were conscious of the dangers of close intermarriage and avoided it.

Thus, there was considerable control over marriage by custom and propaganda, as well as by the elders and the *Werkzeuge*. In the early years marriages between Inspirationists could be entered into only with the consent of God as signified through the *Werkzeuge*. Routine required that the couple declare to the elders their wish to be married. The elders consulted with the *Werkzeuge* as to whether or not permission could be granted. Not all proposed unions were approved. The spiritual standing of the couple was checked carefully and it was impressed upon them that they were choosing a doubtful way of life. If they persisted in wanting to marry, and all was in order, the couple was subjected to a two-year separation, one of them being moved to a different village. They were permitted to see each other only once or twice a month and then only in the presence of a chaperone. If they survived all these tests, permission was granted, but reluctantly.

The separation began when the plan to marry was announced. Before that time, courtship went on secretly. Occasionally the schedule was upset and a child was born before the years of waiting were fulfilled. In such cases the elders held strictly to the rules and refused permission for marriage until the waiting period was over.

When the wedding day finally arrived there was no frivolity involving a special celebration. The common procedure was to call the groom from the field and the bride from the kitchen house with the summons, "now is the time to get married." Then they went to the church, as they were, and stood before the elder, repeating after him the marriage vows. The Corinthian text was read to them, reminding them again that it is better to be unmarried.

The period of separation did not end with the marriage ceremony. It was required that the bride and groom continue to live with their parents for a week or two until a new home could be readied for them.

After the *Werkzeuge* passed away the restrictions were gradually relaxed. By the time mother announced her engagement the premarital separation was no longer required. The couple still had a waiting period of one year after declaring their intentions of marriage, but they did not have to move to separate villages. Those who happened to live in different villages, however, still

175

had problems so far as courtship was concerned. Since they had no cars, or bicycles even, and the horses could only be borrowed occasionally, it meant a long walk to visit in another Amana. One of my uncles walked many trips between Homestead and Middle Amana, a distance of about five miles each way, while courting my aunt.

In those days a minimum age limit was in effect as a condition for marriage; women were required to be twenty-one years of age and men twenty-four. This rule was later also abandoned.

As was mentioned above, public disapproval of marriage required demotion of the couple in church. Bearing children, viewed as further evidence of having yielded to temptation, also called for demotion. Consequently, pregnancy was looked upon as a shameful condition and kept secret as long as possible. When a woman's pregnancy became at all apparent, she went into a true "confinement" and would not be seen in public, especially not in church. I knew of a case where a woman did not speak to her best friend for a long time, simply because the friend questioned her about her pregnant appearance before she was willing to admit it.

Family prejudices presented additional problems for young lovers. Certain families felt that they were superior to others, and especially to outsiders. Thus, parents often had their own objections to proposed marriages.

One family had two daughters, the younger Mathilda being the secret favorite of the father, a proud and righteous elder. The older daughter, Madeline, looked and waited for a husband for years but suitable matches were not easy to find in the Amanas, especially among the "better" families. Finally, Madeline married a man who was much older than she and who was considered to be somewhat beneath her family standards. Her parents were most unhappy about it. The younger Mathilda, pretty, adventurous of spirit, and romantic, came to know one of the outsiders who was employed in Amana. To her this man from the world beyond Amana was exciting and desirable and she wanted to marry him. Naturally, her parents objected violently, feeling that such an association was unthinkable. They forbade her to see her sweetheart but the temptation was so strong that she continued to meet him in secret. Pressure was brought against the match in every possible way and eventually Mathilda's spirit was quite broken. Her father promised to take her on a trip to Chicago on the train if she would give up the idea of marrying the outsider. Mathilda meekly accepted the offer and sealed the agreement. She never married.

Amana wedding

THE MARRIAGE CUSTOMS gradually changed. Demotion in church, though still practiced, seemed silly to me and my friends, and we could only be inclined to make fun of it. Couples began to be married without announcement and eventually without permission from the elders. Some young people even went to outside churches in order to have a fancy wedding and a honeymoon.

While I lived in Amana, I attended only one wedding—that of my cousin, Mary. Children did not go to weddings until they were quite grown and could understand the solemnity of the occasion and the fact that getting married was really yielding to sinful temptation.

Weddings always took place on a Thursday. The kitchen house vibrated with excitement on these occasions, for all the out-of-town guests ate dinner there before the ceremony. The bride had nothing to say about the menu or any of the arrangements. The women in the kitchen house were permitted to serve special food, and wonderful were the menus they put together. On the occasion of Mary's wedding, however, a serious argument came up because Mary objected to the lemon-flavored rice pudding which was to be served as one of the desserts. It was most unorthodox for a bride to be so fractious, but a compromise was reached. The rice pudding was served, but without the lemon flavoring!

During the morning, the horse-drawn black spring wagons, used only for *Liebesmahl*, funerals, and weddings, brought relatives we hardly knew from the neighboring Amanas. After calling at the bride's home where they left their carefully selected gifts on display, the visitors gathered at the kitchen house for dinner.

For this occasion the everyday white oilcloth of the tables was replaced with lovely white linen, taken from the bottom of old storage chests and loaned for the occasion. Though it was Thursday, we all wore our best church costumes. The women, including the bride, with her face flushed and her eyes shining, sat at one table and the men at another. The bride and groom were dressed no differently from the rest of us except that their clothes were new. They sat among us, and no special attention was given them. Everyone ate heartily, then left for church, taking their usual places. The men and the women were separated, as always. The bride and groom, too, sat in their proper order.

After the usual singing, the elder, whose turn it was to preside at a wedding, read from the testimonies and the Bible, not omitting the well-known passage from

180

Corinthians. To the very last, the Inspirationists drove home the idea that "it is better to be unmarried."

At a certain place in the ceremony, the elder called the bride and groom to the front of the church. I looked at them intently, trying to appreciate that this was a climactic moment, but all I could see was Brother Lenz, facing us with his usual inexpressive face and manner, and the back of the groom, his new suit already showing wrinkles, and the back of the bride, her black dress new and stiff. I admired the black satin bow standing out prettily beneath the point of her new black shoulder shawl.

Now that the bride and groom stood before the congregation, they were together for the first time on that day. There were no rings, no flowers, nor any touch of color, and no attendants—only the man and the woman standing before the elder who was to pronounce them man and wife. They repeated the vows, long since familiar to all Christians. When the service was over, they shook hands, thereby publishing to the congregation that they were duly married. Then they separated and returned to their respective places among us and the reading of the testimonies and the singing continued.

After the wedding, we all walked to the kitchen house where coffee, cocoa, and coffee cake were served. Again men and women sat separately. Later we went to the home of the bride for one of the few social gatherings permitted by the elders. Wedding parties were noted for a beautiful collection of luscious, tasty cakes, two and three layers deep, rich with nuts, chocolate, and caramel. We all knew about the cakes before the wedding, for they had been made by the women in the kitchen house. For this occasion, the women were allowed to use whatever supplies were needed to make

181

the cakes as wonderful as they wished, and the bride and her family were permitted to supervise them. There must have been at least thirty cakes at Mary's wedding and they were a memorable display. After baking, it took hours to frost them with drifts of luscious icing. But the culmination of all was the elaborate decoration, all done by one woman. She had made a hobby of beautifying cakes with hearts, flowers, bells, bows, and all manner of delicate, exquisitely formed designs and clever little sayings wishing the bride and groom luck in their new life.

So the cakes were the center of interest at the party, even stealing the spotlight of attention from the bride and groom. There was plenty of beer, too, with crackers and pretzels, and aged wine, saved carefully for years for this very occasion. The general air of the party became more and more lively as the afternoon wore on and a few well-wishers became a little tipsy. We always knew who would need help getting home for they were the same few who liked wine all too well and never failed to take advantage of the free-flowing drinks.

The women were attracted to the room where the gifts were displayed. A lot of the gifts were fancy rather than practical because ordinary housewares were not needed by the new couple. There were many sets of embroidered pillow cases, lace doilies, and scarves of different sizes and shapes. On one table there were sets of cut-glass tumblers and pitchers, colored bowls, and sherbet dishes, all too pretty for everyday use. Fancy china was there, too, although we had little need for "company" dishes. I remembered the dinner for Uncle Albert and how thrilled mother had been to get to use her tableware. I knew Mary would cherish hers and keep them for just such an occasion.

I thought of how wedding practices had changed, my grandmother having no party at all and my mother being separated from my father for two weeks after their wedding. At least this bride and groom were allowed to go directly to their new home—two rooms assigned them by the elders in the bride's former home.

Christian Metz must have rested uneasily during these times when his people gave way to the old German love of conviviality, suppressed though it had been for generations. We had a wonderful time at the wedding. . . .

Unterredung

THE *Unterredung!* I had heard about this annual service of "confession and spiritual examination" all my life, for this was one of Grandpa's favorite topics. He never tired of talking about it, especially as it had been conducted in the days of the *Werkzeuge* when every member had to come, individually, before the *Werkzeuge* and the elders and be examined. My unspeakable dread of it, as a personal experience, came from my mother. Each year, before the service, her nervousness reminded us that she dreaded the moment when she had to make her confession before the assembled congregation. When I grew old enough to attend, Grandpa tried to prepare me.

"Anna, you are a big girl now and it is time you understand about sin and righteousness. Are you ready to tell about your sins at the *Unterredung?*"

"No, Grandpa," I answered truthfully. "I'm not sure what I should say, or what sin to tell about."

Grandpa laid aside his Bible after carefully marking the place he had been reading.

"Anna, surely you can think of some way to please God more than you have?"

But I only stood there, having no idea what was expected of me.

"Come sit by me, and I will read to you about the old time *Unterredung*. *Ja,* the people were more pious in the old days. But even so, Christian Metz had to keep reminding them of their sins—even the elders." He had taken down *Sammlung* 34 from the rows of leatherbound volumes in his high bookcase, and turned quickly to a spot he had marked with a slip of paper.

"The *Unterredung* was a great spiritual experience when Christian Metz was in charge. He listened to confessions and asked questions and then helped the people find better ways. Sometimes he compelled them to be demoted in church in order to repent and again become acceptable to the Lord. But listen, let me read to you."

Grandpa read slowly so that I might understand the big German words:

> 6 November 1859: [This was after the Inspirationists had come to live in Amana.] This morning during the First Church, after the reading of the Scriptures, Christian Metz fell into inspiration. ...He spoke especially to Brother S＿＿ because he had brought suit against Brother J. G. H＿＿ in a Canadian Court, concerning a doubtful claim, and thereby revealed scandal and anger in front of the public eye by not abiding by the rule of brotherhood. ... Brother Christian Metz addressed Brother S＿＿: 'You have done such a great evil against the Lord and your brothers that I would like to break you like a vase and cast you into confusion for your whole lifetime, so that you would have

186

to sink into everlasting despair. ... You continue to live offensively ... even though you have sold your brother short. ... The merciful and compassionate [God] will appease you if you start a new life and go back to the Children's [Third] Church. Come and bow and do not let yourself be asked by your brothers, but let the fear of your soul drive you so that you will receive a new heart and an upright spirit and you will overcome all your crooked ways.'

Grandpa looked at me to see if I had fully appreciated what he had read.

"We need someone who would speak like that today," he said, turning the pages. "In those days it took a long time to hear all the confessions. Christian Metz heard them all himself, the men in the mornings, the women in the afternoons until everyone had been examined."

"It must have taken a long time," was all I could think of.

"Yes, it sometimes lasted seven weeks. Listen to more from the same *Unterredung*, on 12 November to Brother Michael H——:

'Be more alert and careful to overcome your passions. ... Remember how long the wicked spirit possessed your soul. Free yourself. ...'

And to Brother Mathias B——:

'I have sustained you a long time and hoped for something better. What will be your booty? There is definite evidence: whatsoever you have gathered. And it shall all be smoke, fire and finally ashes. ...'

Grandpa paused and continued:

On November 13. ... All came back and the weight of yesterday's service had not lifted. The elders prayed that the Lord would send His Blessing for this work.

187

Thus the Lord opened the hearts and mouths of the brothers so that each one confessed and was accepted and blessed by the elders. . . .

"What do you think of that, Anna? Doesn't that make you feel how wonderful it was to be cleansed of sin by the confessions?"

I said, "Yes, Grandfather," but aside from its sounding very frightening, I could not make much of it. Grandpa seemed to be so pleased about his reading that I sat very still to let him go on.

"Would you like to hear what Christian Metz said to the elders?"

"Yes, Grandfather, read that."

"This 'Conference of Elders' came before the *Unterredung;* it was the spiritual examination of the elders. On October 29, 1859, Metz had an Inspiration and his words were directed especially to Elder Christian W——— because he had fallen into sinful and fleshly living and to Brother E———:

> 'Hear this, W——— and E———. . . . How low have you sunk? Why could righteousness not use her sword and cut the unholy ropes and nets? What is it you are doing that cannot be done in sight of God? And even if you torture yourself to death and work day and night, you are still no longer a servant of God, but your own slave. . . . Wait for a blessing of the Lord, because He will forgive you if you will really repent and better your life. But you have to condemn all your personal rights and your own entanglements.'

"Do you know what that means, Anna?" Grandpa's eyes were shining. He had been reading loudly though he did not know it.

"I think I do," I said to please him. It was strange to see Grandpa so excited.

Grandpa looked at his large watch and said it was time for him to go to the kitchen house for his supper. I knew that if it was time, nothing would keep him, for Grandpa was so punctual about his goings and comings that people even set their clocks by him. I looked for mother in our living room, for now more than ever, the thought of my "confession" seemed like a horrible nightmare.

Mother was sitting in her little low rocker crocheting quietly. The red winter sunset cast a pink glow about her and I suddenly wanted to be near her.

"Mama."

"Yes, Anna."

"What was it like when you went to your first *Unterredung?*"

"Oh, it was ... well, it was something to remember!"

"What did they do to you?" I asked, meaning the elders.

"You see, we no longer had a *Werkzeug* to examine us so the elders helped each other. We had two visiting elders from each village, one an older man who stayed all week, or until all the confessions were over, and a young one who came only for the day. We liked having the visiting elders come, and since my father was an elder, the older one stayed at our house."

"But the confessions, how did they do them and what did you say?"

"Well, I did not like to stand up in front of all the others and make confession, I can tell you! In those days, we sat in a single row facing the elders, who were up in front and each one of us was examined separately. We stood up when it was our turn. I was always afraid

189

of being tongue-tied and unable to speak. That is what I remember most about the *Unterredung*.

"The elders asked us questions after we finished, and even gave personal sermons to some. If they were not pleased with the examination, you could be demoted in church until you repented and changed your ways."

"Did anyone get demoted?"

"Yes, of course, at nearly every *Unterredung* someone was demoted."

"Was it an extra church service?" I asked sympathetically. I always dreaded extra services.

"Yes, it was. The elders started on the first Sunday after New Years in one of the villages. They took all the people of the First *Versammlung* first, starting with small groups of men in the morning; the women confessing in the afternoon," she explained carefully. "Then they kept on, everyday until all had been heard—every man, woman, and child, from all three churches. Then they moved to the next village and heard all the confessions there."

"When I go to *Unterredung,* what shall I say when the elders ask me about my sins?"

"Now, child, where did you get such a notion? The elders will not ask you about your sins."

"But Grandpa has read to me from the Testimonies about how the *Werkzeuge* scolded people and made them repent, and you said you had to. . . ."

"Yes, *Kleine*. That is the way it used to be and Grandpa thinks we should do as our ancestors did. But this is not the way of the elders in Amana nowadays."

"Then what shall I say?"

"You say what all the other children say . . . . 'I did not obey the elders, my mother, and my teacher as I should have done. I will try to do better.' "

She had stuck her crochet hook in the snowy ball of thread and stood up to put it away. The room was now quite dark and the lamp had to be lighted.

"But Mother, I did too obey." I said thoughtfully.

"I know, Anna, but that is what the children say, so you must say it like the others."

"Is that enough to confess in the *Unterredung?*" It seemed to me that such a splendid occasion called for a better performance.

Mother struck the match to light the lamp and the light showed her face, serious and so good to see. The glass chimney in her hand glistened and flashed as she moved it into place, the little frosted stars on the glass showing prettily.

"My dear child. You have not sinned, really. You are too young to know what it means. Now you learn the words so you can say them in the meeting without stumbling. They will do very well and I hope you will always have as much trouble trying to find a sin to confess." She had come close to me and put her arm around my shoulders as I sat at the big round table. This was rather special and very nice, for mama did not usually lay her hands on us in any sort of tender way. It was not fitting to be demonstrative.

Time passed all too quickly as I alternately thrilled with excitement and sank with qualms of dread over the idea of my first *Unterredung*. The day came, and as I started to leave for church, mother prepared to go to the kitchen house.

"Now *Kleine,* say again what you will confess when it is your turn."

191

I repeated the sentence in rehearsed singsong.

"That is good. I am so glad that I had my *Unterredung* yesterday."

"Why, Mama, couldn't you think of anything to confess?"

"Of course I knew what to say, but I like it to be over."

For the life of me, I could not think of one single thing mama could claim as a sin. However, I knew some women who could make real speeches if they wanted to!

I met Elsie in the outer hall of the meeting house and we hung our heavy winter shawls carefully on hooks. Then we went into church as usual. The air was crisp and cold outside on that January day, but inside the large stove had made the room cozy and warm. We could not see out of the windows for they were completely covered with frosty, fairy tale pictures of leaves and castles.

After the regular service was over, Elder Beyer said that the confessions would be heard. The big boy at the head of the row spoke first. No one asked him anything. He just mumbled something and I could not even hear what he said. The boy next to him said:

"I confess that I have not kept the Ten Commandments as I should have done. I will try to do better."

I listened carefully to them all but their confessions were general and not at all truthful. None of them mentioned any real worldly sin, although I knew some of them had been criticized severely by the elders. Already, the small boys were having their turns and I waited for John Hornbeck to confess that he had thrown mud in my face last summer. I thought he was a bully and would have many sins to confess. But he hurried through his "turn" so fast that I did not even recognize what he was talking about.

After the boys had finished without interruption, the girls began with Esther Boehm, whom we knew to be a gossipy troublemaker. She said:

"I confess I have not read the Bible as much as I should have done. I promise to do better." So that was all she was going to say!

As the recitation of confessions progressed rapidly down the line, my thoughts turned to my own speech and I began repeating the words over and over in my mind. All too soon little Louise at the end of my row was saying, "I have been good, I promise to be bad."

I blinked my eyes and wondered if I had heard correctly. Realizing her mistake Louise stammered, "I have been bad, but I promise to be good."

Elsie was shaking with suppressed laughter. She never worried about speaking out in church. I felt frozen with fear lest I, too, mix up my words. Panic seized me. I could not think of a thing to say. The roll of voices came closer. My turn! Everyone seemed to be looking right at me as if a bright light were focused on me. I started with the formula:

"I confess I did not obey the elders, my mother, and my teacher as I should have done. I will try to do better."

I sat down relieved and breathless, feeling that now at last I had entered into the realm of grownups. Their ways were confusing to me but easier to bear than I had hoped. The confessions, general and strictly routine, had not the least hint of sincerity about them. Nor was the service anything like the impressions Grandpa had given me about the old-time *Unterredung* of Christian Metz and Barbara Heinemann, nor even as it was when mother was young. I only felt lucky that time had brought so many changes that I need not submit to questions by a soul-searching *Werkzeug* or an inquisitive elder.

The *Unterredung* was finally over for another year and, as usual, the women had some amusing incidents to tell at the kitchen house. Gretel Stauffer's father had been entertaining a visiting elder as a guest. It was customary to serve some wine and crackers, or cake, or other tidbits before dinner. While Brother Samson was drinking wine with Gretel's father, Gretel came into the room holding a deck of cards in her hands.

"Papa," she said, "will you please play cards with me?"

"Ahem, *mein* Gretel ... go help mama," her father stammered, shoving her out of the room.

As an elder, Gretel's father was not supposed to know anything about cards, much less play card games with his little daughter or even have them in the house. It was obvious that even the elders did not always abide by the rules.

I enjoyed most the story about Sister Martin, a sweet little old lady who was badly crippled with arthritis. Her confession had been:

"I confess that I have not obeyed the will of God as I should have done and I did not go to church enough." Everyone knew that Sister Martin never missed a church service on any day for any reason other than serious illness.

Liebesmahl

THE HOLIEST of all Inspirationist services was the *Liebesmahl* (love feast or communion) celebrating the last supper of our Lord. The following account of the first *Liebesmahl* that was held in Ebenezer shows the importance that was placed on this service. As in all such matters the instructions came from above, through the inspirations of Metz and Heinemann.

Inspirations-Historie (1817-1867)—pp. 362-66:

After the Lord had many times given indications of a pending *Liebesmahl*, He now gave a more definite announcement in several testimonies [by Metz] that He would conduct it during the forthcoming Christmas holidays. For this all members were to prepare themselves. There should first be a personal examination. . . . This was conducted by Brother Christian Metz and Brother G. A. Weber. All elders and all members were

197

interviewed individually and evaluated as to their spiritual standing. . . .

After the necessary preparations had been made in all three communities, Middle, Lower, and Higher Ebenezer, all members, exclusive of the children, were counted and divided into three sections, according to their grading in church. The group designated for the first *Liebesmahl*, 158 members and elders, met on the first Christmas holiday [in 1844] at 8:00 A.M. in the *Saal* at Middle Ebenezer. The service was opened with a hymn . . . and while the congregation knelt for prayer, Brother Christian Metz came under the influence of the Holy Spirit . . . and the work of evaluating the invited guests began, first as a group and then individually. He addressed all the elders present and then also the members. This service lasted all day, with several interruptions for singing and a noon recess.

On the second Christmas Day they all came back, and after the first hymn the examinations were continued by Brother Christian Metz. Then came the selection of the people who were to help with the foot-washing, the serving of the bread and wine, and the supper that followed. There was much kneeling and praying, then the blessing, and the congregation rose and pledged themselves with a loud promise, *"Ja."*

When they came back in the afternoon and the men and women had separated themselves by curtains, the festive work of foot-washing began. This was done along with the singing of hymns and the reading of scripture. Then tables were set up for the token of remembrance. Two hymns were sung while the bread and wine were served. Another hymn and the second chapter of St. Luke was read, followed by a period of silence. Then the designated members served the supper of coffee cake, chocolate and coffee. After this came another hymn and Brother Metz became inspired again and gave his blessing.

On Sunday, December 29, the second *Liebesmahl* was held. This was for one hundred and forty-eight members and lasted only one day, without foot-washing. Again Christian Metz became inspired and gave a long sermon to the group, and then spoke individually to almost all brothers and sisters. This occasion lasted all morning, with intermittent singing. There was a noon recess and then it continued. Blessing was said over bread and wine. Tables were set and bread was broken while Chapter 6 of John was read. After a final hymn, Metz spoke, closing with,

"Remember, your pilgrimage on the earth will end for all of you one by one. You will come together again in the heavenly host, where you will have a real *Supper of Love.*" Then a hymn, and supper was served as before, followed by the blessing and two hymns.

The third *Liebesmahl* was held eight days later on Sunday, January 5, 1845, for one hundred and thirty members. There were the usual hymns, kneeling and prayer. Christian Metz spoke first to the group and then to individuals whereby the Lord asked if they were willing to give themselves up to Him and renew their faith and live to please Him. All agreed with a loud *"Ja."* Then the bread and wine was blessed but not served at that time. Instead, the congregation sang hymns. Members left while tables were set. The bread and wine was served at the tables, along with the reading of Scriptures (John 6) and the singing of hymns. ... Metz concluded with,

"Amen to the Lord for having stood by us with mercy." ... Then supper was served and two hymns of thanksgiving were sung.

The next day fifty children were served in the meeting house.

For years the annual *Liebesmahl* followed the above pattern, Christian Metz designating where and when it should be held. After Christian Metz died, and for as long as Barbara Heinemann lived (1868–1883), she announced when there should be a communion service, according to inspirations she received directly from the Lord. After her death, the elders decided that the celebration should take place every two years, beginning with Ascension Sunday. The service was held in the largest of all the church buildings in Main Amana; even so only a limited number of members could be accommodated at one time. As in the Ebenezer days, the members came according to their "grading" in the First, Second, or Third *Versammlung,* the First Congregation having their service on Ascension Day (Thursday) and the other two groups on succeeding Sundays. Partitions were removed from the big meeting house and tables were set up and covered with white linen cloths. The elders assigned all the duties of preparation well in advance and it was a real honor to be asked to serve in any way. Grandfather had, for years, been chosen to break the bread in the First *Versammlung* meeting; these were the occasions he lived for from year to year.

The year of my first *Liebesmahl* was one to remember. Grandfather was serving as an elder and had charge of the First *Versammlung.* Mother had been promoted from the Second to the First Church and for the first time in her life attended the *Liebesmahl* with the First Church Group. This meant that she could participate in the foot-washing service. I was waiting for the wagons to bring them home on the evening of that day. With my turn coming up soon, I had some questions about *Liebesmahl.*

At last they came, the wagon with mother arriving first. She seemed so very glad to be home, for she hated going to a strange place and being with strange people. She always worked up a severe headache on those days. Then the wagon with Grandpa came and it was plain to see that this had been a big occasion for him. Instead of going directly to his rooms, he stopped by to talk with us. I said—

"How was the *Liebesmahl* this year, Grandpa?"

He folded his hands in his lap as was his habit when deeply moved.

"Not as solemn as it should have been. The people talked all the time, between services and at the kitchen houses, and even laughed, too. This is not the purpose of the most holy *Liebesmahl*." He spoke to me but he looked to mother for a confirmation of his opinion. Mother was quiet for she did not dare say she was glad that the whole thing was over for another two years. Grandfather continued,

"I think the people are no longer pious enough to have the privilege of the *Liebesmahl*."

Mother said, "Times have changed, Father. It is hard for people to feel as they did in the days when Brother Metz and Sister Heinemann had Inspirations about the *Liebesmahl*. You elders do the best you can, but it is not like having a *Werkzeug* to speak for God."

"*Ach,* I know, I know," Grandfather responded.

"But the *Liebesmahl* bread is always so wonderful." Mother was determined to find something cheerful to say. "I thought it the best I had ever tasted. Such a beautiful crust!"

"Yes," said Grandpa, "but it was more Christlike in the old days when the elders broke the bread and passed it around. I never approved of slicing the bread." He pursed his lips together and looked at her over the top of his small glasses.

"But, Father, sliced bread is much easier to serve."

Grandfather did not consider that remark worthy an answer. He was thinking of other problems.

"The elders are talking about not having any more *Liebesmahl*."

201

"Not have a *Liebesmahl!* Why are they saying that?" Mother was as alarmed as if he had said there are to be no more Christmases.

"Something must be done to awaken the people. Many are wavering in their beliefs. Several younger members have left the Society to join other faiths and others go on Sundays to other churches. We need the *Werkzeuge* to tell them how sinful this is. We have worldliness among us and are no longer fit to partake of the most holy sacrament. The matter will be decided soon."

Mother shook her head but said nothing. She was still wearing her church clothes and since this was Sunday, she was not working on any needlework, as was her custom. So she just looked down at her hands, perplexed, as though she, too, wondered about the outcome of the new ways.

Surely one of the most important milestones of all my childhood was that Sunday early in May when I was at last old enough to go to *Liebesmahl!*

Mother helped me dress in my church costume and took much longer than usual as though she would keep me from going away from her for the first time in my life, and for a whole day, too. For of course I belonged to the Third *Versammlung* and could not go with her when she went with the First.

"Mama, let me go. Elsie is waiting."

"Now, Anna, let me be sure you look all right. I want all the people from the other villages to see what a fine girl I have."

202

"But the wagons are already at the kitchen house. I saw them from the window."

"I know, I know, but are you sure you will know what to do?"

"Well, I think so," I said confidently.

"Be sure you do what the others do. Just watch. You don't have to be afraid—and you know you only have to pretend to sip the wine. You must be careful about that or you might choke. But, if you want, take a nice big slice of the bread!"

"I will, Mama, I will." I rushed from the door and ran down the narrow sidewalk to the kitchen house where the *"Liebesmahl"* wagons were waiting. They were spring wagons, painted black, and had four rows of seats, forerunners of modern station wagons, and were used only for *Liebesmahl* journeys, or for weddings or funerals. Each was drawn by an Amana team of horses released from the duties of the field for this special Sunday trip.

On that beautiful May morning at seven o'clock there was a chilliness in the air; birds were singing and the sun was shining. But I was only looking for Elsie. We had agreed that whoever reached the wagon first would save a seat for the other. Brother Rombach was to be the driver, and without the formality of a greeting, he lifted me up into the wagon. This was wonderfully exciting; I had never been for a ride in the big spring wagon before. Elsie jumped up and down saying,

"Here, Anna, sit here."

She had managed a seat in the end next to the driver. I took the place beside her and soon the seats were all filled. The passengers were girls and a few women. Of course the men and boys rode by themselves. I thought it would have been better if all the children could have been in our wagon and I looked around to see where John Hornbeck was going to ride. Driver Rombach waited until the seats were filled, then took his place in the driver's seat. The wagon creaked and groaned as he turned the team into the street and we were off for Main Amana, three miles away.

No one talked much, for even children were aware of the sacred character of this day. Besides, there was so much to see, and I kept looking back as my home and our part of the village slipped farther and farther away. I kept thinking of mother and something seemed to be pulling me back to her. Then we turned the corner at the main road, and Homestead was no longer in view. We came to the river and I stretched for a good look at the rushing muddy water as it all but overflowed the banks. The woods along the way were thick with tall trees and underbrush. Elsie and I began to keep count of the birds. I wondered what the *Liebesmahl* would be like and who would be there from the other villages.

All too soon, we turned off the crossroad and onto the streets of Main Amana. How good to see the houses, looking just like the ones in Homestead, and the shops very similar to those we were familiar with. The school house had a bell tower just like ours, but the building was bigger because there were more children in Main Amana.

The wagon creaked around a corner and, on the next street, it drew up in front of the long, narrow Big Amana Church. The street was crowded with wagons preparing to unload passengers, and some drivers were already taking their teams to the barns for the day. The women clustered at the women's entrance and the men were assembling more slowly at the other end of the building. I took Elsie's hand and together we fell in line behind the women from Homestead. We looked about curiously for children from the other villages but they were shy, as we were, and tried to lose themselves among the women they knew. Just then a woman whom I had seen at Mary's wedding came up to me and said, "*Ach,* here is little Anna, Sophie's daughter. What a fine big girl you are getting to be."

I couldn't remember her name and didn't know what to say to her. Tongue-tied with embarrassment and flushed as red as a poppy, I wanted to move away. At last I managed to say, "It is nice to see you again."

Inside, we looked for places to sit, self-consciously carrying our Bibles and *Psalterspiels.* How big the room appeared with all the partitions removed! We hesitated, not wanting to sit any nearer the elders than need be. The benches were in place for them. Sister Meisner beckoned to us and we sat with her in the second row, for there were many children already seated in the front rows. People took places quickly and all was quiet except for the clomping of the heavy soled shoes on the bare boards. The place was shiny clean, like our churches at home, the benches fairly bleached with much scrubbing. Mama had said that the women worked hard to make the church immaculately clean for the *Liebesmahl.*

I do not recall too well the details of the service. There were so many strange impressions to record, but I could think of only one thing, the serving of the bread and the wine. The service was beginning and I knew the 8:30 hour had arrived. It seemed we had already been away from home for a long, long time. There were endless hymns, sung in the usual chanting manner, without accompaniment, interspersed by much singsong reading by the elders from the Bible and from the Testimonies, the congregation participating at the right places. The service proceeded slowly, as though it might last forever. I wondered how I could manage to sit there until dinner time at eleven o'clock. Only the thought of the *Liebesmahl* in the afternoon kept me in my place. My back hurt from sitting and my legs began stretching and bending and I could not sit still. Just when I thought I could not stand being there for another minute, we were dismissed for dinner. It was a most wonderful relief to follow the Homestead women to the kitchen to which we were assigned for the meal. All the visitors from one village were accommodated at the same kitchen house, so we really did not have much chance to get acquainted with members from other Amanas. Since feeding so many visitors was a large undertaking, the meal was very simple—chicken rice soup and raisin coffee cake with coffee and cocoa. I was so hungry that it seemed to be the best food I had' ever tasted.

All too soon, the one o'clock hour for the afternoon service arrived. Now, surely the "love feast" would take place. Sure enough, the room was now arranged with long tables on each side and these were covered with beautiful snowy linen cloths. Elsie and I sought places at the side of the table not facing the elders, but all those seats were taken. We found ourselves near the front, in good positions to see what was happening, but under the critical eyes of the elders.

The service followed the familiar pattern of our church—we sang hymns and listened to the elders. Then we read from our Bibles, verse by verse until all the passages of the chapter had been read. I listened intently to the passage telling of Christ's last supper with His disciples for I recognized its significance in the service. Then Elder Weber took the cloth off the round loaves of bread, already sliced and placed in large shallow baskets. Elder Bauman and Elder Jung received the baskets handed to them by Elder Weber and, after a short prayer, passed them to each of the tables, the adults being served first. Then they came to the children's tables and finally to me. I took one of the large white slices with its delicious golden crust and laid it on the table in front of me. We had to wait until everyone had been served. At last Elder Weber said, "Eat this in memory of Me." I held the bread in both my hands and tried to remember that this was supposed to be the body of Christ. The time came to bite into the bread and it tasted even better than mother had said it would. No wonder she liked it so much!

Now we would have the wine. Elder Weber placed several large, beautifully shaped glass goblets in front of him on the elders' table. I had heard mother say that one of them had been loaned by my Aunt Eva who lived in Main Amana. All the goblets were loaned by the people, just as were the tablecloths, and finally many of them were left at the church. While I admired the beautiful goblets, Elder Bauman read further from the text saying, "Drink this in remembrance of Me," and the goblets were filled with glistening, red wine from a sparkling flask. One goblet was placed at the head of each table. I watched closely, trying to follow the progress of the goblet at one of the men's tables as each member drank from it and passed it along. It seemed to me that it had to be refilled quite often by Elder Jung who carried the flask.

Serving the wine took much longer than serving the bread. The room was quiet except for the steps of the elders as they moved about with the flasks. A goblet was started with the women on the opposite side of the room from Elsie and me. The first woman on the end, who reminded me of my mother, barely touched the glass to her lips, but the woman beside her drank most of the wine in the glass. The next one emptied the glass and it had to be refilled, and so it passed along the line. Occasionally, someone would choke and quickly cover her mouth with her handkerchief. When the long-awaited moment came for me, I held the glass in both my hands and barely sipped the liquid. How dreadful, the unpleasant bitter taste! I wondered how anybody would want to drain the goblet. And this was supposed to be the choicest wine to be found in Amana, especially made and aged carefully for the *Liebesmahl!* I consoled myself by remembering that the wonderful *Liebesmahl* bread had been all that mother had promised.

Elder Weber was reading from the testimonies that Christian Metz had spoken at the first *Liebesmahl:*

> Beg for yourselves this blessing and don't let any misbehavior or hidden desire live in your hearts any longer but give yourselves up willingly from the heart to discipline and to punishment. Otherwise, you will be overcome with abhorrence and horror. If you give in to sin and shame, the devil in you will cast you into darkness and bind you with chains and fetters.

By the end of the service, I was bone-tired from sitting and it was wonderful relief to stand and move about. The ride home in the late afternoon was one of the best parts of the day. Elsie and I watched eagerly for the first glimpse of Homestead. We talked about the *Liebesmahl* for many weeks.

One of the things I was especially curious about was the ceremony of foot-washing. It was the most sanctified part of the holy *Liebesmahl* and was reserved for adults

208

of the first *Versammlung*. Since I was not old enough, nor pious enough, to attend, I asked mother many questions about it: Who did the washing? Were the women embarrassed about removing their shoes and stockings? How did they manage water and the other mechanical details of the washing? What was the significance of the service?

Mother said the service was derived from the thirteenth chapter of St. John:

> *And supper being ended ... He (Jesus) riseth from supper, and laid aside His garments, and took a towel, and girded Himself.*
>
> *After that He poureth water into a basin and began to wash the disciples' feet, and to wipe them with the towel wherewith He was girded. ....*
>
> *So after He had washed their feet and had taken His garments and was sat down again, He said unto them, "Know ye what I have done to you?"*
>
> *"Ye call me Master and Lord and ye say well; for so I am.*
>
> *"If I then your Master and Lord, have washed your feet, ye also ought to wash one another's feet."*

Mother further explained the foot-washing as follows:

The elders washed the men's feet and only the unmarried women were considered pious enough to wash the women's feet. It was the privilege of these "maidens" to make the necessary preparations for this act of extreme holiness. They had little wooden tubs, made especially for the purpose in the local carpenter shop. The tubs were oblong, not at all bulky, and they were equipped with two neatly placed wooden handles. The washers had to go out to the community washhouse next door to fill their tubs from the big iron kettles of water which had been heated as for laundry. Then they carried them back to the meeting room and washed five or six pairs of feet before renewing the water. Each washer had a towel provided for drying the feet and this also was used for several people. Mother says that by the time it got around to the fifth or sixth person the towel was wet and cold, so the women finished the drying with their own handkerchiefs before replacing the long cumbersome hand-knitted hose and shoes.

When the feet of all members had been washed, the elders washed each other's feet as did the unmarried women washers.

It seemed strange to me that women for whom it was sinful to show an ankle, were at ease about removing their shoes and stockings to have their feet washed in public. The only concern actually, according to mother, was for the hems of their skirts, lest they swish into the water and become wet. A curtain separated the men's side of the church from the women's. A service of hymn-singing, prayer, and scripture reading proceeded during the washing, so members were occupied all the while.

Grandfather's prediction about discontinuing *Liebesmahl* until the people should be more appreciative of their blessings and obligations actually came to be. For some thirty years, no *Liebesmahl* was celebrated in Amana.

Amana traditions had begun to crumble, and the religious beliefs were not observed seriously by the younger generations. There was great alarm among the elders over the loss of members to other faiths and the desertion of others for the worldly attractions offered by the "outside."

In a drastic attempt to hold the old order, the elders decided to deny communion until the community should be more worthy of it. They hoped to emphasize the importance of the old Inspirationist heritage and to combat the weakening influences that threatened the very base of the whole social structure.

So, while I grew up in Amana, there were no other *Liebesmahls*. In 1956 the custom was reestablished and now it is offered every two years. In the alternate years, the elders hold a religious conference, as in the old days.

Members no longer go to Main Amana for this ceremony; instead the elders rotate from village to village on successive Sundays as they do for the *Unterredung*. The service no longer lasts all day, nor does it have the great spiritual significance that was felt in the days of the *Werkzeuge,* or even during my mother's youth. The foot-washing was never resumed.

when death comes to Amana

MY FIRST AWARENESS OF DEATH came when Grandpa Schneider died. Henry and I were still very young and had not grasped the significance of his last illness. One day mother dressed us as if for church, and took us to the home of Grandma and Grandpa Schneider. We liked to go there for we knew that these old people loved us and wanted to have us with them. Theirs was a place of pleasant times and happy hours. Grandpa would make tiny wooden toys for us and Grandma always had a surprise, usually a sweet.

But on this day, before we went in, mother stooped down and took us each by the arm and said, "Now children, be very quiet today." We wondered about this, for mother seldom made such a point of our conduct.

Inside, people stood around and no one talked. It

was strange to find so many people at Grandma's. Uncle Albert was there, but he did not look as jolly as I had remembered him. He barely nodded recognition to Henry and me. The door to the ever-closed parlor stood open and the room was quite dark. I had seldom been in that parlor, so it was as strange as if it belonged to another house. Grandma came forward and took my hand. She did not smile nor make a little joke as was usual for her. She said, "Come with me."

I followed her into the parlor and there, the ends resting on two chairs, was a long, polished, brown wooden box, the largest I had ever seen. Grandma brought me up close and said that I should look.

"Do you know who it is?" she asked. She seemed to be crying.

I could barely see over the edge of the box, by standing on my toes.

"Yes," I answered, "that is my Grandpa Schneider."

When we were home again, I asked mother why Grandpa was sleeping there. Then she repeated to me phrases I was later to learn by heart, for they were from the catechism.

Some days later I stopped in to watch Brother Weber, the cabinet maker, at his work. His shop was on the lower floor of one of the village buildings. It was always full of interesting things, for he repaired chairs and other furniture. The place smelled good—of fresh clean, newly cut lumber. Shavings and sawdust had been swept into neat piles on the floor. Fascinating tools hung in rows over his workbench and I knew no one touched these but Brother Weber. He was jolly and friendly to me so he was a favorite. On the day I recall, he was fitting a lid on a long narrow box like the one I had seen at Grandpa's house.

"And who is that for?" I asked.

"It's a coffin for Sister Louisa Reinbeck who died this morning."

I had heard about Sister Louisa's illness. She had been a very large woman and so the box was large. It was wider than the one for Grandpa, who had been thin.

To make all coffins the same size would have been considered a waste of lumber. The wooden coffins of Amana, stained a rich dark brown and rubbed to a satiny finish, became a familiar object to us, for all were alike in appearance. There was no discrimination in Amana, even in death.

"Do you make a coffin for everyone who dies?" I asked Brother Weber.

"Yes," he replied, "whenever a person dies, I make a coffin for that person."

"And if you made one for me, would it be small like I am?"

"Yes, if you needed it now, but we'll probably wait a long time until you are much older before I make one for you, and then I'll make a big one." He stretched his arms wide apart to show how big.

This was not a comforting thought for by now the lid had been made to fit tightly and the idea of being closed up in such a box was frightening and horrible.

On the day of the funeral, all shops and schools were closed, as was the custom, for everyone was sure to know the deceased—and probably was related to him.

The funerals were dignified affairs. We had no flowers. Flowers were, in fact, unheard of, and even yet the colonists prefer to have no flowers at funerals.

The service was held at the church, though the body was left at the home. The order of worship was much like the regular church service except that the elder who gave the sermon added a biographical sketch of the deceased. This was a sort of eulogy. After the service, all the people came to the home. They filed in and had a last look at the deceased, then stood in the yard, while the coffin was carried out by the pallbearers and placed on an open black spring wagon, drawn by two horses. The wagon was driven very slowly, and the people followed, walking all the way to the cemetery at the edge of town. The men walked in the first part of the procession, in pairs, and then came the women. Never did they walk man and wife together. This procession was a delicate situation for it involved who was to walk nearest the body in the order of relationship. It was important not to hurt anybody's feelings. Behind the relatives walked the children, then young adults and finally the older people, in the same order they sat in church.

At the graveside, the same men who had placed the coffin on the wagon removed it and set it over the grave which had been dug by the farm workers. Ropes across the opening were released slowly to lower the box.

The service here included another hymn and a passage from the Bible. The relatives stayed while the coffin was lowered and covered. Then all returned to their homes, now walking in family groups. There was no unseemly display of grief or loud crying.

All my impressions of the cemetery are not dreary, however. It is still one of the most quiet, peaceful, and pleasant places I know. Originally, it had been an ordinary field, except that evergreens had been planted around it. This was evidently an exception to the testimony of Barbara Heinemann who had decreed that only fruit bearing trees be planted in Amana. The graves were placed in even rows, beginning with the fence row. People were buried in the order of their dying, one after the other, rather than in family groups. We had no family lots, of course, for the cemetery belonged to the society. One section was marked off for children or babes. Maybe the early colonists were too frugal to allow a large plot for small needs. At the opposite end of the graveyard, away from the regular rows, was a place set aside for nonmembers who died in Amana. This was the only discrimination observed in the cemetery.

All members had the same kind of slab—made of cement in the Amana cement yard. No epitaph or family relationship was given on the slab, just the birth and death dates and the full name.

On Decoration Day we brought flowers for the graves of our relatives and this meant that we went from one area to another finding the individual graves which were separated, literally, by time. Each family took care of its own graves. Periodically, during the summer we went with sickle and rake to trim the grass. Some people kept beautiful flowers and vines growing on the graves. The older part of the cemetery was not cared for at all. The elders tried to get someone to cut the grass and weeds, but this was done only once or twice a summer.

The cemetery still stands a silent testament to the days and times of flourishing "True Inspirationism." The names on the older graves match those in the record books of Christian Metz and Gottlieb Scheuner. These were the people who migrated from Germany, built up the Society in Ebenezer and finally came to Amana, enduring many hardships in the name of their faith.

A friendly custom of remembrance was observed in Amana. A few weeks after a person had passed away, personal gifts were given to his friends and relatives. Shoulder shawls for church were a favorite gift for the women. A bolt of cloth was ordered especially for making these shawls. Handkerchiefs, bookmarks with Bible sayings on them, and picture mottoes were often selected as gifts of remembrance. Men received ties or handkerchiefs. We kept these gifts and lovingly treasured them as mementos of the person who had gone.

We had no wills or other documents of inheritance. We owned no property other than a few personal possessions. These were handed down in each family, without any legal intermediary. My grandmother Guyer had died when mother was nine years old and nothing had been done about disposing of her belongings at that time. They were kept intact in a room in Grandpa's part of our house. Every spring and fall, at housecleaning time, mother took the cherished pieces of glassware and china out of the cupboard and admired them as she washed them. Some twenty years after grandmother's death, when I was five years old and Henry was seven, the elders decided that our family needed another room. The time had come for dividing and distributing grandmother's things in order to clear the room.

For this occasion mother and her brothers met in the room where grandmother's things had been kept. Grandpa Guyer was there, too, but more as a listener than an intermediary.

"Sophie, you are the oldest, you should have first choice," Uncle Peter spoke up.

"Thank you, Peter," mother spoke solemnly. "I just want to say that I'd like to keep the set of white Haviland intact. You know it was mother's wedding present from her mother. It should be kept as a set rather than be divided among us. In fact, I don't care whether I get anything else, if I can have the whole set."

I knew that mother had her heart set on those dishes and wondered what would happen if anyone contested her "request," but no one did. She was the oldest and should have first choice.

"All right," said Uncle Peter. "But we will have to make a similar allowance for Paul and me."

"Of course," said mother.

"This grandfather clock—" Uncle Peter had always loved this clock and now he moved around to look at it closely. It stood high in the corner of the room and had been brought from Germany by mother's grandfather when he came to Ebenezer.

"If no one wants it—more than I do—I'd like to have it." Everyone knew that *Tante* Gretel (Uncle Paul's wife) wanted it, too, but Peter was next in line by age and could make his choice next.

"Well, all right," said Paul, "I like the clock, too, but I'll settle for the set of caned chairs."

And so the division proceeded until all grandmother's possessions were distributed.

Afterward, I realized that each of the three had come out with what he (or she) wanted most. A subtle sort of trading had gone on. Mother, as a daughter, received many fine pieces of glass and china without having her right questioned, and her brothers got what they wanted.

Some families did not take care of the division of property as smoothly. In some cases there were minor jealousies and even much bitterness. Occasionally not all of the possessions were brought out. No one knew where they were! This was likely to happen when the mother of a family died after a lingering illness, having lived with one of her children. Some of the choice pieces were put aside before the family division took place.

As individual members of the society, we owned nothing. That is why our family heirlooms were so truly cherished. Many times mother was offered tempting prices for her keepsakes but she would never have thought of parting with them. Daughters, as the home-makers, usually had priority over such pieces. In my mother's family, the old country chest of fine inlaid walnut is traditionally passed along from the oldest daughter to the oldest daughter. With it goes the promise that it should never be sold, but handed to the next in line if someday there should not be an heir. It was understood that when I had my own home, the chest would belong to me and so it has become my most prized possession.

New Horizons

Henry and his paper route

As HENRY AND I GREW UP, we came to resent more and more the restrictions imposed by the elders. We sensed that Grandpa Guyer was even more rigorous than the average elder. Mother proudly referred to him as an "Elder of the old stock," although now and then she, too, was reluctant to inflict his narrow viewpoints upon us.

We hated most being restricted in regard to our Sunday activities. This almost turned into a crisis for **Henry.** . . .

One day Henry sauntered into our living room dejectedly and sat down. He rested his elbows on his knees and twirled his cap in his hands, looking down at the floor. Mother was busy heating the supper she had just brought from the kitchen house. She was watching Henry.

"What's wrong, Henry?"

"Oh, nothing, I guess." But he just kept sitting there not looking up.

"Tell me what it is." Mother always managed to find out about things.

"I need a bicycle, that's all. Martin has one and Emil got a new one today. I'm the only big boy without a bicycle."

Now the troubled expression spread to mother's face, too.

"I know, Henry, but we have no way to make money to buy you a bicycle. We have talked about this enough. Now why don't you think about something else?"

"I could earn money for a bicycle if you would let me." He looked up now to see how things were going.

"Henry, if you mean by delivering papers, I must say 'no.' I can't have you going from door to door peddling papers. I won't have you bothering people like a beggar."

"Mama." Henry sat up straight and assumed a long-suffering, patient attitude. "You don't understand. This is *not* peddling. The people are already getting the paper by mail. The *Cedar Rapids Gazette* wants to better its service and bring the paper directly to Homestead by truck. I would simply deliver it to the people's houses."

"Yes, but you still have to collect the money. Besides, you know that Grandpa will never hear of it," mother replied.

"Oh, Grandpa!" he exclaimed. I knew just how Henry felt for it seemed to me that sooner or later

224

Grandpa got mixed up with everything Henry or I wanted to do.

"Now, Henry, that will do, let's forget the whole thing."

"But, Mama, I can't forget. I told the man I would start on the job next Monday morning."

"Oh, Henry, you haven't promised! Why didn't you tell me?"

"I just could not think of any other way to earn money, so I had to."

No more was said at the time. Mother knew that if Henry had promised to do it, it had to be done. I wondered how she would tell Grandpa.

Henry started carrying the papers on Monday morning. The list of subscribers had been prepared for him by the *Cedar Rapids Gazette* and the papers were delivered to our house. That evening Grandpa came to our living room on his way to the *Sälchen*. Mother had been expecting him. He put his hat on the old chest of drawers and sat down in his favorite rocking chair, his hands clasped in his lap. He said nothing for a while, as though trying to find a good way to bring up a troublesome subject. His clear blue eyes were, to mother, a searching light.

"What's this I hear about Henry carrying papers?" he finally asked.

"Henry wanted to earn a little money." She looked up defensively. "A boy needs money these days," she added.

"I can't see why boys need money now any more than when I was young. In those days, we felt well supplied with the benefits given us by the Society. No one tried to get special things for himself." He rocked a little, and seemed sad as though he knew not how to protect the

225

precious ways of his generation. Mother waited, having no answer for him.

"It was better when no one had money. 'Love of money is the root of all evil,' " he continued.

"But, Father, the society has less money nowadays. The elders give us only a little credit to spend for our needs."

Grandpa would not be diverted from his objective. "I'd have him give it up, Sophie. Better he should stay home. Let the people read the Testimonies instead of the newspaper."

"The man is going to hire someone; it may as well be Henry. We can't keep people from reading papers," mother pointed out. "Besides, Henry has promised to do it. We must let him keep his word."

Grandpa grasped the arm rests of the rocker and gave the smallest sigh of resignation. He rose to go.

That was the end of the discussion with Grandpa. After he had gone, mother was quiet, as she always was when something bothered her. Finally, she turned to Henry, who had listened to the conversation.

"We will just have to make up our own minds whether this is right or not, and decide what to do," she concluded.

"What am I going to do about Sunday morning?"

"Oh, my, Henry, you don't have to do it on *Sunday?*" Now Mama was really alarmed. "You told the man you would do it on Sunday, too?"

"Of course, when you carry papers, you have to do it on Sundays, just like any other day."

"Henry, Henry, that is sinful. Grandpa will never let you do that." Then as an immediate afterthought, she added, "He must not know."

"I guess he will know all right. I have to carry the papers past his window."

"No, you must not do that. We will find a way." Fine wrinkles of worry began to show on mother's face.

I don't know when or how the details were arranged. But when Sunday morning came, I heard mother get up just after the paper truck went by out in front. Then I woke up enough to see her come in from the back porch, dragging a bundle of papers. This was not easy for mother, for she was a small woman and not very strong. She took the papers to the window and waited. Then, as if from nowhere, Henry appeared, and I jumped to her side to help her boost the papers through the window to Henry. He must have sneaked out the back door, bending low under Grandpa's window, to get around the house for the papers. It was most exciting to be in on such a dangerous game!

When Grandpa came in later, bringing our breakfast in the familiar long basket, Henry and I were busy reading our catechism and mother was setting the table. No one mentioned the Sunday paper. Grandpa must have known, because he did not have much to say to us.

As long as he lived, Grandpa never read a paper on Sunday. His son, my Uncle Paul, sometimes visited us on Sunday and brought a paper, but Grandpa would not touch it until Monday morning.

I was pleased with the way Henry's paper business turned out, for this meant that I could have a chance to earn money, too. As he grew prosperous, Henry often sublet some of his jobs to me. When he was too busy with the paper route to do his chores he paid me to carry wood or haul out the ashes. On Saturdays when he played baseball, I carried the papers for him. And eventually I inherited the paper route. I needed money, too!

227

money matters

As MOTHER HAD POINTED OUT, problems of money and credit were becoming everyday considerations. By the 1920's the flourishing prosperity of the early years was showing signs of serious deterioration. As before, items produced in the colonies were in plentiful supply but the limited sales for cash did not produce sufficient capital to satisfy the increasing "wants" of the members. The elders doled out credit less and less generously. Even though their policy and the need for limiting credit was understood, members still could not ignore the temptations offered by the "outside" through mail order books, tourists, and visiting salesmen. The whole subject of money and credit began creating unfamiliar feelings of dissatisfaction among the True Inspirationists. Even I was affected. . . .

"Mama, when will you come with me to buy my new shoes? See, these are worn all the way through on the side."

"Not now, Anna. I must pick the grapes for Dr. Breck. You know he ordered two bushels. Maybe you are big enough to go by yourself."

This was too wonderful. Never before had I been allowed to take our little brown credit book and go to the store alone. Mother kept the little book in a secret place because it was our only way to get things from the general store. The elders decided how much credit we should have. Each year mother had to sign in a big book before they gave her our credit. I often went with her to the store to buy thread, or yard goods, or shoes, or any of the things that were not made in Amana or supplied to us. Each time the cost of the item was written in the little book and thus charged against our account.

"How much credit have we left?" I asked, thinking of my possibilities.

"Only $16.00 and that must do for everything until next year when the elders make the new allotments. Part of it is credit we saved from last year. I want to save enough to buy a bathtub."

"A bathtub! Why do we need a bathtub?" I couldn't imagine saving our money for something like that.

"Now, Anna, you know we need a bathtub, or . . ." Mother hesitated. "It would be nice to have a big white one. Wouldn't you like to take your baths in a bathroom instead of in a little tin tub in the sitting room?"

"Well, yes," I agreed. "I hope the elders give us more money next year. I'm bigger now and so is Henry and we need more."

"The elders will think of that." Mother never permitted Henry or me to criticize the elders.

She had gone into the next room where she kept the book in a secret compartment of our big "Old-Country" chest.

"Now, you be sure the shoes fit well and don't get them too small. And mind you, don't lose our book. Henry needs underwear and will need the book next."

"When can I have a book of my own?"

"Oh, my, not until you are twenty-one or married."

"But there are so many things I want. In Elsie's mail order book . . . ."

"Now, now, Anna, there is nothing you *need*. Maybe you should not look at the mail order book so much."

Armed with the magic credit book, I started to run— then decided walking was more appropriate for a big girl going shopping alone at the general store.

I knew every inch of the merchandise by heart. Yet it was good to be there with the power to choose something for myself. I inspected the candies, the tobacco, the yard goods in bolts on a shelf, and the beautiful colored threads, though these were not for me. Sister Henrietta, the clerk, interrupted my shopping:

"Did you want to buy something, Anna?"

"Yes, I have come for a pair of shoes," I said as mother might have done.

"Now, think of that, and alone, too. Brother Herman will help you."

I marched past her to the little room where the shoes were kept. Brother Herman took care of supplying the shoes for all the people in our village, though he never had many pairs in stock at any one time. He turned from putting boxes of new shoes on the shelves.

"Well, Anna," he smiled pleasantly. "You want to buy shoes, yes?"

I nodded my head, feeling as important as any grownup.

"What size do you wear?"

I hesitated, stammering a bit. "I guess I don't know." Mother had always decided.

"So, then we shall try. You want shoes for school?"

"Well, yes," I answered, "but really more for church."

"Well, let's see. I think these are the kind your mother would buy for you. They cost $2.00. Do you like them?"

A quick glance told me they were just plain old school shoes. I remembered a pair we had tried on when I had been in the store with mother. I had noticed them in an open box as I came in. They were the most beautiful shoes I had ever seen, trimmed with shiny black leather. It seemed to me that I just had to have those shoes, though mother had decided they were too expensive.

"I like those in that box better," I pointed toward the counter.

"But, my child, that pair costs a lot more credit— $4.00."

Credit meant nothing to me then. I just wanted the shoes.

"Will you please let me try them, Brother Herman?" I begged.

He shrugged his shoulders a little and reached for the shoes. Even though Brother Herman was an elder, all the children liked him for he was friendly and paid attention to us.

He carefully fit the shoe on my foot. Though it was rather loose, it was beautiful. While I admired it, he took out the other shoe and soon I was standing up feeling that the shoes were already mine.

"I want this pair," I said.

"Do you think your mother will want you to have them?"

"I think she will," I answered with much more confidence than I felt.

On the way home, I tried and tried to find some way to tell mother I had spent much more of our credit than I should have for my shoes. I was sure that she would not have me take them back in exchange for a less expensive pair, for she was too proud for that and would think such a business degrading. When I reached home, she was knitting a long woolen stocking. She looked up and said, "Anna, what shoes did you buy?"

"I bought those pretty ones. I wanted them so much, Mama."

"Don't tell me you bought those expensive ones I said you should not have? You know we cannot afford them."

"Yes, Mama. I bought them."

"And how much did you pay?"

"Four dollars."

"Anna, what were you thinking of? You are becoming worldly and vain. What am I going to do with you?" Then mother thought about Brother Herman. "Why did Brother Herman let you have them? He is an elder and knows how little credit we have, and yet he lets a child spend it foolishly!" I was relieved now, because I felt that mother was blaming Brother Herman more than me. Not long afterward, she, too, made a worldly purchase . . . .

One day we were at Elsie's house looking at her mail order book. It was full of the most wonderful dolls, clothes, and toys. There was one doll she wanted and one that I wanted more than anything in the world.

"I wish we had some money," I said longingly.

"Me too," said Elsie. "Maybe we can get our mothers to buy the dolls."

"I don't think so. My mother makes only a little from her garden and she has been saving that for years to buy a bathtub."

"Why don't the elders let us have some money like other people?"

"Mother says that they provide us with all our *needs* and that we should be very thankful we don't have to earn all our money to pay for our houses, and our food and clothes. Do you know what she told me? That in towns like Cedar Rapids, the people have to pay to go to church!"

"I know, and they even have to pay to have the doctor come or to have their houses painted or to have a funeral."

"This communal plan would not be so bad if the elders would keep a bigger variety of things in the general store."

"That would not help because we have to save our store credit for our *needs*."

"Well, just the same, I wish I had that doll." We were quiet while we tried to think of a way.

"You know what? I think I will ask mama to buy it for me. I have 65¢ Henry paid me for carrying his paper route for him. Maybe she will give me enough of her bathtub money to buy my doll."

"I'm going to ask my dad for some of his money. He

got some for furs he trapped that he's saving for a gun he wants. See, here is a picture of it," said Elsie.

"Well, it takes so much money to buy a bathtub and a shotgun that they should not mind letting us get the dolls first."

We put the book away hurriedly. I ran home to ask mother about the money and Elsie went to the mill to ask her father.

Mother was in a happy mood. She was humming a tune as she sprinkled clothes to iron. I thought I had better tell her about the doll before asking for the money.

"Mama, Elsie has a new mail order book and it has the most beautiful dolls in it."

"Now, Anna, you know we do not have money for dolls."

"Sometimes I wish I lived 'outside' so that I could earn money to buy things."

"What a sinful thing to say, with the elders providing everything for you!"

"How do people earn money on the 'outside?' "

"Oh, they work in factories."

"Like our woolen mill?"

"Yes, like our woolen mill."

"Then why don't Uncle Peter and Elsie's father earn money? They work at the mill."

"Anna, I have told you many times. No one is paid for working in Amana. We all work for the society and the elders arrange for us all to receive what we need. We don't get paid in money but we get taken care of so we do not need money."

"I need money," I persisted although it seemed I was getting nowhere. "You need money too; when are you going to get the bathtub?"

235

"Real soon. I have already had Uncle Jacob order it from a catalogue he has at the store." Mother looked more thrilled than I had ever seen her. I knew then that she wanted the bathtub even more than I wanted the doll. I decided not to persist any longer.

"Is the tub very large?"

"Yes, it is five feet long and stands on four little legs. You might even have some trouble getting into it." She winked at me playfully.

"It must hold lots of water." This bathtub would be nice to have. "When will it get here?"

"Maybe we will have it in a week or two."

There went my hopes for some money, but mama was so happy that I really did not mind.

"Two weeks! That's a long time to wait. Who gets the first bath?"

"Now, my child, don't get so excited. You know it will take time to get it in place. You must not count on it right away."

I left to report to Elsie. It seemed that at that moment I had come off with no doll and with no bathtub.

But when the bathtub did come we really had excitement at our house!

Not many people in Amana had a big white bathtub. That was one reason why mother wanted one. It made her feel important that she had been able to save some of her credit. It also pleased her to know that outsiders liked her handiwork and garden products enough to come back year after year until she had accumulated enough money to buy a big item. It was all the more satisfying, because being a widow, she had done it all by herself.

Long before the tub was ordered mother began making over a small bedroom into a bathroom. I don't know where she got the oilcloth paper for the wall, next to the tub, but she planned that George could help her put it on when he came to whitewash the room. He made a lot of remarks:

"Well, Sister Schneider, how does it happen that blue whitewashing is not good enough for you anymore?"

"Be still, George, and hurry so we can finish today." Mother did not want to talk about the wallpaper.

"What are you going to do with this room, anyway? Make a kitchen of your own, maybe? The elders will never stand for that." George was curious about all the preparation.

"I have some wine for you as soon as you finish," Mother bribed.

"*Ach*, so? Sister Schneider, you know that I am doing you a special favor when I help you put paper on your walls. Remember, I am a whitewasher and am not supposed to do anything but put on whitewash."

"*Ja*, I know, I know." Mother was willing to agree as long as he kept doing what she asked him to.

"I guess nobody in Amana has paper on their walls. Did you ask the elders?" George wanted to know. George did not like this business but he knew that mother would give him a generous drink of wine when he finished, so he tried to please her.

Now George, you must be careful about matching. Make the blue designs come out together." She pretended not to have heard the question about the elders.

"Worldly, that's what I call it. Give me good old Amana blue whitewashing any day."

At last the papering was done and mother was so pleased that she would sneak off and look at it several times a day. She had made new curtains of blue checked gingham for the window. She had actually considered ordering a green check, or even a red, but her adventurous spirit stopped short of introducing a new color to Amana. Blue was the color for decorating the interiors of houses and that was that. But the curtains were very pretty, for she had made white cross-stitch trimming along the hems and blue crocheting around the edges. The old potbellied stove had been polished until it shone, and the floor was scrubbed shiny clean. Next she put down strips of handwoven carpet and we were ready for the bathtub. Neither Henry nor I had said a word about it to anyone because we knew it was distinctly out of the ordinary and we were afraid of what the people would say about it. We were sure that they would talk, for whenever anything happened to anybody, everyone had something to say about it—usually not good.

One day when I came home from school, there stood the tub in the hall. I thought, "How wonderful. This will be a happy day for mama!" I ran into our living room calling:

"Mama, Mama, it's beautiful." But mama did not answer. I called again and wondered, for mother never failed to meet me when I came home from school. I looked in the bedroom. There she sat alone in her little rocker by the window and she had been crying. I had never seen her cry before except when *Tante* Maria died.

"Mama, who died?" I was afraid and alarmed.

"No one died, Anna."

"Then why do you feel so bad?"

"It's the bathtub." And she began wiping her eyes again. I did not know what to do or say. She looked so little and unhappy, sitting there.

"Don't you like it? I think it's beautiful." I looked at her closely.

"Anna, Uncle Jacob came here with Brother Schultz and they made an official elder call. They said terrible things to me. They made me feel so ashamed." Tears came again and she could hardly talk. "Never in my life have I been reprimanded by an elder before."

"What's wrong about a bathtub?" I was puzzled by the ways of elders.

"They said it was extravagant." She wiped her eyes, "But I only used the credit that we had saved for years." Indignation rose up in her. "And my own money from selling my garden things and tablecloths!" Mother was becoming angrier as she talked.

"Those Schultzes use every penny of their credit every year, long before the year is over." She stood up. "And then they borrow on the next year's allowance besides. We have never overspent our allowance in our lives. So *he* comes to my house to scold me about being extravagant!" She began pacing up and down the room.

"I don't think you're extravagant," I was fighting mad too. "Let's get it hooked up so we can all take a bath."

"That's when the trouble began—when I went to the elders to ask for a plumber." Mother was drying her eyes on her apron and I knew she was not going to cry anymore.

"Now, I'm going to ask them again. If that Brother Schultz says anything, I'll tell him he can't have any more of our wine, ever again. I have let him use most of our wine allowance since your father died." Mother was smoothing her hair with quick angry pats. It was exciting to see her so *mad*.

"And every year since prohibition I have been giving him some of our leftover wine. Him and his *Peistengel!* Maybe he even bootlegs it!"

I never heard what happened, but the next week the plumbers came and put the tub just where mother wanted it. After the drain pipe was connected, mother let us have baths in the new tub. We still had to heat water on the potbellied stove, until the water was boiling so that it would warm up the cold water that ran into the tub from the new shiny faucet. But we no longer needed to carry the water in buckets, up and down the stairs. Just pull out the plug, and swishhh, away went the water.

I felt like a sinful "outsider" as I slithered and floated and turned in the great white "tank," my pigtails pinned high on my head.

Never again did I bathe in one of those old-fashioned, common little tin tubs, made by the Amana tinner. Mama was happy to be the owner of a white bathtub, even though it was extravagant.

the Brecks, our friends from "outside"

THE COLONISTS were so self-sufficient they had very little to do with outsiders. However, there was no veterinarian and one was called from nearby Marengo whenever there was need. Since Uncle John was in charge of the farms, he was the man who dealt with the Marengo veterinarian, Dr. Breck.

Uncle John and Dr. Breck became very close friends and Dr. Breck fell into the habit of bringing his wife with him so that she could visit with *Tante* Lina. As Henry and I were often at Uncle John's, we too became acquainted with the Brecks, and then mother came to know them.

The Brecks won our admiration for many reasons. They paid attention to Henry and me and were sympathetic, friendly people. They knew the glamorous world "outside"; and they brought us presents at Christmas and for our birthdays. Most important of all, they had an automobile.

For a long time, the Breck's car was the only automobile that came to Homestead and it was a wheezy, balky, saucy little touring type Ford. We all felt that it was worldly and sinfully extravagant but, oh, so exciting. On several occasions, the Brecks had taken Uncle John and his family to visit with them in their home at Marengo. The more the boys told us about these visits, the more Henry and I wanted to go there ourselves.

It was summer when the Brecks finally invited mother, Henry, and me to come with Uncle John's family on one of these visits. Mother didn't object, knowing that Henry and I were so eager to go. We all neglected to mention our plans to Grandpa, and so we "happened" to meet at Uncle John's house where the Brecks came for us at an appointed time. As their auto came snorting down the road, making more noise than had ever been heard in Homestead before or since, we wondered how three more adults and four children were supposed to fit in the car. It came to a jerky stop, engine roaring, and Dr. Breck jumped out. He was a stocky Irishman with a round, ruddy face and for this special occasion, he was wearing a white linen "duster" and a large motor cap, making him look very funny.

"Hello, everybody," he shouted above the noise.

"Good afternoon, Dr. Breck," we answered.

"Are you all ready for a spin in my 'tin lizzy'?"

"We sure are," yelled Henry, and mother put a restraining hand on him.

Portly Mrs. Breck sat smugly in the front seat, showing every sign of pride and good taste, even though the vibration of the machine made her shake all over as though she were possessed by some evil demon.

Uncle John was walking around the car, kicking at the tires, inspecting the shiny headlights, and fairly beaming at the wonderful machine. The boys imitated him. Mother and *Tante* Lina seemed to draw back from it. I was impatient to get in.

"We can go right away if you're ready," shouted Dr. Breck.

We all nodded eagerly and waited to be told to get in.

"John, you can sit in front with us. I guess the kids will have to sit on top of somebody," was Dr. Breck's solution for the seating problem. So Uncle John helped mother and *Tante* Lina into the back seat and then there was barely room for Henry, William, Walter, and me to pack in on top of them. Dr. Breck turned around gayly.

"Stick your feet outside, son, if there's not enough room inside." He laughed heartily at his little joke and pushed his way into the small space left for him. The doors were finally made to stay shut after several hard slams, and he yelled, "All ready?"

We all nodded 'yes.' Then without known cause, the motor died—dead. After the terrific din, the ensuing silence hurt our ears. In a quiet, normal voice, Dr. Breck said—

"I'll have to crank her." He looked at Mrs. Breck and Uncle John, "Sorry, folks, I have to take the seat out to get the crank."

"Oh, bother," grumbled Mrs. Breck, but obligingly she pulled herself out of the seat. I had been trying to "sit light" on mama's lap but the letdown was so tiresome I slumped to wait patiently. Dr. Breck had taken

243

off his fancy duster and now in shirtsleeves and suspenders, he carefully set the spark and the gas and fitted the crank onto the shaft. He gave several ferocious turns. Nothing happened. He re-set the spark and tried again, but nothing happened, except that it "kicked" back and the crank flew off. He brushed the back of his hand across his perspiring forehead and gave the crank a series of quick turns. As the engine coughed a little, he jumped to the wheel and gave it more gas. The motor roared and sent chills of vibrations through us, shaking us until our teeth chattered.

Quickly he shoved the crank under the seat and the passengers reloaded. Then he donned his jaunty costume, his smudged, wet face as happy as a child's. The auto sputtered like a wild monster and finally, after a series of jerks that kept our heads bobbing, it gave a lunge and we were off up the road as if released by some enormous invisible spring. We hung on wherever we could with one hand and clutched our hats with the other. However, Henry let go of his hat for a second, and off it flew like a bird. It took quite a while to get the car stopped so that Henry could go after it, and I began to feel a little sick from the gasoline fumes rising around us.

On our way once more, we came to a flock of white chickens passing the time of day on the road. I closed my eyes as we mowed through them and by the time I could see through the cloud of dust in back of us, we were too far away to tell how many we had hit.

Then it came again—that horrible feeling in my stomach. Quickly I leaned over the edge of the car and all unknown to the driver, underwent one of my most embarrassing moments. The remainder of the ride was a blur and a nightmare, but in time it came to an end and was forgotten in the enchantment of discovering the new world we had entered.

Cars did not come to Amana for some time after they were fairly popular elsewhere. Like other outside influences, they were forbidden by the elders. But once people had ridden in a car, their outlook on life was never the same. A new influence, compelling and significant, was creeping in to stay.

when Mama went away

"ANNA AND HENRY, come here." Mother closed the door behind her. She seemed to be out of breath from hurrying. Henry dropped his wood carving and I laid down my knitting. When mother called us that way, she had something special to tell.

"What happened?" Henry wanted to know. Mother hung up her shawl in the big wardrobe and waited until she was sure we were listening, then she continued.

"Uncle Albert died."

"Uncle Albert!" He was just about the most important relative we had, though Henry and I had not seen him since Grandpa Schneider died.

"Now listen carefully." Mother was speaking quickly and seriously. "I'm going to the funeral with Uncle John and *Tante* Lina."

247

"But, Mama, how can you? Uncle Albert didn't even live here." Everyone knew that only people who lived in Amana could be buried there.

"Be patient, Anna. That's what I'm trying to tell you. Uncle John is borrowing Dr. Breck's car and we will drive to Sioux City. The funeral will be there."

"Uncle Albert was rich, wasn't he?" Henry was remembering the wonderful presents Grandma and the aunts received from him each Christmas.

"Yes, he had lots of money, but that is not why we are going to the funeral. Remember, Uncle Albert was your Grandpa Schneider's brother, and once he lived in Amana and was one of us."

"Why did he leave?" This was one of Henry's favorite subjects.

"He thought Amana was not good enough for him. He wanted his own business, and he wanted to make lots of money."

"I'd like that too," said Henry. Mother let the remark pass.

"Now don't bother me with silly questions. I must find a way to borrow a hat and coat for the funeral."

"Isn't your church costume all right?" That was what we wore to funerals in Amana.

"Not for a funeral on the 'outside.' Women wear hats and coats, and *Tante* Lina and I want to dress like the others."

Neither Henry nor I had any suggestions for that problem. None of the women in Amana owned a hat or a coat.

"Maybe you can make a hat," I finally offered.

"No, Anna, I have nothing to make one of, and besides there is no time. *Tante* Lina is trying to borrow some things from Mrs. Breck. She and Uncle John have gone to see about it. Now we must get your things ready so you can stay with Grandma Schneider at Uncle John's house while I'm away."

This was turning into a big affair. Mother had never left us before, nor had we ever stayed all night in any house but our own. Now we were to take clothes and make a three-day visit. I forgot about the funeral in the thought of adventuring with Walter and William, my favorite cousins. Of all the places we might go, Grandma Schneider's house was the best. This was because Uncle John was the farm manager for our village and lived in the house nearest the barns. From his house and yard we could watch the farm workers. We were told never to go inside the barnyard alone. At milking time farm hands would bring in the large herds of cows, and we were awed by the mooing and the tromping of heavy hoofs as they took their turn at the stock tank before they went in the barn for milking. The cats were waiting for their "squirts" from the hands of the milkers. Sometimes a bull would be brought in, pulling in all directions at once, raving and roaring like a tornado. Several men would be holding him with many ropes and there would be much shouting until he was finally coaxed into his stall. Once in a while Uncle John would take us to the corrals where the horses were kept. They were broad-backed and heavy for pulling wagons and machinery. I used to wish for a pony to ride, but we had none at Amana because they were "worldly" and not "useful" like the other horses. Farthest away from Grandma's house were the pig barns. We did not go there often because they were too smelly and ugly.

There was an extra attraction for Henry at Grandma Schneider's; Uncle John owned the only dog in Homestead.

249

"I'll play with Kasper all the time," said Henry.

"Then you'll play without me. I hate that dog."

"You don't understand a dog." Henry was superior. "I wish I had a dog more than anything in the whole world."

"That's foolish, Henry, you know that pets have never been allowed in Amana. There was probably a testimony about it from Barbara Heinemann," I said.

"I don't see why. Do you know I saw a picture in a book that showed dozens of dogs, some big and some small. How many kinds of dogs are there, anyway?"

"I don't know, Henry. Ask Uncle John." Mother had taken her Sunday church dress from the wardrobe and was looking it over.

"What kind of a dog is Kasper?"

"I think Uncle John said he is an Airedale."

"I'd sure like a dog." As usual, Henry was trying to carve one from a piece of wood.

"Cats are better." I was mortally afraid of Kasper. "Especially the ones around the kitchen house. The ones around the barns are too wild. I wish I could have a kitten here in this house for my very own."

"People on the outside have pets in their houses, Uncle John told me."

"Anna and Henry, will you please be still. You should be studying your catechism or doing something useful. We have no pets in Amana." Mother spoke emphatically. I think she was secretly glad. Mother didn't like cats and she was afraid of dogs.

The next morning mother and the others left for the funeral. Everyone got up early in the morning, though we had made neat bundles of our clothes the night before. Mother put on the coat Mrs. Breck had sent for her. It was dark and plain like a man's and seemed to swallow her in its deep folds and large sleeves. The hat was black and had a heavy black veil. I did not tell mother but I thought she looked much better in her Amana church costume.

As we watched the car drive away, three days seemed ever so long and I began to wish for Saturday night when mother would be home again. But with school each day and the novelty of staying at Grandma's at night, and with Walter and William for company, Saturday morning soon came around. This was the day we really waited for because there was no school and we had all day to play.

We agreed that the first activity would be an excursion with Henry to check his traps. This was an expedition across the pastures, along the river and into the woods. The morning was crisp and cold and the sun shone brightly in a wintry sky. I tagged along behind the boys, keeping quiet so they would not remember that I was a girl.

"When I grow up I'm going to move away and be rich like Uncle Albert," said Henry.

"Me too," said William.

"Not me," Walter was always the careful one. "I want to be an elder and tell people what to do."

"I wouldn't want to sit up in front of everybody." I joined in.

"It's mighty different—on the outside." William was the oldest and acted as if he knew more than we did. Since he was to become a teacher he would have a chance to learn about the outside.

"Yah. Cars, radios, fancy clothes, and lots of things we have never even seen."

"I want to be a doctor." This was from Henry.

"How are you going to be a doctor? We've got Dr.

Miller, and you know the elders won't send anyone out to learn doctoring until he is old. Everybody knows we need only one doctor."

"They need doctors outside."

I felt like crying when the boys talked of leaving Amana. How could they? We had everything in Amana.

We walked a mile or so across an alfalfa field and came to a woodsy spot with a little stream. Here Henry had set a trap for muskrats. Beyond in the pasture, he had traps for raccoons, gophers, and other small animals. We all knew where to look, for we had been with him before. Henry said, "I smell a polecat."

"That's nothing; there are always polecats around here," said William, who was dashing off to check the trap by the big tree. Henry and Kasper were ahead of us.

"I told you so," yelled Henry.

"What is it?" We all ran to see.

"Phew-w-w." We backed off and held our noses. A skunk! It was dead but it still smelled like a skunk.

"You take it out." Henry suggested to William. "You're the oldest."

"Yes, but it's your trap. The fellow who owns the traps always takes out the game."

"All right," Henry agreed. "But some of you will have to carry it. I already have the gophers."

So Henry carefully pulled the jaws of the trap apart and released the large carcass of a male skunk.

"Are you going to skin him?" I asked, dreading the business.

"Of course," said Walter. "That pelt's worth two dollars."

Swinging the dead skunk, Walter led the way back

252

to Uncle John's work shed. Here were knives and stretching boards for preparing the pelt.

"It's a nice big one," Walter observed when the job was finished. "What will we do with the carcass? The ground's too hard to dig a hole to bury it."

We all pondered the problem.

"I know. Let's burn it in *Tante* Lina's stove. It has a real strong draft," Henry suggested.

"Well, it might make a smell."

"Not if we make a big fire. It will burn up in no time."

That seemed a good idea so Walter stuffed the carcass in an old bucket and we moved in on *Tante* Lina's "Comfort Heater" with its squares of isinglass. *Tante* Lina was proud of that stove because it was a fancy one purchased with her savings, and not just a plain old potbellied one.

Grandma Schneider was upstairs in her rooms and no one was around. We figured we'd have the burning over before anyone came back. A few pieces of wood were smoldering in the firepot, so we shoved the carcass in the stove, then piled a lot of wood on top of it, opened the draft wide and waited for the remains to go up the chimney in smoke. Almost at once there was a sizzling as of heat and water. Then one of the most horrible odors I ever hope to smell began to fill the room. It was like nothing we knew—musky, burnt flesh and bone, altogether sickening.

"Open the door," ordered Walter but Henry was already outside. I put on my coat and followed. Grandma Schneider came down from upstairs.

"Whatever are you doing?" She stood in the doorway.

"We're burning something." Henry tried to be brief about it and assumed an air of nonchalance.

"And what are you burning?" Grandma opened the door and looked into the stove, which was now red hot. The odor of steaming skunk swept out into her face and she slammed the door shut. We stood out in the hall, holding our noses, and looked on.

Grandma was holding her apron over her nose. "What *is* that?"

"It's the body of a skunk." Henry could think of nothing to say but the truth.

"You are burning a *skunk* in *Tante* Lina's new stove?" Grandma could not believe that this horrible thing was true.

"It will soon be gone. We made a big fire." Walter tried to sound confident.

"Not before your father gets home. Walter, why did you do such a thing?" Grandma looked as if she were going to cry. "Do you boys know how long it will take to burn that body?"

I was beginning to feel a little sick and had to move out into the yard. The heat of the room made the smell all the more horrible.

"Now don't put any more wood on the fire. When it cools down a little you will have to take that smelly thing far, far away. I just hope we get it done before your mother comes home."

We began waiting. We had to stay outside for we could not bear to be near the smell. It was now permeating the air and being carried by the wind so that people who passed by came sniffing up, then held their noses as they asked what was wrong at Uncle John's house. We would say no more than that they were burning

254

something in the stove. No one blamed anyone. We all wondered how this would turn out.

About four o'clock, we saw the Breck's car come up the street, and though we were so very glad to have mother and the others back, we remembered at once that we had a problem. As they rode up in front of Uncle John's house, mother, Uncle John and *Tante* Lina were all holding their noses, mother and *Tante* Lina looking like strangers in their borrowed clothes. The car stopped and as they scrambled for the doors they all asked the same question. Henry, William, Walter, and I stood around waiting for William to speak.

"Papa, we caught a skunk. And we skinned it."

"But what is that smell?"

"And we tried to burn the carcass in the stove."

"Not in my lovely new stove!" *Tante* Lina was about to cry.

Uncle John was in the house asking no more questions. He had the air of a man facing an urgent emergency.

"All right. Now, Walter, go to the blacksmith and borrow a big iron tongs. Hurry."

Walter was gone as if shot from a gun.

"William, get an old tarp from the woodshed and put it down in front of the stove. Henry and Anna, get an ash pail from the woodshed."

Grateful for a job, Henry and I hauled in an old pail used to carry ashes. Uncle John went to change his clothes. When all was ready, Uncle John stopped holding his nose long enough to fix the tongs around the body and carefully lifted it to the pail. Mama and *Tante* Lina stayed outside looking grim and unhappy.

Just then several neighbors who had seen the car come in, sauntered over to hear about the funeral—and

255

to find out what was going on. Poor Uncle John was the center of attention and whereas he would have liked a chance to discuss the funeral in an important way, this other business was too embarrassing. He worked quickly. Soon he had the smoking, blackened, smelly carcass delivered to the pail.

"Now, William and Walter, take it away, far, far away."

Henry and I followed the foul odor—as if by doing so we might escape further punishment. Way behind the barns we dumped the remains and came contritely back to Uncle John's house. We could still smell the odor; in fact, it lingered all winter long. Poor *Tante* Lina aired and scrubbed but it was no use. I always wondered why Uncle John never punished us. It was a most unhappy winter for the boys and me, for wherever we went, everyone made fun of us. No greater punishment can be given in Amana, not even the reprimanding of the elders in church.

new adventures

IT WAS THE BRECKS who thought that William, Walter, Henry, and I needed more experiences outside Amana and they urged our parents to let us have a ride on a train. The Rock Island trains passed through Homestead and all our lives we had watched them—the flashy passenger trains that flew by without stopping, whistles shrieking, and the long freight trains, usually coming through at night, wakening us with their sustained roar. The unpretentious locals also came through, bringing freight to Homestead and taking it away, usually with a passenger car or two attached.

The Brecks, reinforced by our repeated pleading that we might have a ride on the train, eventually won permission to take us as far as Marengo in their car so that we could travel back the twelve miles to Homestead on a real, steam-puffing, rail-grinding train. Mother dressed us in our best everyday clothes, not our church clothes, and we left with the Brecks in their famous auto so that we could catch the train at Marengo. Mother told us "good-by" as if we were leaving for New York and our only disappointment was that we had no excuse for carrying luggage like the salesmen who got off the train at Homestead.

"Now watch for Homestead, and don't ride all the way to Iowa City," cautioned Dr. Breck humorously, as we scrambled from his car to the depot.

"We won't," we promised.

"Now I'll buy the tickets and each of you may carry your own," said Dr. Breck as he left us standing in the middle of the small dingy waiting room. Mrs. Breck drew her skirts close to her to be sure they did not swish against some out-of-place cuspidor. It was plain to see that she could hardly stand this dirty place with its bolted-down benches, its bare, grimy windows, its unscrubbed floor, and the big blast stove in the center of the room. The stove was the worst of all for it was covered with dried tobacco juice.

After Dr. Breck had the tickets, he beckoned to us to come outside. Then he said, "I'm afraid I have bad news for you. You see, there are no passenger cars on the train today."

"But Dr. Breck, we have to ride the train home," I reminded him.

"Of course you do, Anna. So the man is going to let you have a very special ride."

"How can we have a special ride, if there are no passenger cars?" William wanted to know. We were all sick with disappointment.

"Do you know what a caboose is?"

"I do," said Walter, "it's the tail end of the freight train."

"Well, yes, I guess you could call it that," conceded Dr. Breck. "Anyway, the station master says that since there is no passenger car today, you can ride in the caboose."

"The caboose. Hurray!" William slapped his knee with delight and the other two boys beamed. I did not know whether to join the jubilee or not.

But it was too late to back out, and besides, whatever the boys did, I would have to do. The noisy, puffy, black engine was already steaming around the bend, dragging a nondescript set of freight cars, and a rickety caboose. The brakes gripped the wheels as the train slid to a stop. I saw the trainmaster talking to the engineer and then come to us.

"You can get right on the caboose now, kids."

All three boys flew to the caboose and without waiting for the courtesy of a step box, dragged themselves up onto the car platform. I looked helplessly at the step, high off the ground, and wondered how I would ever get up there. Just then someone lifted me from behind and set my feet on the platform. The boys were already inside, making an inspection. William, acting as if he owned the place, was lying on the bunk bed, with its dirty fringed couch cover rumpled under him. Henry was sitting in the one "Captain's" chair and pretending to be a trainman. Walter was peering out the window and waving to the Brecks. I looked at the messy potbellied stove which took up the whole center of the train and wondered apprehensively how we were ever to get to Homestead in this rickety outfit. The noise of the chugging engine discouraged conversation but made pantomime appropriate. The boys made exaggerated

259

faces and acted out crazy ideas. That is, they did so until the train gave a sudden jerk that sent us sprawling, chair and all, toward the back of the caboose. William, who was relatively stationary on the bunk, rolled with laughter while Henry grabbed for the stove in mock despair and Walter and I collided, ending up in a heap on the floor. The train slowly shoved off and all four of us scampered up to wave to the Brecks. Thus began our journey by train from Marengo to Homestead.

The setting somehow brought out the high jinks in all of us and we had a hilarious time. It was fun to watch the trees and farmhouses whiz by with what seemed like tremendous speed. We counted telephone poles until we ran out of numbers. The boys bounced on the couch and flopped on top of each other, with the shaking of the train.

Soon we began to notice familiar landmarks. The train slowed down as it went through South Amana. We stretched our necks to see if we might see someone we knew. Somehow an Amana village looked good to us after our adventure on the outside. We saw several women with baskets of food come out of one of the kitchen houses. Suddenly we were hungry and glad to know that our trip would soon be over.

Next we darted past the barnyards and along the Amana fields. It seemed that the corn stood proud and straight in the rich black soil. We had been told that our forefathers had chosen this very land because of the richness of the soil.

Suddenly we plunged into the shadow of a deep woods. Off in a distance we could see the "ice pond" where we had gone fishing and the picnic area we had often hiked to.

Back out in the sunlight, we could see Homestead in the distance. We rumbled over a railroad trestle and wondered if we were scaring somebody on the road below.

"There's our house," said William, as we rolled into town. Sure enough, we could spot it easily from the train window.

"And there's our Grandma!" I shouted with glee, as I waved wildly back to the little blackclothed figure waving at us.

"There's the church," said Henry. "And the schoolhouse. Soon we'll come to the depot. I hope the train doesn't forget to stop at Homestead."

But he needn't have worried. Just then we heard the squeaking of the brakes and felt our legs give out from under us. We fell in a heap on the dirty floor. This time the empty chair slid clear across the caboose, bumping into the stove. We lay there till the train came to a stop. Then we quickly brushed our clothes and darted for the window. There stood mother and *Tante* Lina, watching eagerly for us.

I shall never forget mother's look of shocked surprise as she saw us descend, not from the usual passenger train, but from the caboose of a freight train, our faces smudged, our hands dirty as coal miners, our clothes rumpled and soiled, but our spirits riding high.

It was the most wonderful train trip I ever hope to have! Just how little the Brecks had succeeded in showing us worldly travel we understood only much, much later.

Uncle John's surprise

ONE SUNDAY, mother, Henry, and I had come home from afternoon church service and had changed our clothes when the telephone rang. It was *Tante* Lina, who often called mother. She said we were to come over to her house right away as Uncle John had a surprise for us. We could not imagine what it might be. Henry was sure that the Brecks had come to take us for a ride. I thought Uncle John wanted to show us a new colt, or a calf, I hoped.

We hurried over to Uncle John's as fast as we could and he and the boys met us at the door. They had their hats on and seemed ready to go somewhere. Henry said, "Where's the surprise?"

"You will have to come for a walk with us first," said Uncle John mysteriously. *Tante* Lina had her bonnet on, too, so the six of us trudged along after Uncle John as he led us to the road that stretched out into the country. There was no conversation to speak of as we walked along, more curious than ever about what the surprise could be. We walked by the patch of woods where we had gone mushrooming in the spring. I remembered how I had panicked when I had strayed too far and had thought I was lost. I was glad the surprise was not leading us back into those woods. Finally we climbed a small hill and Uncle John paused to wait for us. "Well, do you see anything?" He asked. Then Henry spotted it—an automobile standing discreetly under a tall and solitary elm at the bend of the road below!

"A car! You're taking us for a ride! Whose car is it?"

"It's mine!" Uncle John swelled with pride.

The Breck's automobile had had a far-reaching influence on Uncle John. From the beginning he had liked it better than anything he had seen anywhere. To make matters worse, one of the transient workers around the barn had arrived from Florida in the most dashing little red runabout imaginable, adding further to the temptation of Uncle John.

So now he had a car!

Henry and I were already far ahead of the others as we ran down the hill. This was a brand new, shiny, black Ford, similar to Dr. Breck's, but a later model. The canvas top was neatly folded back and the machine looked as though it had just been dusted and polished.

"Will you take us for a ride?" I wanted to know.

"Sure," said Uncle John, "but only in the country. We can't go near the village because the elders might have something to say." He winked slyly.

We all knew that was true, but at the moment, who

cared about the elders? Henry had been inspecting the car without saying anything, then he looked at Uncle John and began,

"But, Uncle John, how did you . . .?"

Mother was making signs to him. He started again.

"I mean, where did you . . .?"

Mother could not let him bring out the embarrassing question of where the money came from. She interrupted quickly.

"Now, Henry, don't ask inquisitive questions."

Uncle John said, "Let's have a ride."

This was the beginning of many rides we had with Uncle John. For the rest of the season, he kept the car hidden out along the country roads. Finally, he decided that everyone knew he had it so he brought it in to the barns, the inference being that the head of the farms needed a car.

It was only a matter of a few months before Uncle John wanted to take us on a long trip—75 miles each way, to Newton. He chose Newton because by this time, the Brecks had moved there and wanted us all to come for a visit. Henry was most excited about it. I remembered how I had been car-sick on the way to Marengo and could not be too thrilled, and mother never liked to go even a little way from home. Perhaps I shared her dislike for the strange food and the unaccustomed places. She usually had a headache even after visiting in one of the Amanas. However, she did want to see the Brecks and she did not want Uncle John to stop asking Henry and me to go places. So we prepared for the long journey.

I cannot remember too much about the trip, except that it took forever. We started very early in the morning and arrived at the Brecks shortly before noon.

First we made a tour of the Breck's apartment, admiring all the luxuries of the outside world. We were especially fascinated by the electric lights and the radio. The boys squatted on the floor with the headphones on their ears. I continued the tour with the ladies. While mother and *Tante* Lina admired the shiny enameled stove, I spotted on the kitchen table a pan of the most unappetizing things I had ever seen—slimy, shapeless, gray. Apparently, this was for lunch and I could bear no more. I ran out of the room searching for a place to hide and settled for a spot far under a bed. When mother called me for lunch I did not answer. I could not bear the thought of having to eat anything so horrible. They all searched and finally found me. Mother made me tell her my trouble. They all laughed and explained that we were having oysters. This was supposed to be a special treat, because we were never served anything like it in the kitchen house. I remembered that salsify was supposed to taste like oysters and wanted nothing to do with them. Mother promised me I need not eat them, thereby making a very un-Amana-like concession to me, an Amana child. My tears were dried and the lunch was soon over.

In the afternoon we took a tour of the city. I found Newton a fascinating place, with all its buildings, vehicles, crowds, and best of all its beautiful school buildings. The windows had been decorated with pumpkin faces in preparation for Halloween. They looked so different from the drab, small-paned school windows I had been accustomed to. I suddenly felt the urge that William and Henry had expressed so many times—to become an outsider and learn and maybe even teach in schools like these.

forebodings

GRANDPA GUYER'S MORNING VISITS had become as much a part of the daily ritual at our house as breakfast and morning prayers. Each morning, through the years, he came, carefully balancing the familiar long willow basket. We knew he came not just to bring our morning meal to us, but rather to share the beginning of a new day and to keep an affectionate eye on us. His visits reflected the seasons and their peculiar activities as well as the current topics of community interest. We all felt a sense of pleasant expectancy about Grandpa's coming, though each of us had a different reason. Mother, in a casual sort of way, managed to bring up topics which troubled her or about which she wanted Grandpa's opinion. Henry and I counted on him for news gleaned from the workers at the woolen mills, or from eating at

267

the common dining room. I do not know just when the pleasantness of the morning visits subtly changed to unpleasantness, to talk about the problems of the society and the way things in Amana were no longer as Christian Metz had wanted them to be. I came to dread seeing Grandpa so worried and I could not remember when last he had smiled and called me *Kleine*.

I especially recall one unhappy day in the March of 1930, not knowing then that Grandpa would not live to see another spring. He came, seeming suddenly slightly bent and very old. As I opened the door for him, Henry took the basket, placing it on a chair, as he had done so often before. Mother turned to look at her father, his stern silence casting a shadow over our spirits. She asked anxiously,

"Father, do you feel well?"

"Sophie, why does the Lord not send us a living *Werkzeug*—another Christian Metz to tell us what to do?" He ignored her question and spoke as though to himself.

"I don't know, Father." Then, as though sensing the cause of his distress, she tried to comfort him. "Maybe next month's sales will be better."

"No, Sophie." He shook his head sadly. "Martin, our best woolen salesman for twenty-five years, came back from Chicago yesterday. Not a single sale! And his stories about the depression are heartbreaking. Millions of people have no jobs, no money, and no food. No wonder the stores don't want to buy Amana woolens! Some of them are even cancelling their orders and we cannot move our present stock."

After a long pause, mother said, "That's bad, very bad. But we in Amana must thank the Lord that we have food and fuel and roofs over our heads."

"*Ach*, Sophie, you don't understand. The society must have money, too. Without money, we cannot buy dyes, chemicals, bindings—all the things we cannot produce in Amana. We can't get along without money." He was grimly silent and no one had anything to say. At last he continued—

"One day we may not even have our homes." His voice sounded like a cry of anguish. "Worst of all, the people are talking of changing our society. This we must never permit."

"How do you mean, change our society?" Mother looked baffled.

"They say we must discontinue our communal system. That would be wrong—so wrong."

"How could we change our communal system? Doesn't our constitution say we must live as a community?" These ideas were completely foreign to mother.

"That's just it, Sophie. For ten years the society's attorney has told us we should form a corporation. This has been discussed many times by the Council of the Brethren, and of course they would not hear of it. But gradually the older, more pious elders have passed away. Suddenly I am in the minority. I just had a big argument with Brother Wilhelm at the breakfast table. He is the head elder for Homestead and now he, too, talks of changing." His voice broke off into a dry sob.

"Brother Wilhelm is the Store *Baas*. He must know how badly we need money. Maybe we will make more profit as a corporation," said mother simply. She still did not comprehend the meaning of all this.

"*Nein, nein*, we must mend our ways. Brother Metz spoke for the Lord when he made our constitution. He said, 'As truly as I live, says the Lord, it is at no time My will to dissolve the ties of the Community . . . or to

269

suffer its dissolution, neither through artful devices, or skill and diplomacy, or cunning or power of men.' " Grandpa had studied the testimonies of Christian Metz so much he could quote from them freely. "We need another leader who is pious enough to get a message from the Lord and who will direct us in the right way. Perhaps we should move onward, away from the outside influences, like they did in the old days. When the society was facing ruin in Ebenezer, Brother Metz once spoke at an elders' meeting and said:

" 'The Lord has yet another solution to this downfall, this collapsing, if it can no longer be taken in hand; He will change His station, and there shall be a battle, a suffering, and a parting. You will have to leave your homes and will have to be transported into bleakness and barrenness.'

"Times were bad in those day, too, Sophie, and Brother Metz kept us together. We must go again and start anew somewhere." He looked to the heavens as if to beg for instruction.

"But it's different now," mother protested. "The people would not leave their homes and go to another land. There is no frontier left in this country."

Grandpa stood up and moved quietly toward the door. It was as if he knew it was useless to say more.

After he was gone, mother shook her head and said, "I just don't think things can be as bad as Grandpa says. We have always had plenty in Amana. We still have our homes and crops. Isn't this enough?"

Henry had listened in silence. Now he spoke, not as a lad of fifteen but as a man—a thoughtful man.

"No, Mama. Grandpa is right. The men speak of nothing but the big deficit." Henry had been working

270

as a clerk in the store and as a packing hand at the woolen warehouse since he was fourteen.

"What does that mean, 'the big deficit'?" Mother was reaching for the reality of the foreboding now smothering Amana like locusts from the sky.

"We owe thousands of dollars, and every year we borrow more. Soon we'll have nothing to borrow on," he told her simply.

Mother only looked at Henry as though she could not believe that he, her son, could speak and know such things which she could in no way understand.

The time soon came when the rumblings of economic disaster could no longer be ignored. Wherever people gathered together, talk concerned problems of production, lack of markets, and needed cash for debts or necessary outside purchases. It affected each of us personally when we received our annual credit allotment from the elders. With Henry now fifteen and me thirteen, mother should have received an increased allowance. Instead, we were given less than we had ever had before, as were all members of the society. Henry, a lanky 155 pound six-footer, had outgrown all his clothes.

One day mother took some of father's suits that had been hanging in the big walnut wardrobe all these years and looked them over carefully.

"I'm so glad I have protected them with moth balls," she reflected. "Maybe they will fit you now, Henry."

Henry took one look at the drab, striped materials and the narrow lapels on the coats. "You expect me to wear those!" he exclaimed.

Mother broke into tears. "No child of mine has ever worn hand-me-downs. I never even cut my dresses down to fit Anna like some people do. I didn't think it would

271

ever come to this." She shook her head sadly. "But a suit of clothes costs so much money."

She took the little brown book from its hiding place and looked at it helplessly. As she held it in her hands we felt a strange new fear, one never before known by the True Inspirationists. The little brown book could no longer provide us with our needs.

After seventy-four years of unique prosperity, hard times had come to Amana.

the "change" is upon us

As the spring turned to summer Grandpa Guyer became ever more concerned. He would stay later and later at the kitchen house and argue with Brother Wilhelm, then come home all ruddy and excited. Mother's main concern was for Grandpa's health. He was known to have high blood pressure and she knew he should not become so upset. But there was no stopping him.

Then one day in August a worker from the woolen warehouse where Grandpa worked, came running to our house to tell mother that Grandpa had collapsed. Hastily, she prepared a bed and several men carried him in on a stretcher. I learned afterward he had suffered a serious stroke. It left him speechless and paralyzed for a ghastly week. Then the doctor told mother that Grandpa would not live.

All his close relatives came to be with Grandpa at the end. Of course, mother was there with Henry and me, though I was only thirteen. My uncles and cousins and great uncles and aunts came and we all sat in Grandpa's bedroom, waiting for his last breath. It was a shocking experience. I shall never forget the crowded room and the sickening odor of the overheated people mixed with the repulsive smells of a sick room. Nor can I forget the poor old man, no longer recognizable, breathing noisily, his mouth open, his cheeks and eyes sunken. For weeks afterward I was haunted by this nightmare.

Finally it was over. When the last breath had been drawn, someone stopped the clock so that the time of death might be confirmed. Besides, it would not do to have a clock strike in a room with a dead person. Maybe the idea of the timelessness of eternity made the keeping of time seem unimportant.

On the first day, the body was measured and laid out on a couch for viewing, while the coffin was being made. The next day, it was placed in the coffin by the cabinet maker, who was also the undertaker. The body was kept in Grandpa's sitting room until time for the burial. Friends and relatives came to the house to pay their respects. At night the room had a truly eerie atmosphere, for it was only dimly lighted by a low-burning lamp. Two men, not close relatives, watched through the night.

I remember distinctly feeling the presence of death in the house as I awakened in a sweat every time the clock struck in our rooms. The stopping of the clock downstairs had made a great impression. It was awe-inspiring to know that Grandpa was dead, and that he was in his coffin downstairs. Since this had happened in the summertime, ice packs were kept around the body. We had no embalming facilities in Amana.

During the days before the funeral, I thought often of Grandpa and what he had meant to all of us. He was, in many ways, a typical Inspirationist of the past generation. Piety was for him a way of life, and he seemed always to be set apart as an elder, even when Henry and I were alone with him. We had great respect for him though it was not unmixed with fear. Surely he was not one for gaiety, nor did he encourage it in us. He was stern with himself in his efforts to be godly and he expected us to follow his example. Poor Grandpa had studied piety so long that he could not see any other way.

Yet we were all truly fond of Grandpa. He was a meticulous worker and would have no part of anything that was poorly done. He was neat, careful, and frugal. To this day, I never put a hoe away without cleaning it well, for Grandpa taught me that this is the way to take care of a hoe. He was a patient and thorough teacher and I marvel now at how much I learned from him about the ways of nature. He was never happier than when he could be out working with the growing things of spring. He looked forward and planned for this time of year all through the winter months.

During the months following Grandpa Guyer's death in August, 1930, our old Amana security seemed to collapse all about us. With each new economic disaster, our anxiety deepened. Mother would say again and again— "I'm so glad Father did not live to see this," or "It's good Father did not know."

The experiences of that dreadful winter left us with little doubt that a day of dealing openly with our problems had to come soon. So when a meeting was called in each village on a certain noon in March, 1931, to decide what was to be done, no one was surprised. We even welcomed the ordeal ahead, for at least it would show what might be expected in the future. Anything would be better than the miserable uncertainty we endured.

The meetings were open to all members who were twenty-one or older. Of course, only mother could attend for our family. Henry and I watched her reluctantly put her shawl over her head and walk toward the door. Though she had often rebelled against the restrictions of Grandpa's generation, she had little enthusiasm for any plan aiming to change the old Amana way of life. Quietly she left us, without a word, as though she would say "good-by" forever to something dear, and fine, and wonderful. Henry and I, at that moment, doubted our own convictions, which had been for an all-out change. Picking up his cap, Henry said,

"Let's wait outside with the others."

Without further conversation, we hurried to join the other young people whose fate was likewise being decided at the noon meeting. They had gathered outside the meeting house door as though they could not wait for the answer. Everyone seemed to have a definite opinion about what should be done.

"They should have let us come, too. We're the ones who will have to take over in the next few years," said William who was always first with a suggestion.

"I'm glad I don't have to decide," said Walter, the careful one.

"I hope we don't lose our homes," was my opinion. I remembered Grandpa's prophecy.

We waited and watched impatiently for signs that the meeting was over, and thought it would never end. At last the doors opened and the people came out, solemnly, the men from their entrance and the women from theirs. We all hurried to our homes where the news would be told us.

A committee of four, chosen for the specific duty, had carefully explained the current problems facing the people of the Amanas. Even mother, who had always taken the old way for granted and who was instinctively opposed to any change, understood the explanation of the committee. The facts presented were simple and altogether familiar to all of us. Production had fallen off so drastically that inventories of goods for sale were very low. Present-day members, many of them unacquainted with the old time Inspirationists, felt no allegiance to the ideals of Christian Metz. This meant that some members were taking much from the society in benefits but putting little in as a repayment. Other members coveted the possessions of people on the outside, such as cars, radios, and various appliances not provided by the society. These members were guilty of using Amana property and time to earn money for personal accounts—a practice strictly forbidden in the old days. The big deficit Grandpa Guyer had worried about kept increasing and the Board of Trustees borrowed more and more money in an effort to pay for supplies not produced locally. At the close of the meeting, the consensus was that something had to be done and done quickly, if the Amana Society was to escape going into receivership.

A second meeting was called for the evening of that day. Although we all went back to our jobs that afternoon, we could talk and think only about the possible new plan that would make us self-supporting but would also free us from Amana restrictions and open doors to the outside. I was working at the kitchen house at the time and reactions there, as elsewhere, varied according to the age and condition of the person speaking. Mina

277

the *Baas,* now in her sixties, was glum about the whole affair.

"Too many people these days have forsaken the ways of Christian Metz. They don't even know what 'True Inspiration' and 'Piety' mean," she grumbled.

"I can't say about that," said Sister Alma, "but I can think of several brethren and sisters who never do an honest day's work, yet they always come to the kitchen house with their baskets." No one missed the edge of accusation in her voice. We all knew who the loafers were.

"In the old days, no one earned money for himself," continued Mina. "If we received money for anything, even from an inheritance, we gave it to the society. We truly shared and shared alike."

"Yes," added Sister Mathilda, seventy and unmarried, "And the Lord gave us living *Werkzeuge* to lead us. Now we are not pious enough, and we are being punished. God does not listen to us." She shook her head sadly.

"The old days are gone, Mathilda," rejoined Sister Alma, pointing to her children at play in a corner of the room. "Now we must think of the children. They must be educated to live in the new times."

At last someone had spoken my own thoughts. Along with all the youth of Amana, I wanted to learn about the world outside and above all, I wanted to go on to high school and maybe even to college.

At the evening meeting of that momentous day, plans were discussed for electing local committees who in turn would start working on the problem of formulating a new plan. Election of the "Committee of 47," as it was called, followed promptly. On April 23, 1931, each village elected its own representatives, the number being determined on a basis of population. Homestead elected five members, including Uncle John, who was still farm manager of our village.

Already one of the basic laws of the old order was broken. We were all surprised that very few members of this most important committee were elders. Some were young men who had refused invitations to become elders and others came from families who had not been held in high enough esteem to be considered worthy of eldership.

Reactions of the different villages varied; Homestead, located on a railroad and a highway, had been subjected to many outside influences. This may explain why our committee members favored a change to a new plan. They were to find opposition in the meetings from members representing the more secluded Amanas whose members favored "repairing" or "patching up" the old system in the hope that prosperity would return in due time.

By common consent, in order to function more efficiently, the "Committee of 47" was reduced to a working committee of 23, chosen from the members who had received the most votes in the local elections. And again, the number was finally reduced to ten, including the chairman, the vice-chairman and the secretary of the Committee of 47, and one member elected from each of the seven local committees. This committee of ten was subsequently empowered to draft a new plan for the operation of the colonies.

No need to say that we all waited anxiously for the formal proposal for reorganization. In the meantime, personal planning took many a fancy flight. Henry thought in terms of Uncle Albert, a business of his own,

279

a car, and lots of travel. I thought of high school, for already Elsie and the others were planning a car pool for our daily trip to Marengo. Even mother was eager for the new life. To her this meant being able to cook the food we liked and to concentrate her time and efforts in producing fancywork and garden products to sell. Only a few older members were reluctant to give up the old ways.

The committee, at work on the enormous task of finding an answer to the many problems growing out of their planning, discovered the need for an expression of the wishes of the members themselves.

Accordingly, a two-page printed circular was sent out to each member, setting forth the problems and on a separate page, requesting a signed vote indicating the course favored for the future. This simply stated, factual explanation, translated from the German, reads in part as follows:

"Dear Brethren and Sisters:

It is the wish of the recently chosen committee, to work as much as possible with the consent and agreement of the members, and we naturally hope thereby to gain their support and cooperation, because without unity and good cooperation, very little can be worked out for the good of the universal welfare. In order to work towards this mutual cooperation, the committee has found it wise again to inform the members about the facts that were laid before them at the recent meeting, that they might think about them quietly, and thus come to an open, honest conclusion as to which way would be the best for our future mutual welfare... The committee felt obligated to act one way or another, but has not taken definite action, because the thought hindered them that many members had not had the time or the opportunity to weigh the matter from all sides and thus come to an intelligent conclusion. However, since something has to be done and we can no longer go about our ways with indecision, we thus beseech every one of you to think the matter over earnestly, to discuss it with the members of the local committee... so that some of the ambiguous points might be discussed at the next meeting. The enclosed questionnaire should then be filled out and signed and delivered to the committee. Before this is done, the members must weigh all sides with careful and impartial consideration, and not fall into hasty, biased or selfishly designed conclusions. . . .

In the first place, the fact has been established that we no longer have an income as a corporate body and that every year we go backward and become poorer, and thus, in the foreseeable future, if no changes are made, we will become insolvent and will be reduced to poverty. It must be clear to everyone that we can no longer go on in this manner. . . .

After we grasp this idea, a second question arises: What can we do? Or better; what can be done? To this we might answer: There are only two ways that can be entered upon . . . either we have to be willing to go back entirely to the old way in which the community was originally set in operation, to give up many conveniences that have become dear to us, and to assume a standard of living that is below that of the outside world; or on the other hand, we must give up our communal system and reorganize our community, as is outlined for us in our constitution. Now there are many members who believe the easiest way is to improve our system a little bit here and there, to do away with certain abuses, especially those that do not particularly pertain to them, and then wait quietly for times to get better and for God to help us onward. Little can be accomplished by patching and repairing. This has been tried for many years by our elders without results, as we can see. If going back to the old way is to bring results, we must do it thoroughly and live entirely as the old folks did. And here we must consider what would be involved if we were to go back to the practices of self denial of our founders. . . .

Have we really thoroughly contemplated what all would have to be considered in order to go back to the old ways? We want to touch briefly on a few points that would have to be positively carried out if we were to have any results at all:

With our spending, we would have to stay entirely within the limits of our communal credit.

Private earnings, by whatever means they might be, would not be permitted. Included in this would be the sale of fruit and other garden products, such as tobacco, etc., as well as the sale of women's handiwork and finishing of

281

furniture and other objects for private sale, and also all other forms of private enterprises.

Any money earned on the outside, which is really a breach of contract against the constitution of the Society, would have to be collected and given to the treasury of the Society. Many of you do not consider how unfair it is to earn money on the side in consideration of those members who have contributed to the Society for 80 years and have not brought in any private income and through whom it was made possible that we could exist as a communal enterprise. If all the money had been given to the Society, that by rights belonged to the Society, it would often not have been necessary to borrow money and pay a high rate of interest on it.

There shall be no pay for any service administered. Even if someone works overtime, he must do it willingly and without extra pay, for the good of the whole.

We must be willing to reduce to the utmost the number of paid outside laborers and do the work ourselves.

Any purchases that can not be made with money provided by the community, must not be made. This includes radios, stylish clothing, silk stockings, coats, etc.

Not one cent of community money can be used for private means.

No community car can be had for personal use or pleasure trips. To have private cars would be entirely out of the question. . . .

No former members may be kept and supported by the community even for a short time, without express permission of the Council of the Brethren. . . .

Purchase of luxury items, tidbits, cigars, cigarettes, tobacco, etc., is forbidden, if we are to get along with our communal funds . . ."

And so on for yet another page this painstaking account continues. The items were so pertinent that few members could avoid recognizing the finger of guilt pointing at them.

The questions that were to be answered by the members were:

1. Is it in your opinion possible to go back to the old life of denial exactly as it is prescribed, and are you and your family willing to lead this life without reservation?

    Answer "Yes" or "No."   Answer _____

2. Is it in your opinion possible that by reorganization (which is described as fully as can be at this time in the additional sheet), the building-up of our community can be effected according to Article V of our present Constitution, and are you and your family willing to present your plans and views before the Committee and to cooperate in carrying out the plan approved by the Trustees and the majority of the members?

Answer "Yes" or "No." Answer _____

Signature _____

Henry and I read mother's copy carefully. She, like many other members, scarcely looked at it, knowing the contents from hearsay.

"How will you vote?" Henry wanted to know.

"Is there any way but *for?*" mother responded immediately. She had already accepted the inevitable while Henry and I still thought in terms of choices between the old way, complete dissolution, and a middle course.

"I hope they break it up entirely and give us each our share," was Henry's first choice.

"I don't want Amana broken up, but I want to go outside," was my choice.

Mother only commented, "The old days of Christian Metz and Grandpa are gone."

On one point we all agreed. The "Change" had already come.

By June 10, 1931, as requested on the questionnaire, all returns were in. No lukewarm response was given here for it held the key to the future fortunes for all residents of Amana. Seventy-five per cent of the votes were *for* reorganization. Only one village, with an elder

283

of the old stock for a leader, called a church meeting and suggested to "take it to the Lord in prayer."

The Committee now set to work in earnest on the tremendous task of dissolving the old communal organization which had been in operation for seventy-five years, and subsequently converting it into a modern business corporation, run for profit and owned by stockholders. During that summer of 1931, they met in session after session. Appraisers were called in to inspect our houses, shops, accounts, woolen mills, farm lands, and livestock. The attorney general of the State of Iowa and his associates helped with the legal tangles, as did a corporation lawyer. Minutes of these meetings reveal the struggle between the old idealism of share and share alike and the new adventure of every man for himself. Occasional meetings were marked by tense silences and eloquent expressions of deep-seated disagreement. But no meeting was marred by discourteous outbursts or lack of consideration for another's point of view. The habitual discipline of the True Inspirationists ruled the committee until at last the final plan was ready and submitted for vote by the members on February 1, 1932.

More than 90 per cent of the voting members promptly approved the plan (only 75 per cent being required by Iowa law). The formality of signing by the individual members sealed the contract and the new order had replaced the old.

The Parting

the new economy
in Amana

WE IN THE AMANAS during the month of May, 1932, will always remember the period of transition as one of enormous expectation. We were beguiled by the idea of moving from a system of elder-imposed restrictions to one of personal freedom always symbolized for us by the "outside." Inclined to judge the new freedoms in terms of benefits rather than of responsibilities, we tended to lose track of the good embodied in the old. However, wise old heads on the committee had no thought of letting go of their present blessings on a mere prospect of gaining others.

The plan for reorganization, as finally adopted, was a masterpiece of compromise, being highly ingenious, and devised to accomplish carefully the eventual transfer of the community assets to the individual members.

It provided also for the evolution of a standard stock corporation. The actual conversion of this communal estate, valued at $2,078,300, including real estate, livestock, shops, and industries, into a potentially income-producing enterprise with excellent expansion possibilities, is unique in the history of our country. It posed legal and social problems never before encountered by the experts who worked out the solutions. It involved not only the communal property, which was vast, but our homes, our futures, and our livelihood. In the end, it managed to preserve many of the Inspirationist traditions and benefits of the welfare state while establishing a modern business to be owned and operated by the members—for profit.

Therefore the plan was a transitional one, subject to renewal after twenty years. At that time possible modifications were planned which would move the ownership and management more and more in the direction of an orthodox corporation.

As a starting place for unraveling the tangled Amana affairs, two separate and distinct units were instituted —THE AMANA CHURCH SOCIETY and THE AMANA SOCIETY, each duly incorporated under Iowa law, and each having its own constitution and by-laws.

The Amana Church Society became legally responsible for the affairs of the church and for the benevolent activities of the community. It held jurisdiction over all church property such as church buildings, schools, and cemeteries. A Board of Trustees replaced the Great Council of the Brethren, the former governing body of the community, and represented all that remained of the old Inspirationist authority.

The Church Society was a wise provision by the planners, for it left the colonists many of their most cherished church customs and responsibilities along with many of the welfare benefits they had always known.

Of the two societies, the more important division from the standpoint of operation, was the *Amana Society,* a modified stock corporation. A brief summary of the stock provisions is essential for an understanding of the "Change":

The society's $2,078,300 worth of assets were divided in the following manner:

> 1200 shares of Class A Common Stock at $50 per share
> 32,366 Prior Distributive Shares (Years-of-Service Stock) at $50 per share
> 4,000 shares Preferred Stock at $50 per share
> 4,000 shares Class B Participating Stock at $50 per share.

The most important of the stock was the Class A Common Stock, which was the voting stock. Class A shares were issued on the basis of one share to each member over 21 years of age and a resident of the colonies. This stock, with a par value of $50, might be retained only so long as the member lived in the community. If he wished to live elsewhere, he had to relinquish his share, receiving true value for it. If a member died, his share of stock was bought back by the society. New shares were sold to young members as they became of age or, rarely, to a newly accepted member. In other words, these voting shares were under no conditions transferable, even by will, and they were salable only to the corporation itself.

Thus the committee, in an honest effort to be loyal to the members of the society, intended that the control of the Amana Society should rest with the resident members. By exercising their legal franchise, they could prevent outsiders from coming in, and they could govern all important decisions.

In our family, only mother received a Class A share.

According to the new constitution and by-laws, Class A stockholders and their families were still eligible for free medical and dental care, and free burial. The indigent aged and orphaned were also duly provided for, if they were unable from their own means or by their own industry to support themselves. By this device were many of the old welfare benefits preserved.

Next in importance came the Prior Distributive Shares known as the Years-of-Service Stock, also having a par value of $50. These were issued to members according to the years of service they had given to the society after they had come of age and signed the constitution. No allowance was made for the type or quality of service. Some of the really old people received as many as sixty shares. These were the source of ready money with which homes, shops, and businesses were purchased from the society. For this purpose a $65 value was given per share. Also, elderly people with no other means of income might cash one share per year for subsistence, receiving $50. This was expected to be sufficient to meet their needs for a whole year. Any charges outstanding were deducted from the amount paid.

This stock was transferable and could even be sold to outsiders. From the beginning, we were urged not to cash our Years-of-Service stock other than for our needs, especially since this stock represented our estate, inherited from our forefathers, and we were told to keep it as an investment in our community which we ourselves owned. There were those among us, however, who had waited too long for cars, radios, and other luxuries. They sold their shares at a considerable loss in order to get immediate cash.

The third type of stock was the Class B Participating Stock of which four thousand shares were set aside, with a par value of $50. This stock was held by the company to be sold later, as cash was needed, and was to be issued only on a two-thirds vote of the Class A stockholders.

The fourth category was Preferred Stock, four thousand shares with a par value of $50, to be issued by the vote of the directors without action of the stockholders. It should be mentioned here that only holders of Class A stock could serve as directors on the Board. The Preferred stock could be purchased by the members, was transferable, and carried no voting privileges.

The society retained stock assets representing the corporation interests, since the corporation would now operate the local enterprises for profit. Details of management were turned over to a duly empowered business manager, an outsider.

The conversion itself was a smooth, methodical process. Even before the actual inauguration of the new plan, groundwork was laid to start the wheels rolling. We all knew that on June 1, no food would be served from the communal kitchens. We were keenly aware of the need for money, and consequently of jobs where the money could be earned. We spent a busy time from February, when the plan was adopted, to June, when it went into full operation, negotiating as best we could for homes, businesses, jobs, and arrangements for single people who had no family homes. Suddenly, we were coming face to face with problems of taxes, abstracts, deeds, and insurance—matters never before heard of in the Amanas.

No more could we call the village plumber, carpenter, or locksmith when we needed a repair job done—unless we were prepared to pay. Our woodpiles would no longer replenish themselves in the proper season, nor would our henhouses automatically provide us with chickens. It would take more than a jug of wine to entice George, the whitewasher, to give us a bit of an extra touch. Never before had we fully appreciated all the ready service at our beckon. Nor did we have tools, cooking utensils, or equipment of any kind. These must all be purchased by money obtained from cashing shares of the precious Years-of-Service stock.

Many people could not forbear buying tempting goods so long as the cash held out. However, it must be said that most of the members of the society carried on under the new direction in a spirit of wholehearted cooperation with the new management, just as the followers of Christian Metz had offered allegiance to his system in which they had believed. This fine spirit of cooperation, born of a long-time discipline of considering the common good, helped carry the newborn organization through the hazardous and truly testing years of the Thirties.

At the suggestion of the business manager, it was decided that new businesses should be started. Several oil stations were built along the highway. One of the members had established a refrigeration and air conditioning business and he was willing to sell it to the society. This eventually was to become a major enterprise. Several members were sent away to learn the fundamentals of this new program. The woolen mills were in the red, so one of the factories was converted for the refrigeration plant.

Many of the old enterprises were rejuvenated and modernized. New fabrics and patterns were introduced by the woolen mills. Amana craftsmanship was offered to the public in the form of beautiful handmade furniture. The bakeries expanded and began to deliver the famous Amana bread to nearby towns. The meat markets also sought outside markets for the choice Amana hams and sausages. Some of the more venturesome members bought places, like the old kitchen houses and hotels, and turned them into restaurants. Today these represent one of the thriving activities of the colonies and attract thousands of visitors each year. The modern methods succeeded. When the depression finally faded from the land, the Amanas boasted the highest standard of living of any similar rural community in the United States. There were no homeless, or poverty stricken, or criminal people. There were no slums and none of the social problems associated with low standards of living.

As the new system gathered momentum, the corporation began making money. During World War II the refrigeration department and the woolen mills became especially prosperous because they sold their goods to the government in large quantities. The people soon acknowledged that the "Change" offered many advantages. The general standard of living was exceptionally high. The villages were pictures of prosperity and everyone was abundantly provided for. The corporation continued to offer medical, dental, and burial services without cost. The church remained free to its members. They not only had everything they needed, as in the old days, but most of them had everything they wanted as well. Younger members worked for the corporation and older people lived off their shares. In time, the business manager was dismissed and local men assumed leadership in the industries.

Uncle John explains

MEMBERS OF THE ORIGINAL "COMMITTEE OF 47" served as go-betweens for the "Committee of Ten" and the villagers, keeping us informed about the working out of the details of the new system.

Wherever people gathered together, talk was of nothing but "The Change." Everyone had an opinion about everything. The lawyers who came to help the committee with legal problems were outsiders. "Can we trust them?" The appraisers who came to inspect our houses were "snoopy." They were eager to give advice and suggestions. The women talked most about desserts, recipes, and their plans for their first kitchens. However, the question of greatest concern to each family was the matter of jobs whereby essential income might be provided. Since we had no man over twenty-one in our family, Uncle John kept us informed. One day he sent us a message that he had news for us and asked us to come over to his house that night. This meant that the committee had made definite decisions about us. As soon as evening church was over, we three walked through the cold spring twilight to Uncle John's house. The farm animals were quiet for the night, and the peaceful landscape with a lone star looking down on us belied the excitement we all felt as we stood waiting for *Tante* Lina to open the door.

"Come in, Sophie, come in, *Kinder*," she beamed in her usual jolly way. Then in mock distress she covered her mouth with both hands. "*Ach!* No more can I say '*Kinder.*' Look how tall Henry is now, a full-grown man." Henry who was very serious, blushed with embarrassment. "And Anna, you, too, are growing up. I haven't seen much of you since you've started working at the kitchen house. You have grown a whole inch, I believe. But just the same you will always be small like your mother."

"I don't feel small," I replied defensively, as she patted my shoulder gently.

Now we were inside and Uncle John had come in. "Hello, everybody, come let's sit by the table. I have news for everyone." He spoke as a master of ceremonies. Uncle John always liked a chance to grandstand. *Tante* Lina excused herself and we four took our places around the beautiful walnut table—a drop-leaf one, made in the Amana Shop.

"Sophie," Uncle John lost no time getting down to business, "you will be glad. The committee says you won't need to buy your house. If you will take care of the *Sälchen* as you do now, your family can live in the house without paying."

"Oh," said mother. "I had planned to cash stock and buy the house, as others will do."

"You won't need to do that," explained Uncle John in a conciliatory manner. "You just hang on to your stock."

"But I will need cash to live on," mother persisted. "Why have stock if you cannot exchange it for money?"

"Sophie, you know they have told us we must go easy on cashing the stock. If everyone cashed his stock now, before we get our corporation on its feet, we'll all be bankrupt. We don't have that kind of money."

"You mean I can't cash stock to live on?" mother asked, not believing.

"That's what the committee decided. They claim you don't need to cash stock because you have a son and daughter who can support you."

Mother clasped her workworn hands in front of her on the table and we all looked at them as she did, seeing as if for the first time, the prominent joints and the deeply cut lines, mute witnesses of a lifetime of toil in the fields and kitchens of the community. She spoke with a tinge of anger. "Why, they are mere children!" Then she looked up accusingly, "It used to be the elders, now it's the committee who tells us what to do."

"Well, of course, if you need to cash a share of stock, I'm sure it can be done." Uncle John tried to calm the storm, then he turned his attention toward Henry.

"And you, Henry. There are plans for you, too." Henry moved restlessly, seeming to have extra hands and feet.

"Since I'm too old to go to high school, I am thinking of getting a job on the outside," he announced firmly, squaring his shoulders and looking Uncle John directly in the eye.

"The outside! How could you do that? You'd have to have a car to get to your job if you worked outside." Uncle John's voice indicated how foolish he considered such a plan to be.

"I plan to buy a car," Henry responded.

"And how do you plan to pay for a car? They cost a lot of money, you know."

"Henry, why do you talk so?" mother cut into the conversation pleadingly. "You know I need a man in my house."

Henry said no more that evening. He seemed to recognize defeat and accepted it because there was nothing else to do. Sensing his crushing disappointment and his helplessness in the face of mother's claim on him, I wondered if he even heard what Uncle John was telling him.

"Henry, I want you to work with the farm crew. You know I'm still to be the farm manager for Homestead. You'll be paid the same as the other men, ten cents an hour." This last was intended to make Henry feel good. Henry did not answer, but just sat there, not moving, his hands in his lap. I had not seen Henry cry since he was very small, but just then, as I looked at him closely, I thought there must be tears in his eyes.

"What about my job at the store and the warehouse?" Henry was not eager to work in the field.

"There are enough older men to do the work there. We need you young fellows on the farm crew." Uncle John persisted.

"And, Anna," Uncle John spoke my name and the attention of all was focused on me. "What would you like to do?" he asked playfully, as if he did not know.

"I want to go to high school," I told him respectfully.

"That will be for next fall. This summer we must find a job for you."

"Uncle Adolph has already asked to have Anna work for him at the hotel," mother spoke up.

"I guess that will be all right," Uncle John answered. "It will be like working at the kitchen house, except you will wait on tables besides."

"For outsiders?" The thought of being closely associated with outsiders was almost frightening.

"Well, if you are going outside to school, you will have to get used to strangers," he added logically. "And just think, you will be earning money, too!"

"How much will I be paid?" I asked eagerly.

"You will receive about $4.50 a week because your hours will be longer than other people's," mother spoke up. "You will work seven days a week from seven in the morning till one or two in the afternoon. Then from five to eight in the evening, depending on the amount of business they have."

"What about Sundays? Won't I go to church?"

"Well, whenever Uncle Adolph can spare you, you can go. They will try to arrange the work so that you will get to church almost every Sunday, and sometimes to prayer meeting. I don't like that part of it," said mother solemnly; then as an afterthought, she added, "but you must have a job."

"That is very good salary." Uncle John insisted on being optimistic. "It's more than some of the men will make when they work the short shift at the woolen mills." We all knew the woolen mills were in the red, but in order to keep everybody employed they kept it going and divided the work among the men.

"I guess it's all right," I said, never having had any-

299

thing to do with so much money before, and having no basis for comparison.

"Now then, that takes us to Sophie—you want to work, too, don't you, Sophie?"

"Yes, I want to work," said mother.

"Well, I thought I would like to have you as head of the garden crew. We will operate the kitchen gardens as we did before. Only now we sell the produce for the corporation so they can pay us our salaries. How about it, Sophie?"

"Yes, I would like that," said mother but still without enthusiasm.

"You will get paid ten cents an hour, like all the other workers." Uncle John had pushed his chair back as though his duties were done.

"I guess we will get along," said mother, beginning to wonder just how much the new system was going to differ from the old, so far as she was concerned.

On the way home through the pitch black darkness our thick-soled shoes beat a clatter on the wooden walks, our feet knowing the way as if by instinct. We had little to say. Although I had come off quite well, I could think only of Henry and wished for a way to make things right for him. If only he had been a few years younger so he could go to high school with us.

emancipation summer

HENRY WASTED LITTLE TIME in disappointment over not
being free to work outside the Amanas and accepted the
job with the farm crew at the standard wage of ten cents
an hour. He was still determined to earn extra money
and buy a car as soon as enough money accumulated. No
one knows where Henry picked up his ideas for capitalistic enterprise but his projects kept our household in a
haze of confusion for years.

First there were the guinea pigs, a pair, whose "in-
crease" nearly moved us off the premises. We had cages
and fences all over our yard. Of course, they helped
"mow" the lawn in the summer, but when winter came
they had to be transferred to the cellar. It seemed they
filled every nook and cranny of the unexcavated part of
our cellar. I lived in constant horror of meeting the

weasel whenever I had to help do the chores. And then there was that lovely "perfume" that permeated through the house. I began to be ashamed to bring my friends home. But Henry had a market for his pets at the experimental laboratories of the University of Iowa at Iowa City, and that helped swell his pocketbook and his ego. The demands were sporadic and minor, however, and finally Henry decided the guinea pigs were not worth their keep.

After the guinea pigs were abandoned, we had rabbits. As I remember, the rabbits smelled even worse than the guinea pigs and multiplied almost as fast. Henry had hoped to sell the rabbits as breeding stock, but again the demand was not overwhelming. All this time he was working with the farm crew, carrying his paper route, and saving every penny, after paying mother for his board.

Henry's needs for money increased much faster than he could acquire it. He yearned to take a correspondence course in electronics so that he could get a better-paying job and maybe someday go outside to work. He kept trying one thing after another. I can't remember just when the pigeons joined us, but we had pigeons, and some of them were good "homers," too. Dr. Breck helped Henry take them away to stations miles outside so that they could "practice" coming home. And they helped supplement the meat supply when squirrel and other game was out of season.

Then there was the goat. Everyone remembers the goat Henry brought home from a farm as a tiny snowy white kid. This goat was supposed to grow up and give milk, and at the same time "mow" our lawn. But before long, Henry had to admit that his goat would never cooperate on the milk business, being a billy. The new pet

304

flattered Henry, though, following him around devotedly.

Mother and I had been tolerant of all the other experiments but we had no time for this ornery little pest. We were told that when the wind was in the right direction, people could smell it all over Homestead. The rule was that the goat must be kept staked in the back yard when Henry wasn't around and this was easy to do at first. As the kid grew older, chains were for breaking. One day I came home to find the goat grazing in the garden beside the house. There it stood facing me as I slowly and carefully edged toward the front door. By the time I reached it, the goat had his head down and was ready to charge. The screen door was locked. Frantically, I decided to try the back door. Knowing where I was going gave me a little advantage over the goat, so I flew around the corner of the house and made a dash for the back porch. Just a shade ahead of the charging beast, I rushed up the back steps and opened the screen door. The goat was following so closely and so violently that the screen door did not stop him—at least not until his head was sticking through. He stood there puffing, his teeth bared as if in laughter. I was *not* laughing!

Henry had the screen to fix and since he had no good argument for keeping a billy goat, mother and I voted that the goat was ready for butchering. Thus ended another of Henry's projects.

By now Henry had acquired a reputation of being a quite enterprising young man. In August he was invited to join the office force at the Main Office in Amana, one of the more desirable local places to work. He now had a real excuse to buy a car, for he would have to commute. He took the $60 he had accumulated over the years, including his paper route money, his trapping bounties, and the coins that Dr. Breck or Uncle Albert had slipped in his pocket whenever they visited. This made the down payment on the most beautiful second-hand Nash that $100 could buy. How proud he was of that car and how he kept it shining!

I, too, had my troubles during this first summer of emancipation. In the first place, I exchanged a ten-hour day in the kitchen house for a ten-hour day at the Homestead Hotel. The chief difference was, as Uncle John had indicated, I now served outsiders. At first my hands shook as I placed dishes before these strangers, who looked at me critically and who listened to my speech, finding it full of flaws and quaintnesses. They teased me and made me feel embarrassed and "different."

One of my first customers in the hotel dining room was a salesman who stayed three weeks. I served him all his meals and helped clean his room and make his bed every day. He had been kind and courteous, not nearly as critical and demanding as most people were during those depression years, when a purchaser of a fifty-cent meal could have all the coffee he could drink and all the meat, potatoes, and wonderful Amana bread he could eat. His remarks too were friendly, though impersonal, and I came to feel at ease with him. On the day he was to leave Homestead he spoke to me at breakfast.

"Anna, you are a good waitress. I shall miss you."

"Thank you," I stammered, blushing but grateful.

"I'd like to leave you a little something." He handed me an envelope.

Not knowing what to do, I took it. After he had gone, I opened it and found a dollar bill! Embarrassed and chagrined, I could think of no good reason why a salesman would give me a dollar. Miserable, I felt compromised in some terrible way. When I showed it to the other waitress she told me it was a tip and that it was perfectly proper.

After that first tip I found an occasional nickel or a dime under certain plates. I would slip them quietly into my shoe, still not quite believing that this was money I had earned. On some busy Sundays my shoes would get so full my feet hurt. I saved most of my tips in a special fund for school. Some of the coins I kept for souvenirs. One of my proudest possessions was a fifty-cent tip from Henry Wallace, then a young Iowa politician with his eyes already on Washington.

As the summer progressed, I assumed the various duties of a hotel maid without complaint, thinking only of the fall when I would go away to school. However, I had one experience which threatened my future plans and it still stands out as the worst ordeal of all for me. It concerned Henry's car.

As a part of the school plan, arrangements had to be made for commuting to Marengo, twelve miles away. It would be necessary for me to take my turn with the driving, for five of us were to share in a "pool." Henry, surprisingly enough, agreed that his was the family car, and that I could use it if I could learn to drive. He would ride to the Main Office with some of the others on the day it was my turn to drive. No brother should ever teach his sister to drive! Henry had never been very patient with me, his kid sister. I knew he did not really want to teach me because he considered me a stupid girl. These circumstances did not make for an easy learning situation. I was terrified just thinking about it.

On our first venture I sat stiffly beside Henry as we

zoomed out of Homestead in search of a quiet country road for my training. He explained the "shifting" and braking system on the way out. It all looked so easy. At a lonely spot he stopped the car and I took over. He left the motor running.

"Now, as you release the brake, put the clutch in, and give her gas," he yelled over the roar of the engine. I fairly shivered with "nerves."

I released the brake and tried to make my feet do the right things. Suddenly the car bolted forward as though shot from a firing range. Henry grabbed the wheel frantically, forcing the car to the left. My foot pressed harder and harder on the accelerator. In no time at all, the car was off the road and down an incline, resting upright in a muddy ditch. Too stunned for tears, I still frozenly gripped the steering wheel. Henry sat holding his head and did not even ask me if I was hurt. At last, in a roar of anger, he yelled at me,

"See what you did! I told you to *brake.*"

"I tried," I sobbed weakly. "I'll never drive your old car again."

"I'll say you won't," snapped Henry. By this time, he waded through the oozy mud to my side of the car and opened the door.

"Come on. Let's go. We'll have to call a farmer to pull it out."

"Can't you get it out?" I ventured hopefully.

"Can't I get it out...?" he asked with unflattering exasperation. "Look at it. The wheels are in mud up to the hubs and there's no way to get up that bank. I'm not even sure a tractor can do it."

"Will you *have* to call a tractor? I mean can't I help you...?"

"How else do you get out of a ditch? I hope you

realize tractors cost money. And what's more, it looks as if the axle is broken and probably some other things too."

"I'll pay—out of my wages—and my tips, too." I offered everything, saying a mental "good-by" to high school.

"You probably won't have enough," Henry scoffed. I could see all the precious money I had saved, dime by dime, eaten up to put the car in shape again. Worst of all, I hadn't learned to drive.

I waited tearfully for Henry to go to the nearest farmhouse. As the tractor approached, Henry and the farmer were obviously joking about my driving. I tried to hide behind the car, but finally came out of my retreat when Henry yelled, "Be careful, or the car will fall on you."

The chains were attached and after much grinding and chugging, up came the Nash.

"See if she'll start," the farmer prompted.

If the heavens had opened and I had heard a choir of angels I would not have thrilled any more than I did to the sound of that motor!

As all things pass away in time, so did the effects of the accident. By the end of the summer the bill was paid, though most of my earnings were gone. Mother insisted that Henry continue to give me driving lessons. Had it not been for driving to school, I should never have touched a steering wheel again, I am sure. But perseverance held out, even though Henry's patience did not, and by September I was ready to take my turn with the rest of them.

a new life for Mother

FOR EACH OF US, the "Change" had a special, personal meaning. With Grandpa gone, mother was free as she had always longed to be, to go along with new ideas. The first sign we noticed of her enjoyment of her emancipation was her quiet excitement about her kitchen plans and of making wonderful desserts—mostly of chocolate. Mother had never known real satisfaction where sweets were concerned. Now she studied recipes for rich devil's food cake, chocolate pie, chocolate waffles, chocolate cream puffs, fudge, and just plain chocolate cake. "If we could only grow a chocolate tree," she would say when the other women were making plans for their gardens.

Recipes were not easy to find. Occasionally a good one appeared in a newspaper, or Mrs. Breck would send one. *Baas* Mina helped her and the other women as best she could. During the years, Mina had kept her own recipe book, in her own handwriting, for the kitchen house. But few were the desserts in Mina's book, and the cakes were the cheap one-egg variety. And there was another problem—the proportions. Mina's recipes called for measurements like, "a kettle of potatoes, four sifters of flour, a handful of salt, a dozen eggs." Cutting the Amana proportions down to family size was a favorite preoccupation in those days. Many families wanted to follow the familiar menus, and to this day they serve *Mehlspeise* on Tuesday, cottage cheese on Saturday, etc. But not mother. She wanted new, exciting food. Long before June 1, mother had a first-rate collection of recipe books, her favorite being the one she sent for from the Baker Chocolate Company.

Then there was the question of kitchen equipment. To start with, we had our small kerosene-burning stove, used in summer for reheating our food. We also had a squat table type, flat-topped wood-burning stove, used in winter to heat our kitchen-dining room and also to reheat the food from the kitchen house. This little stove, standing about thirty inches high, had two round "lid" openings used for placing kettles over direct heat.

Now that women were minded to equip their kitchens, salesmen from the outside were quick to sense a market bonanza. Being totally unacquainted with shopping on the outside, we favored buying in our own community.

There was a man called "Herman," a friend of Uncle John's, who came to our house one day, casually, as if it were his habit to drop in every day. Mother let him in and offered him a chair. Soon he worked the conversation around to the subject of stoves—and this was not hard to do. He said,

"Sister Schneider, how will you manage when you must do all the cooking for your family?"

"I have recipes," replied mother, as though this took care of everything.

"But how can you cook on these stoves?" He took a sudden interest in our kerosene-burning stove and our wood burner. "These stoves are good for reheating food from the kitchen house, but you can never bake a good cake with them." He waved a disparaging hand.

"I have a small oven on my kerosene stove," mother nodded casually. "I have always baked the children's birthday cakes in it."

"No, Sister Schneider," he said emphatically, turning the corners of his mouth downward. "For those fine new recipes, you should have a bottled gas stove."

"No, Brother Herman, I don't need another stove." It was mother's turn to be emphatic.

"Let me show you. I just happen to have a picture of one with me. A friend of mine sells them." He made it all sound very plausible, as he took from his pocket a salesman's folder describing a bottled gas range.

"See, Sister Schneider, it is all white enameled—beautiful—and how it can bake cakes and pies!" His eyes lit up as he extolled the wonders of the gas stove. Mother studied the pictures, finally taking them to the window for better light. The descriptions, in English, meant nothing to her, but it was easy to see that she was impressed.

"And so easy to operate," continued Herman. "All you do is turn it on and light a match—just like you do with the kerosene stove, except that you don't have any smelly kerosene to bother with."

Still no comment from mother.

"And such wonderful cakes it bakes. See this beautiful cookbook you get with it, with all new recipes. Sister Schneider, you should have a bottled gas stove. Besides, it is the very latest model."

That last remark did the trick. "I don't know anyone who has a bottled gas stove." Mother had that "bathtub" look in her eyes—the one that had to do with her need for something out of the ordinary once in awhile, being a widow and excluded from all the married women's boasting.

"It will last for years and years and give you pleasure every day." The salesman closed in on his sale.

"How much does it cost?" mother asked at last.

"Only sixty dollars—not much for such a beautiful stove."

Mother's enthusiasm wilted. "It would take me many, many months to save sixty dollars," she said wistfully.

"Maybe you can sell a share or two of your stock—since this is for a 'necessity.' There are many people wanting to buy Amana stock."

"I will see," said mother, thereby capitulating entirely.

"Good, good, Sister Schneider. You will never regret it," said Herman blandly, as he folded his salesman's illustrations, all ready for the next eager would-be cook.

Thus it was, that when the time came for us to do our own cooking, we had three stoves in our kitchen-dining room.

Mother evolved a pattern for using them—the kerosene burner was for jelly making and canning, or any "messy" job. The wood stove served most of our cooking needs in winter, since it also heated the room. The bottled gas stove was largely for display purposes, being seldom used, because gas was expensive and because mother loved to keep it bright and polished, like new.

Mother planned her cooking chores carefully. Never did she light the oven unless she had enough baking to fill it. The family swears that the first tank of gas, and only a small one, at that, lasted her for a whole year—but she insists this is not so.

Mother recently confessed to me that Herman turned out to be working for an outside salesman and so "earned" a stove and other benefits for himself by selling stoves to his "friends" in Amana.

Before salesmen from the outside came to the colonies and stocked the stores with modern kitchen gadgets, the women of Amana knew only the type of utensils they had used in the kitchen houses. Most of them, made locally by the tinsmith or imported from Ebenezer in the Sixties, bore little resemblance to those being used outside Amana. Thus it was that the women all had their secret design on certain familiar equipment from the kitchen house.

The closing of the community kitchens and the consequent disposal of the equipment was a point of high interest. The committee made a ruling about it—that the kitchen *Baas* should have first choice of the articles there, since they had not even a tentative arrangement for cooking in their own rooms. After they had what they wanted, other women might buy the remaining equipment from their kitchen houses. Finally, everything left went to public auction. Mother wanted some cherry pitters the worst way. They had been made by

Paul, the tinner, and were quite ingenious gadgets for poking the pit out of the cherry without squashing the fruit. Mother was sure she could not find a similar item anywhere. Every day when she came home, we would ask,

"Did *Baas* Mina buy the cherry pitters today?"

"Not yet," she would say cannily.

Finally one day she said, "The cherry pitters are gone. I must wait to see if there will be any at the public auction."

When the day for the auction came, mother, armed with the proceeds left from the shares of stock she had cashed for the stove, was one of the first women there. Henry and I went too, for this was a new and exciting adventure. Never before had we been to an auction.

Brother Martin, who seemed to know about auctions, was in charge. "Now first we take the big pieces," he said in German, for this was an auction for Amana residents only. He rested his hand on one of those businesslike potato ricers which stood about three feet high. "How much am I bid?" He began an auctioneer's routine. "This ricer will handle a peck of potatoes at one time. You all know how to use the wooden masher—it is very easy to operate." He gave the wooden "pusher" a twist.

No bid could he entice.

"Someone must want this wonderful ricer, made in our own Homestead tin shop. How can you have good *Mehlspeise* without a good ricer?"

"Fifty cents." The bid came from Uncle John. Henry and I knew he was probably going to use it for something around the farm buildings.

"Fifty cents—who'll make it a dollar," Brother Martin tried to stir up another bid. At last he just shrugged his shoulders and said, "Sold to Brother Schneider for fifty cents."

Next came the huge, black, cast iron kettles with the little iron pegs for "legs" and the round bottoms for fitting into the holes of the large ranges. A few conservative bids took them away. Mother bought one which she later gave me for an antique. As the afternoon wore on, we saw all the familiar items knocked down for little or nothing, as people bought things, mostly for souvenirs.

We thought the auctioneer would never be ready for the cherry pitters, but at last they came up for sale.

"How much am I bid?" yelled the crier, holding up four at the same time.

Henry and I whispered to mother, "Fifty cents, say fifty cents."

"No, that's too much—twenty-five cents." As mother stood there, her hand half raised and her mouth open, Sister Miller spoke out loud and clear.

"Fifty cents!"

"Seventy-five cents! But they're not worth it!" Mother took a stand like a seasoned capitalist.

"Who will give more, come on give me a dollar," yelled the man.

"Going, going, gone—for seventy-five cents to the lady by the table."

Article after article, well known to all of us who had spent much of our waking time in the kitchen, passed over the block, and time and again Henry and I urged mother to bid but she only took a firmer grip on her pocket book and said "no." Finally, nearly everything was gone—the ladles, the spoons, the tin covers, the huge bread-mixing boards, the cabbage cutters, the potato slicers, the bean shredders, the vats for making soap, and the crocks for preserving eggs and sauerkraut. There

317

remained only a few odds and ends. Among them was a stack of dilapidated wooden lap trays that had been used by the women when preparing vegetables.

"Twenty-five cents," mother sang out without prompting from anyone.

"Twenty-five cents bid by Sister Schneider. Give me fifty, who'll make it fifty?"

No-one bid against mother. Slowly she moved forward to claim her purchases. Then we started for home, Henry carrying the wooden trays, mother with the iron kettle in hand, and I proudly clutching the cherry pitters.

Eventually, mother tucked one of the cherry pitters into my hope chest and I confess this ingenious little gadget is one of my most cherished—and useful—possessions.

In adjusting to the "Change," it was mother's instinct for self-preservation that gave her the most trouble. Besides being definitely frugal in the spending of money, she wanted to be well provisioned against the coming winter. That first summer, she planted a large garden in back of our house, the seeds having been given away at the time of the auction. Her expert care, combined with Iowa's rich earth and beneficent weather, produced enough garden truck to supply a regiment. We used it for our table, canned it, and sold what we could. We lived only a few doors from the village store so mother had a handy market. She must have been something of a politician, too, when she made a good friend of John Weiss, the man who handled the produce. The secret of her success probably was that she listened while he talked, which was all the time. Being a vegetarian himself, he was something of a connoisseur, and those vegetables from mother's garden were as beautiful as pictures in seed catalogues. Henry and I could not abide John and his ever-present garlic breath but mother wanted to sell her vegetables. She even let him come to her garden whenever he needed supplies, and help himself. Many a green pepper and red tomato was marketed by John for mother that summer.

The Lord blessed us abundantly with food. There were always bushels of apples, pears, plums, grapes, potatoes, onions, cabbage, beans, tomatoes, and anything an Iowa garden will produce.

Mother misjudged our needs that first year for she intended that we should not go hungry during the winter. Also, in line with the thrifty training of the elders, she could not bear to let any food go to waste. We wrapped bushels of apples and pears, one by one, and ate them all winter long. When the fall found us with a large pile of unwanted cabbage, she made us store it carefully in a dark corner in the cellar. Even though she was always serving cabbage, we made only a slight impression on the pile during the winter and finally threw most of it away in the spring.

In many ways, mother's life went on much as it was before the "Change." She followed the old pattern rather closely. Perhaps it was freedom from Grandpa's austere discipline that meant more to her than the new economy. She continued to go to all church services, wearing her church costume, including the heavy shoulder shawl in winter. She worked as hard under the new system, if not harder, than she had done under the old, for she took charge of the garden crew for the corporation and supervised the cultivation and harvesting of

319

acres of onions and potatoes. She has never known an idle moment, habitually improving the time with hand work or by doing household tasks. Nor has she ever traveled far from home.

Mother belongs to Amana, as one becomes a part of the place where one was born and has spent a lifetime, never having lived away. She loves Amana for all it ever stood for. In her heart she is proud of her True Inspirationist heritage and she will always "believe faithfully."

becoming an outsider

As THE APPROACH OF FALL brought Marengo closer and
closer, I wondered what this new life would be like.
A feeling of vague uneasiness alternated with one of
pure exhilaration. The five of us who would be students
at the high school, had made a visit there to apply for
admission. The matter-of-fact principal had been
friendly and helpful. She had even let us see the class-
rooms with their rows of desks, their wide windows overlooking the town, the blackboards, ready with chalk
and erasers, and many unfamiliar items like colored
charts on the walls, a globe of the world, pictures, book-
cases filled with brightly bound books. There was a
room for cooking, a room for sewing, and one for
manual training. Best of all was the large gymnasium,
with a stage and an auditorium. Here we had come to

see Cousin William perform in the senior play the previous spring and I had been so thrilled I determined nothing would stop me from going to high school.

So long as my thoughts dwelt on finding out about all those alluring prospects I had seen at school, and the joy it would be to learn about them, I was in a heaven of expectation. But when I thought of actual associations with the teachers, and students, and other outsiders, a panic of fear chilled me.

But first I had other preoccupations. Girls must get ready to go away to school, and I was no exception. Mother and I had made two new dresses for my wardrobe. They were both of dark backgrounds with a small floral design and were cut according to a simple pattern for women's dresses. I even had new shoes—a pair of plain black, "sensible" oxfords, to wear with my long ugly stockings. I had no problem of hats, gloves, purses, or jewelry, for I owned none of these accessories. I wanted ever so much to cut my hair as other Amana girls were doing, but fear of being struck by a bolt of lightning, or of being haunted by Grandpa's ghost, prevented such worldliness and I continued to twist my long, blond hair into a "bun" at the back of my neck.

The weather was hot as only an Iowa September can be, but I dressed in my new clothes for that first day of school. As I waited impatiently by the window for the car to take me away, mother hovered about, trying to say "good-by."

"Anna, are you sure you want to go?"

"Yes, Mama."

"Do as the others do and you won't feel strange."

As she looked at me with the reassuring affection I had known during all the crises of my childhood, I sensed her pride and satisfaction at the thought of my getting to go. Perhaps she, too, had known moments of wonder and wishing for a world beyond the barriers of Amana. Be that as it may, if she felt any regret at my leaving the old way she gave no sign.

I answered her, "I will, Mama," but my own thoughts were even then far, far away.

Five of us drove back and forth to Marengo that first year—Elsie and her brother Joseph, Walter Stoppel, John Hornbeck, and myself. Only John, whose mother had insisted he go a year ahead of schedule, had attended high school before. He might have prepared us a little, but he gave information only on request.

"What will we study?" I wanted to know.

"Well, there's algebra, history, Latin,—manual training or home economics, gym,—and English," he recalled slowly, as if he had taken those subjects years ago instead of recently.

English, that was what interested me most! My limited contacts with outsiders at the hotel had made me keenly aware of my German-accented speech. "Does it take long to learn to speak good English like outsiders?"

"It took me not long," John answered smugly.

"What do we do when we get there?" My thoughts flew ahead of the car.

"You just wait for the bell to ring, then you freshmen go to the assembly."

"Will you show us how to get there?" I worried.

"Aw, it's in the auditorium on the first floor." John's patience was giving out. As soon as we arrived, he deserted us and acted as though he didn't know us.

While we waited for the bell, Joseph and Walter joined the fringes of a large group of boys clustered in a corner of the hall. It did not seem to take them long to get acquainted.

Elsie and I stood alone in an out-of-the-way spot, trying to make ourselves invisible. Already, I felt that most dreadful of all youthful terrors; I was different and did not belong. No girl but me wore long stockings and oxfords. No girl but me had long hair. Even Elsie had bobbed her hair. All the girls wore pretty, colored, "store-bought" dresses, much shorter than mine, or bright colored sweaters and skirts. I was glad Grandpa could not see their bare knees and legs and short socks.

As if by hypnotic suggestion, when the bell rang, we found our way into the auditorium. A plain, neat-looking, middle-aged lady teacher with glasses smiled a pleasant greeting as we hurried to the nearest seats just inside the door. She stood quietly, waiting for everyone to find a place, and as if by miracle, a hush settled over the noisy room. When all were silent and you could hear the clock ticking on the wall, she spoke.

"I am Miss Calhoun, your freshman adviser," she announced easily. "I am also your teacher of English I. This is a mighty fine looking freshman class, and I have seen quite a few," she bragged a little. "I'm sure you will like high school. There are many exciting things for you to learn and do here." She turned to pick up her class book. "Now, I am going to call the roll so that we can know who is who. Let me know if I do not pronounce your name correctly or do not call your name. Otherwise, just answer "present.""

The roll call proceeded and I had the feeling of being in church and of waiting for my turn to read from the Bible.

"Anna Schneider."

"Bresent," I answered. There was a ripple, as of amusement, through the room, and I felt myself shrinking under the chair. Miss Calhoun paused a little as if she would say something, but she passed on to the next name. When she had finished she laid the roll book on her chair and faced us, her arms folded.

"Maybe some of you do not know, but we at Marengo are lucky this year in having some very special newcomers join our classes. You are all familiar with the Amanas, the community of seven villages a few miles east of here. For seventy-five years, the people there have worked and lived in a world of their own. They have had little or no contact with other communities. The reason has been that they wanted to worship God as their forefathers had done. Only last year, they decided to change their whole plan of living. Now for the first time, young people from Amana have come to our high school." Everyone in the room seemed to be looking at Elsie and me, as if they could spot us by our oddness.

"I know you will all want to help these students get acquainted. Imagine how it would be if everything were new and different for you."

As Miss Calhoun looked at us in her kindly way, I wondered how she knew. She continued, smiling graciously.

"Maybe they will help us learn about Amana, too."

Hence a sympathetic teacher with a gentle heart had smoothed the way for some adventurers in a strange world. She had openly struck the keynote that was to be accepted at Marengo High School. It echoed afterward in all our relationships there.

What might have been a devastating experience turned into a year of solid, interesting accomplishment for us all, thanks to Miss Calhoun and the other teachers. I shall always be personally grateful for her endless patience as she helped me with my greatest problem—speaking English correctly.

"Say it again, Anna: *Just,* not 'chust'; *people,* not 'beeple'; *think,* not 'tink'; *loved,* not 'luft'; *God,* not 'Gott.' "

I said them over and over, day after endless day. Finally Miss Calhoun suggested I enter the declamatory contest in order to have a real incentive to articulate precisely. For one of the practice sessions she had six of us go on the stage at once, all of us saying our pieces at the same time. I was pleased when she told me she could distinguish mine through all the bedlam. And when the night of the contest came, I spoke easily, without any shyness or stage fright. My piece received honorable mention.

However, it took more than Miss Calhoun's efforts and training for me to overcome Brother Schlegel's English. People would still say to me, "You speak with an accent." Once at a masquerade party I was the first one to be identified. "That's Anna Schneider," someone said as soon as I opened my mouth. I knew they recognized me by my speech.

No need to go into all the details of those high school days. As we progressed through the curriculum, we students from Amana with meager backgrounds were leading the class academically. Starved for learning and sensitive to the wonderful opportunity which had come to us by chance, we fairly devoured assignments and waited for more.

Socially we fared less well. We still felt strange in groups of young people, and avoided school parties or any contacts where conversation was necessary with outsiders. (My one attempt under masquerade had failed.) We did not know how to dance. That is, none of us did except John, the outgoing one. He had learned the previous year when he had stayed at Marengo, though he was careful not to mention this talent in Homestead. The old inhibitions kept me from even trying to dance. I knew Grandpa would not have approved. My "dates" during my high school days quite naturally were with Amana boys, since we commuted and spent our evenings and week ends with the other young people at the local Welfare Club.

College likewise was both painful and glorious. Elsie and I chose the same Iowa college. I think I would have perished those first few weeks had it not been for Elsie. We were not together much, for she stayed at the dormitory and I worked for my room and board in town. And yet it was knowing she was there that helped. Also she was freer to go home on week ends than I was, and she brought back local news and sometimes a box of cookies from mother.

As time went on, Elsie and I grew further and further apart. Our curricula were different and we were asked to join different social organizations. I was still shy and ill at ease socially, but I made more of an effort to participate. After all, I argued, people must like me or they would not ask me to join. And I no longer had the Homestead Welfare Club to fall back on.

The group I felt most at home with was the German Club. Here, no doubt, I was sought after because I was a real asset to the group, for I spoke German fluently. At least I felt useful and wanted.

327

Here I met a young man, a graduate student doing a thesis on the subject of German dialects, who offered to help me with my speech difficulty. He pointed out to me that the "j" sound was especially hard for me. He was of Pennsylvania Dutch origin and had had similar trouble.

For the first time in my life I learned that "j" and "ch" were not pronounced the same, as Brother Schlegel had instructed us. My friend taught me how to say them right. Together we would go up and down the stairs, reciting "jacket," "Joseph," "Jerusalem," etc. until people stared us into quitting. The theory was that one uses more breath and hence more effort in speaking while walking and climbing than while standing and sitting.

Sometimes we would go out for coffee and quote "Jack and Jill went up the hill" across the table from each other. It became an obsession with me to master the "j" sound. I wonder if that is why years later when my children were born I named them "James" and "Jacolyn!"

One year the German Club decided to take an excursion to Amana. How proud I felt when I was asked to arrange the program. We had dinner at the Homestead Hotel, which had by now become a second home to me, for I had continued to work there every summer. Uncle Adolph and his wife prepared a regular feast with *Sauerbraten* and potato dumplings. I arranged for a tour through the woolen mills, and we saw the lily lake and the canal that my great grandfather had engineered. We visited my home and I proudly showed off mother's needlework and rugs.

Everyone was gay and jovial. Here was a good place to practice the German we had learned in class. One of the first-year students, Ernest Bolte, shook mother's hand with a flourish and spoke in awkward German,

"I am Ernest, what are you?"

He had meant to say, "My name is Ernest, what is yours?"

Mother was baffled, but in an effort to be gracious, she said,

"I am earnest, too."

We all giggled at the little joke.

We spent the evening around my old reed organ, singing gay German songs. The walls fairly rang. Never before had our house known such gaiety. Mother had made *Marzipan* and *Lebkuchen* so that all might sample such German delicacies. The excursion was a tremendous success.

I suddenly realized that I, an Amana daughter, had a heritage to be proud of. People were interested in me and my Amana background. I need no longer feel ashamed and quaint, instead I must blend the old with the new life and draw from both to find the real *me*.

Even my religious background began to fall into place. I had studied Old and New Testament History in college and had become quite interested in comparative religions. It had been hard to reconcile some of Christian Metz' doctrines and Grandpa's restrictions in this modern world. Some of my courses in science had made me wonder about the Heaven and Hell I had learned about in the catechism.

Suddenly there was room for every religion in this wonderful world of ours. Even if I had been taught certain things I could no longer abide by, I need not feel ashamed, or compromised, or guilty. I remembered what mother had said to Henry when he started the paper route,

"We must decide for ourselves."

I understood that to each of us every thought and action can be either good or sinful depending on our intention, whether it be bobbing our hair, exposing our knees by rolling our stockings, dancing, or reading the newspaper on Sunday. We must "decide for ourselves" and then "believe faithfully."

Amana wedding, June 1942

ONE GLORIOUS JUNE DAY in 1942 I found myself skipping
across a neatly cut lawn, past newly bedded cedars with
fresh green tips and graciously blooming tea roses, to
the front door of Henry's new home. Only last month
he had moved into this thoroughly modern cottage on
the main street of Homestead. He had been married
some five years previously to Ruth Graber from South
Amana and they had moved in with mother and me,
as was the Amana custom. But from the beginning they
planned to build a new home. So they purchased a
piece of property across the street from our old home on
land that had formerly been the kitchen garden. Now
it was completed, the first new house to be built in
Amana in decades. And just in time for my wedding.

In a large box under one arm I carried my wedding

dress; under the other, another box containing my veil. Ruth was standing in the door, holding in her hand a tall candelabrum of the type commonly used for weddings.

"Anna, I thought you'd never get here—we have so many questions." She was a picture of flushed excitement, her shiny blond hair pinned here and there with a bobby pin and her brightly figured housedress showing signs of her busy day.

"We had to alter the veil; the headband was a little large," I explained.

"I can hardly wait to see you in your wedding gown. I so wanted a white one myself, but Henry thought it might offend the elders." Ruth paused to reflect wistfully.

"Yes, I know. Now ten years after the 'Change,' no one cares or notices. Besides, I know only the weddings of my friends on the outside and do not remember Amana weddings, except the cakes."

"All right, then tell me how would your friends put these candelabra—in front of the fireplace, or off to one side? The baskets of gladioli you sent from the florists are in the kitchen and must be near the fireplace, too. I left them in the kitchen for you to place. What do you think?" Ruth still held one of the stands, testing it in different locations.

"Let me see the flowers." I was on my way to the kitchen. "Lovely! I've never seen prettier basket arrangements." I could hardly speak for sheer joy over all these wonderful happenings of this day.

"They are pretty. You know Mother Schneider wanted to use some of the peonies from the garden, but I knew you preferred the greenhouse glads."

"They seem more like a wedding," I answered

334

lamely, unable to say just why I felt that the flowers had to come from a professional florist.

Mother had entered by the back door, in her quiet unobtrusive way.

"Mama, wait till you see my wedding dress!" I could talk of nothing else.

"Ruth told me about it. I hope it's not too fancy," she remarked.

"Wait and see." I carried a basket of pink and white gladioli in each hand and took them to the living room to decide where they should go.

"Do you think there will be room for all the relatives?" Ruth looked over the room wondering. "With the furniture all out, the room looks larger than it really is. Will it hold thirty chairs without crowding too much?"

"It will be large enough," was my calculating appraisal.

"Where is Tom?" Mother remembered the bridegroom.

"He will come later—with his folks, and they will bring the bridal bouquet and the corsages from Cedar Rapids. We have such a pretty corsage for you, Mama."

"You should not have flowers for me. I don't know how to wear them."

"Don't you worry, we will show you," I told her.

"How does the room look now? Do you like the flowers near the center of the fireplace?" Ruth concentrated on the arrangements.

"I think it's all just right." I could only admire the general effect. "I'm glad you and Henry finished this pretty house before Tom and I needed it for a wedding."

"A house is blessed by a wedding," Ruth beamed

with pride, and unnoticed, Henry had come in and smiled his approval.

"Henry, are you ready to give me away?" I greeted him.

"Most any time," he answered too willingly, but with that old teasing look in his eye.

"Then, as soon as I catch 'Little Henry' and tell him again what he is to do with the ring, the Schneider family will be ready for Anna's wedding. Teaching a three-year-old how to be a ring bearer is the hardest job of all."

Mother picked up little bits of leaves and litter from the carpet. Ruth gave a last touch to the flowers. Henry stood in the corner of the spacious room, obviously enjoying being host for such a pleasant occasion.

"You may use the guest room for dressing, and I suppose you will want to start soon," Ruth was saying practically. "We have been sending all the relatives to the neighbors' but they will start coming here early—you know the Amana way."

"It's too bad we can only invite the relatives to the house," said Henry regretfully.

"I like this part to be just for the family," I answered. "Most everyone in Homestead will be at the reception." I moved about, viewing the room from different angles.

"I'll dress now; then come to help you," said Ruth who would be matron of honor.

Henry left to get the folding chairs at the Welfare Club. Mother went to check the cakes. She had made thirty luscious cakes and had them all frosted and decorated; the reception was to be as elaborate as Mary's had been. I was left alone in the spacious living room

336

turned wedding chapel, and my thoughts began playing overtones to the events taking place about me.

After many years of striving to be an outsider, I now was about to marry a man from the outside, and not one of my people. Realizing that I would be leaving my Amana home and my family, I wanted desperately to cling to something that was here and in no other place. Like other True Inspirationists, we were not given to demonstrations of affection but we had always known deep and abiding feelings, one for the other. It showed itself in quiet, true, sincere little ways and could be relied upon like the rising of tomorrow's sun. I had come home to be married; but where was the Amana of my childhood? Surely not here in this typically modern cottage with its painted exterior, its attractive open fireplace, its expansive beige broadloomed carpeting. Where was the simple Amana interior with its blue whitewashed walls, its hot-blast stove, its rag-strip carpeting? My unexpressed yearning for my childhood home found no fulfillment here, yet I felt a distinct element of satisfaction in being able to have a wedding like my outside friends would have.

With the mood of nostalgia still upon me, I gathered up my two boxes and climbed the stairs to the guest room. Alone still, I carefully slipped the white, lacy bride's dress over my head and waited for Ruth who would fasten the tiny buttons and so fit the dress closely to the lines of my body. There on the bed lay the cloud-like veil, object of my dreams since I had first seen one worn by a college friend. I lifted it gently and turned it tenderly in my hands.

There was a knock on the door and Ruth asked, "May I come in?"

"Please do, and help me."

337

"Anna," she put her hands to her face. "How beautiful!"

"All brides are beautiful, they say," I answered happily.

"Do you suppose our grandmas were when Barbara Heinemann called them in from the fields and told them, 'This is the day for you to marry?'" Ruth wondered.

"I don't know. I never thought much of the old marriage customs." I was grateful for a real wedding day.

"At least you won't have to sit up front in church for a year, for sinning, as I had to." Ruth seemed amused at the thought.

"Yes, but it did not have much meaning any more for you and Henry."

"Maybe not, but it made me feel dreadfully foolish, as if the people were thinking about us."

"And that part about living apart for a while after marriage, as mother and father did." We had heard the story many times.

"I sometimes wonder how they made the people do all those unnatural things." Ruth took the veil from my hands to set it on my head.

There was another knock at the door, and there stood mother with a florist's box in her arms.

"My bouquet!" I forgot about the old marriage customs and tore impatiently at the wrappings. "Just what we ordered, rose corsages, and my bouquet." I posed with it, looking in the mirror, and Ruth and mother stood by admiringly. Mother said nothing but seemed somehow to be playing a strange part in a strange play.

"Tom's here!" I suddenly remembered, for he must have brought the flowers.

"Yes, and his folks, too. We must hurry and get ready," said mother.

"Don't let him see me now, in my wedding dress. It's bad luck, you know. And I want him to be surprised." Tom had heard us tell about the old Amana wedding customs, and I knew he must have been a little skeptical of what was coming off. Even though he had overheard some of our plans, he gave up trying to figure them out, because our chatter habitually drifted into German whenever we lost ourselves in all the preparation. So he was wont to withdraw with a book and pay no attention.

I had met Tom in college and we had dated steadily my senior year. We often visited in Homestead together. From the beginning he had been fascinated by Amana customs and Amana ways.

"I'm glad Brother Hermann would come," my thoughts skipped back to the preparations. "I wanted an Amana elder to perform our ceremony." Another wish was to come true.

"He was happy to do it. Here he is now, driving up in his new car," Mother saw through the window.

"Anna, you should see all the gifts in the playroom, most of them not even opened." Ruth had gone downstairs to welcome the guests.

"For me?" Could all this be for me?

Ruth adjusted the little crown that held my veil in place. Mother stood quietly watching, as if seeing a vision. She held her corsage of red roses in her hands, waiting for someone to pin it to her dress. In that instant, I saw her as I had not seen her before. Her hair, now mostly gray, was still combed in the old familiar style, with a "bun" at the neck. Her face, lined by the passing years, shone with happiness, reflecting my hap-

339

piness. But I saw sadness, too, the same that I felt deep inside me, having to do with the "parting." Her dress, simple and dark as might befit a woman of Amana, missed the traditional by being modish and attractive. She wore it with her habitual simple dignity. As Ruth pinned the bright corsage in place, Sophie Schneider looked the conventional mother of the bride, and no one would have suspected that she was a daughter of one of the sternest of the True Inspirationist elders.

One impression seemed to melt into another until at last I stood before the flower-decorated fireplace. Tom appeared as if from nowhere and took my hand. We faced my good and long-time friend, Brother Hermann. He held a small black testament in his hand, but no book of Inspirationist testimonies. He shook my hand warmly and said, "Anna, I have come to read the wedding text for you and this young man who will be your husband."

"I'm glad you have come." I smiled my gratitude.

Ruth stood beside me and as I handed her my bouquet, I thought no bride ever had a lovelier bridesmaid than pretty, womanly, winsome Ruth.

When the rustle of excitement had quieted down, Brother Hermann began to speak.

"Dearly beloved, we are gathered together in the presence of God and these witnesses to join this man and this woman in holy matrimony." I had a feeling that this was no elder speaking, for he spoke in English, not in German as was his usual custom. The words "holy matrimony" stuck in my mind, too, as being new and not a part of the lines used at Amana weddings.

My thoughts were interrupted by the voice of Little Henry, "Do I take the ring now?"

A ripple of amusement passed across the room.

"Who giveth this woman to be married?" the ceremony proceeded.

"I do," Henry stepped forward, handsome and very proper in his navy blue suit. I felt a wave of pride and affection for Henry.

Brother Hermann was saying, "Do you, Tom, take this woman, Anna, to be your lawful wedded wife?" ... And then it was my turn. "Do you, Anna, take this man, Tom, to be your lawful wedded husband?" ... The moment came when the ring was needed.

And there was Little Henry, a small edition of his father, self conscious in his new suit of blue trousers and white shirt, carrying the ring on a white satin pillow. He was lovable and completely charming as he looked up at his father for approval. Henry bent down and untied the ring and then led Little Henry to the edge of the crowd.

After Brother Hermann read the words, "I now pronounce you man and wife," and Tom and I were truly wed, I realized that I had not heard the phrase most important in the marriage ceremonies of the past: "It is better to be unmarried"!

Now I was really an "outsider." Tears came to my eyes as I turned to face Uncle John and *Tante* Lina and all my other relatives who had made my childhood such a memorable one. Yes, I was an "outsider." But as they rushed up to "kiss the bride," I knew that I would always be an Amana Daughter, proud of my unique and wonderful heritage.

the dream passes

"I REMEMBER THE FACE . . . . *Ach,* shure, it's Anna."

It was a June evening and I had taken my friends to visit Friedrich Mannheim, one of the oldest residents of present-day Amana. When I was a girl, he was one of the salesmen who traveled for the woolen mills. Now he was the keeper of the records for the society.

For some time I had wanted to know what had survived of the religious heritage of Christian Metz and the True Inspirationists in changed Amana. I wanted also to know more exactly the real nature of the "Gift of Inspiration," that power strong enough to move families from Europe to unknown homes in a foreign country, compelling enough to hold them and their descendants steadfast for seventy-five years and more.

On this evening we found Friedrich in his home

343

village passing the time with an old friend, the two of them seated comfortably on a bench on the cool side of an old Amana house in an old Amana garden. He came toward us, his short, heavy-set figure nearly lost beneath a large-brimmed straw hat. With his denim trousers held up by aged suspenders and his blue shirt open at the neck he was a prototype of an Amana gardener. He removed his hat graciously and peered at us over the top of his plastic-rimmed glasses searching for recognition. Then with a friendly handshake he said,

"*Ach,* shure, it *is* Anna."

He took us to his own home and we were quick to accept his invitation to be seated on a bench in his garden. As the evening wore on, we led him around to talk of the old days.

"Was Christian Metz a large man?"

"No," said Friedrich, and he seemed startled by the question. "You know, just today, I had his *very own* cane in my hand. My friend Louis has it—a rare keepsake. It came just to here." He showed us a distance of about three feet from the ground.

"Metz used it for walking in the Old Country— and here too. No, he was not large. All of the Metzes were small people."

"What did people think of him, did they like him?" I asked next.

"Oh, they loved him! He was a wonderful man, and he worked hard. When they were building the church in High Amana, Metz planed the whole floor, all by himself. You know he was a carpenter, and the son of a carpenter." Friedrich looked at us to be sure that we did know.

"But if he was such an important *Werkzeug,* did he work, too, as others worked?"

344

"Yes, he worked." Friedrich had been standing all the while.

"Sit down on the bench with us," we invited.

"No, no—I stand. I like to gestulate." Speaking English was a little difficult for him but he spoke with much animation, punctuating his remarks with pronounced gestures, suggesting an old time revivalist. He went on to tell more about the Inspirations of Metz.

"Oh, he had the 'Gift of Inspiration' all right," he said. Anyone hearing Friedrich and seeing him acclaim about it could sense the miracle. "The Gift was no small favor conferred by the Lord—but a special power granted only to those who could use It well." Friedrich's dramatic emotion made me wonder if I could have resisted the powerful presence of Christian Metz, had I known him.

"Was Metz a good speaker?" asked Ruth.

"He was a wonderful speaker. He had a fine voice. People listened when he spoke and remembered what he said."

"Did he ever marry?" I wanted to know, remembering his granddaughter.

"No, Metz was never married."

Friedrich was lost in memories and we followed his recollections.

"Metz' poetry was beautiful. Ah—." He shook his head, searching for words fine enough to describe it. "Do you know the funeral hymn, '*Ich Will die Welt Verlassen?*' Listen!" He began to recite in German:

> I wish to leave this world
> And grasp hold of my Loved One,
> Who bled for me at the cross,
> Who has given Himself up for me
> In death, that I might live,
> And took upon Himself
> My great misery.

345

I wish, in my great suffering,
To reach out with both arms
To Him who has sought
My salvation and my life;
This shall be my endeavor:
To follow after Him.

I rush toward the end;
Lord, send Your angel to me,
That he may lead me out of misery,
To be my comfort and joy.
I am still afraid
Of the coldness of death. . . .

The body sinks into the earth
That it may become earth again
From which it has come;
Whatever is temporal, must perish.
That, which God has chosen for Himself,
Will arise, as did my dear Lord,
Jesus Christ.

Here we sow into the earth
That it might decompose
And spring up anew.
In the same way the Godly
Who come to this world,
Will arise from the dead.
This we believe!

He paused after the solemn speaking of the words of the hymn. "That is the best hymn for a funeral. Metz could make funerals good—and, you know, funerals can be cold, cold." Friedrich hunched his shoulders together as he recalled how cold a funeral can be. He seemed to sense his power to hold our attention, and he continued thoughtfully,

"And that other hymn, 'Gott der Wird's Wohl Machen,' God Will Take Care of Things, that was inspired, too. Neither Metz nor Barbara Heinemann was educated. So they could not have told such wonderful things if they had not been inspired by God!"

We nodded in silent agreement. I wanted to know more about Metz, the man.

"Where did Metz live?"

Friedrich explained which house in Amana had been the home of Metz. Then he thought of a picture he wanted to show us of Metz' home in Ebenezer, so we followed him inside to his "office." Darkness had fallen without our noticing. Friedrich switched on a lamp, obviously a former kerosene burner, revealing a table with one end set against the wall. A fine old grandfather's clock hung above the table high against the wall. A confusion of papers, books, magazines, and things covered the table. An old ceiling-high Amana bookcase dominated the opposite side of the room with its fine polished walnut doors standing open to reveal volume after volume of black leather-bound books. Friedrich asked us to be seated and I chose a colonial caned rocker; Linda and Ruth sat in the heavy edged "captain's" chairs like the one Friedrich evidently used for his office chair.

Said Friedrich with a flourish of the hand—"Everything is a mess—but I don't care. I don't care!" He had fought the good fight for order too long and had given up only to find a new peace of mind.

"I work here. I keep the records, and such a business!" He threw up his hands. "I have to pay an oil bill for the church. *Ach!* So many bills!"

He was searching through an aged cardboard box and in no time had the desired pictures. We marveled at his deftness in finding anything he wanted in the apparently unorganized quantities of books and papers.

"Here it is! Metz' home in Ebenezer. See how much

347

it looks like our houses? They built houses in this country like the ones they had in the old country." In here somewhere Friedrich had added a second pair of plastic-rimmed glasses to the ones he had been wearing. I watched curiously as he manipulated first one, then the other, then the two together.

He began bringing out other treasures—more photographs, and remarkably old, precious books, some bearing the dates of 1713, 1715, printed in German, and bound in parchment or leather. He talked of the early Inspirationists and how the first ones, according to him, came from England, even before the Pott Brothers began preaching in Saxony.

He began talking of many subjects, including jokes about New England folk which he had us read while he chuckled over them. Then came his funeral record book. Friedrich was proud to show his records, but he shook his head as he considered how many former Inspirationists now had their names in the funeral records.

A question about when the "Inspirationists" started sent Friedrich to his crowded bookcase. Standing on tiptoe, he brought down book after book—all collector's items for one reason or another. He had one with Rock's signature on the flyleaf—printed in 1717. He had the complete *Inspirations-Historie* of Metz and Heinemann along with many others. Since a *Werkzeug* like Metz gave over 3,000 testimonies, these volumes amounted to many books. Some of the bindings were gone but Friedrich explained that he kept them because "They got my 'Fadder's' notes on them."

Ask anything you would about the history of the True Inspirationists and Friedrich could find a reference for you, and without delay. This literature he knew nearly by heart, for all his life's thinking had been

348

focused on it. Now I understood why much of the conversation by my older relatives had been about the testimonies and genealogies of different families who had followed the inspired ones from Germany.

Friedrich was speaking again.

"The *Werkzeuge* had to live like Apostles," he told us a simple statement of fact, looking us in the eye expecting confirmation of this great truth by which he, too, had lived.

But let us not give the impression that Friedrich was without a sense of humor. Speaking of Metz, he explained that Metz kept his eyes open for what was going on around him. "He had a wonderful insight! He had to have," said he, with a knowing gesture. "He was strict, too, when he had to be." Then he raised his hand signifying recollection.

"Once there was a woman who was shooting darts at a man and the man did not even know it. Metz knew the woman was trying to start the fire of love," Friedrich winked slyly. "So Metz told the man about it before he knew he was in trouble. Then the man was careful." Clearly Friedrich felt that the man had come off quite well. We laughed spontaneously at his satisfaction that this hussy had been thwarted. (Friedrich had never married. . . . He had abided by the Inspirationist philosophy that "It is better to be unmarried.")

Finally, we turned Friedrich's attention to Barbara Heinemann, the last of the *Werkzeuge*.

"Tell us, Brother Mannheim, what was Barbara Heinemann like?" I asked.

He picked up the cue eagerly. "She was a heavy-set woman," he beamed. "When I was a little boy, I sat on her lap and she had to hold on to me because she had so little place for me to sit."

We laughed at that bit of comedy. "And was she a large woman—tall?"

"I could not say how tall," he replied.

"Was she friendly? Did the people like her?" I remembered that I had heard from my grandmother that the people were all afraid of her, because she became very personal in her "Inspirations" and embarrassed the members in public.

"Yes," said Friedrich. "She was friendly and warm, except when she had to be otherwise. Shure, some people did not like her and even left the community because of her testimonies, but they *should* have gone, maybe. We were better off without them. And she worked hard, too. She worked very hard. All the people did. There were two words for life in those days—*work* and *pray*."

Now for the big question. "Did you ever hear one of her testimonies?"

"Oh, yes, but I was quite small. I remember. She spoke in a deep harsh voice, not at all like her natural voice. You knew that the words were inspired and it gave you a feeling of being in the very presence of God." Friedrich drew his lips together and peered serenely over the top of his spectacles.

We had stayed a long time and the hour was growing late, yet I still had questions to ask.

"Barbara was married to George Landmann? What became of him?"

"He is here," said Friedrich, rising a little from his chair. "He is buried in the Homestead cemetery."

"Then Barbara lived in Homestead?" I had never heard of that.

"No," he explained, "she lived in Main Amana. She

was associated with Christian Metz as a *Werkzeug* and could do her work best by living near him, so she did."

"And George Landmann, what did he do?"

"He taught school in Homestead."

Seeing Ruth's involuntary surprise, Friedrich continued.

"They did not live together as man and wife, but they loved each other," he said earnestly. "Barbara even sacrificed being with her husband so that she could better serve the Lord. She had her work and he had his, and everyone understood."

Linda rose to signal time for leaving. "We must go, Brother Mannheim. It has been so good to hear you talk about the Inspirationists."

"*Ja,* I like it. But nobody cares any more. So few are left to remember."

We bade good-by to Friedrich and stepped out into the dark night. The evening had passed quickly and Friedrich had enjoyed talking about his favorite subject as much as we had enjoyed listening. He had brought to life, ever so briefly, the vivid, dynamic presence of the *Werkzeuge*. He had given us a new insight into the faith of our fathers.

I still visit Amana frequently; with each visit, it seems that less and less remains of the old communities of Christian Metz and the True Inspirationists. The buildings are there but many of the wooden structures, formerly unpainted, now wear bright colors as if they belonged to any rural Iowa town. The main streets, formerly dusty or muddy roads, have been "blacktopped" the better to accommodate high-powered cars which have replaced the horse-drawn vehicles. The village store continues to do business in the old building but now money is the stock medium of exchange; the old coupon books showing credit allowable for Amana families are no more. Instead of the limited supply of merchandise furnished by the elders, all types of modern manufactured goods are there—latex bathing suits, Amana freezers, souvenirs from Japan. The woolen mill, famous for its blankets and handsome woolen yardage, still operates on the banks of the canal, but like any other modern factory, for profit. The winery sells *"Peistengel"* to tourists. Antique shops do a big business with imported antiques, and a museum displays artifacts of the early colonists. And modern ranch-style homes strike a sharp contrast with the simple, dignified, brick and stone buildings of Old Amana. Since the communal organization was discontinued in 1932, there have been many changes.

"So few are left to remember." Friedrich had been right. Our visit with him had given us new insight into the faith of our fathers. New insight and new understanding, but not acceptance. For the power that had sustained Friedrich and all the others—the power that had made them "believe faithfully" through the years has somehow failed to reach our generation.

The dream of the True Inspirationists is gone forever.

Appendix

THE TWENTY-FOUR RULES OF TRUE GODLINESS

Hear, then, what I say to you:

I, the Lord your God, am holy and, therefore, you, too, shall be and become a holy community, if I am to abide in your midst as you desire. And, therefore, you shall henceforth resolve:

1. Cast all foreign gods out of your hearts so they will not infatuate you and lead you into fornication and profanity against your God. ....

2. Have nothing more to do with the unfruitful works of darkness. For My holy temple can have nothing to do with the temples of haughtiness, uncleanliness, ambition, lust for power, jest, and unnecessary, exuberant, critical or idle talk that would steal time that should be devoted to Me. If you are to be children of the Light you cannot mingle with the unholy, the liars and their works, the scoffers and the slanderers, who are nothing but darkness.

3. When you mingle with outsiders, you must conduct yourselves so that the outsiders have no reason for slander or to shame My Holy Name. It is better to suffer unfairness and to be cheated by them. But mainly avoid such company that might destroy your interest in the Lord. Avoid all mockers, scoffers, and those who fill you full of vanity.

4. You must conduct your outside activities more and more according to your conscience and give up willingly what My Spirit considers sinful (you must not worry about your individual harm, for I am the Lord your God who can and will provide for you), so that you will not fall into the criticism of mockers. The time

355

that I give you on the earth is short. Therefore, see to it that My Hand will create something worthwhile in you.

5. Refrain from all falsehood, lies, and hypocrisy. I will give this, My Servant, this elder, the intellect of a judge so that the truth shall be revealed to you through him and through My Spirit. See, My Children, I have chosen you from many, many, many in these days, and I have promised you that I will be a fiery barricade for you against the defiance of your inward and outward enemies. Truly, truly, I will keep My Promise! So you must faithfully keep what you have promised and are promising Me.

6. You should, therefore, strive toward certain gifts and be envious of those to whom I shall grant certain gifts of prayer or wisdom. For the enemy is constantly trying to poison you. If you are humble and patient you will all in time be filled with My pure and holy Spirit. When that time comes you will speak with other tongues than now. Then I shall be able to communicate with you most intimately.

7. Put far away from you all slander and all malice toward each other, which you are accustomed to. Nobody is free of it! Behold, I will command that the spirit of My Love shall be in your midst whenever you are gathered together in humble prayer so My Love shall be sent directly to the hearts that are empty.

8. You must be resigned to endure suffering, both from without and within because Belial will not refrain from proving his spite through his hidden forces. Therefore, it is pleasing to Me and it becomes unavoidably necessary that I should constantly prove you through suffering and affliction, to make you firm and precious and to fabricate you in My Crucible. And whosoever does not dare to exert all outer and inner forces to the honor of My Kingdom and My Name (and he must not be lazy about it) must step aside, so that he would not be a blemish on My Honor.

9. Therefore, do not listen to any surmises or suspicions in the future and do not get angry at each other over

any deficiencies you might have. Each one of you should strive to become a mirror for the other one. And you should all strive daily and hourly to stand as an individual before the Lord, as a city, or a light on a mountain, that shines bright and pure, nearby and far away.

10. In the meantime, busy yourself with outward and inner calmness, the more the better. Strive constantly in humility to become overwhelmed with the innermost and most lowly depths of your own nothingness, even though it will cause the death of your own personality, so that I might bring My Holy Seed to grow in your ground, where I have buried it.

11. See, My People! On this day I make a covenant with you, which I bid you to keep faithfully and reverently! I will personally mingle with you daily and will visit your station, so that I can see how you are proving yourself.

12. Beware, Say I, Your Lord, of belittling this covenant, and of neglect, indolence, and sluggishness, which up to now has been your master and has ruled your heart. I will never again leave your side, or go from your midst; instead I will reveal myself much more intensely and forcefully, more holy and more beautifully through the light of My Countenance in and under you, as long as you will fill Me with your faithful and sincere desires. This will be the bond, with which you will bind Me and hold Me. See, I choose you today to be slaves of My Love, freeholders of My Kingdom and possessors of My Heart. So let yourselves be bound willingly with the ropes of My Love, and you will never be lacking in powers of love.

13. [This one was starred in the text, probably by my grandfather, whose copy I was using.]

And you, who are leaders and fathers of families, hear what I say to you; The Lord has chosen you to be members of His Society, with whom He will mingle daily. So see to it that you will truly act as leaders who constantly stand under the true sovereign, your king, and manifest yourselves as lights in your houses, so that your members will be brought to strict discipline and true piety, through your example, which you should constantly seek to make more irreproachable, more earnest, and more valiant.

14. Your children, you who have any, you should strive with all your abilities to dedicate them to Me and to lead them to Me. If you hold yourselves close to Me, I will give you sufficient wisdom, courage, intelligence, fortitude, and sternness mixed with love, so that you yourself can be an example of piety to them, and that your method of rearing them shall be blest. ... But those that ignore you and do not listen to My Voice and My Discipline given through you, their blood shall be upon you!

15. Now go and do that which I have assigned to you and do not give in, just as I Myself do not tire of working with you sinners; thus you will remain in My Grace and will save your souls. And may those wives and children endure their own crimes, who will not submit to you and to Me. I will not tolerate the scandalous behaviour among you and in your households that the world and the children of unbelief and passion have so much to say about; instead, I have ordered the spirit of My Living Breath that it should go through all your homes and will inflame every soul that does not willfully shut itself away from Me. ...

16. And none of your grown children shall be permitted to come to church who have not had a proper example and direction by their parents and also from the elders ... who, with their fellow workers, must watch over the training of the children ... with earnestness and love, but without all severity and harshness. And should the parents be negligent and the case require it, they shall be temporarily excluded (from church) for their humiliation.

17. Therefore, prove yourself to be the ones, whom I have set aside as an eternal monument and whom I will press upon My Heart as a permanent seal so that the

358

spirit of My Love may rest and work in and among you at will.

18. And this is the word which the Lord speaks of these strangers who so often visit you and cause so much disturbance; none, whom you find to be a scoffer, hypocrite, mocker, sneerer, derider, and unrepenting sinner, shall you admit to your community and prayer meetings. Once and for all, they are to be excluded, that My Refreshing Dew and the shadow of My Love may never be prevented from manifesting themselves among you. But if some should come to you with honest intentions who are not knowingly scoffers ... then you may well admit him. I shall give you ... the spirit of discrimination and give you an exact feeling, whether they are sincere and come with honest intentions or otherwise.

19. If they then desire to visit you more frequently, you shall first acquaint them with your rules and ask them whether they will submit to them and to the test of the elders. ... But if a scoffer or mocker declares that he repents, him you should only admit after considerable time and close scrutiny and examination of his conduct, to see if he be righteous. ...

20. And those who pledge themselves with hand and mouth after the aforesaid manner ... you shall watch closely, whether they live according to their profession and promise or not, lest the dragon defile your garments with his drivel.

21. (To the elders) Therefore, shall My Elders and their helpers go out among the members of the congregation to see how they keep their houses, and of what nature are their hearts. I will give to you, My Servant, (E. L. Gruber), and your brethren, eyes with which to see this, if you ask for them. And, if you shall find that someone has any unnecessary grief, or is living in indolence, shamelessness, and wantoness, and similar circumstances, and therefore, is being slandered by the enemy, you shall draw attention to this in a pleasant way. If he improves, you shall rejoice. But if he will

359

not improve after several reminders, *you shall shame him openly before the congregation and if he will still not improve, you shall cast him out for a while.* ...

22. And while you are all together, you shall be informed of this; that there is not one among you who can withdraw from this brotherly punishment and admonition, so that no secret haughtiness may sink like a thorn into any member to disturb and poison his innermost thoughts.

23. And you shall not let any duties or practices which you are to perform away from the Society become a habit or you will find it necessary to deny them for yourself all over again; instead your meetings and assemblies shall make you ever more ardent, fervent, and passionate in a true innocent love for each other. ...

24. The members of this Society and this church shall give the promise honestly and openly, before the congregation, to My Elders, with their hand, mouth, and heart, after they have given this due consideration, and it shall be kept reverently!

—Jahrbücher der Wahren Inspirations-Gemeinden,
(Published by the Amana Society 1819-1823) pp.
13-22.

glossary

Einsprach—A written message of protest
Lebkuchen—A cookie made with honey
Liebesmahl—The *Love Feast* or communion service of the church
Marzipan—A pressed cookie, originally made with almonds
Mehlspeise—Main dish of flour or potatoes
Peistengel—Rhubarb wine
Psalterspiel—Hymnal
Saal—Meeting hall (church)
Sälchen—Small church or meeting hall
Sammlung—Collection of the testimonies of Christian Metz and Barbara Heinemann
Tagebuch—Diary
Unterredung—Confessional, spiritual examination
Versammlung—Church gathering
Werkzeug—Instrument of the Lord